Contemporary Issues in Taxation Research

Volume 3

Contemporary Issues in Taxation Research

Volume 3

Emer Mulligan and Lynne Oats

Contemporary Issues in Taxation Research, Volume 3
Copyright © Emer Mulligan & Lynne Oats 2019

For more information, contact Fiscal Publications, Unit 100, The Guildhall Edgbaston Park Road, Birmingham, B15 2TU, UK or visit: http://www.fiscalpublications.com

All rights reserved by AccountingEducation.com Ltd 2019. The text of this publication, or any part thereof, may not be reproduced or transmitted in any form or by any means, electronic or mechanical, including photocopying, recording, storage in an information retrieval system, or otherwise, without prior permission of the publisher.

While the Publisher has taken all reasonable care in the preparation of this book the publishers make no representation, express or implied, with regard to the accuracy of the information contained in this book and cannot accept any legal responsibility or liability for any errors or omissions from the book or the consequences thereof.

Products and services that are referred to in this book may be either trademarks and/or registered trademarks of their respective owners. The publishers and authors make no claim to these trademarks.

ISBN 978-1-906201-39-5

 Typesetting by Mac Bride.

Cover design by Filter Design Ltd

Printed in Great Britain by Lightning Source, Milton Keynes, UK

Contents

1 Contemporary Issues in Taxation Research: An Overview   1
   Emer Mulligan and Lynne Oats

2 Sweden: Failure of a Cooperative Compliance Project?   7
   Lotta Björklund Larsen

3 Aggressive Tax Planning and Corporate Social Irresponsibility: Managerial discretion in the light of corporate governance   51
   Ave-Geidi Jallai and Hans Gribnau

4 Alternative Methods for Resolving Tax Disputes in Poland: The odds of success   87
   Hanna Filipczyk

5 How Effective is Islam on Tax Compliance Decisions of Muslims?   121
   Recep Yucedogru

6 The Role of Software Systems in Tax: An Empirical Evaluation   140
   Menno van Werkhoven, Reinout Kok and Felienne Hermans

7 The Role of Social Norms in Tax Compliance Decisions   160
   Riad Cheikh, Emer Mulligan and Breda Sweeney

8 Tax and Social Policy: The Case of the Irish Pension System   175
   Dinali Wijeratne, Emer Mulligan and Michelle Maher

9 The EU Notion of Abuse of Law and the Italian Tax Legal System: Towards an Enhanced Horizontal Interaction among National GAARs?   197
   Daniele de Carolis

10 The EU Directive against Tax Avoidance (ATAD-1)   210
   Marco Greggi

11 **Key Stakeholders' Perceptions of Introducing a General Anti-Avoidance Rule (GAAR) for Tackling Aggressive Tax Planning in Indonesia** 234
Niken Evi Suryani and Ken Devos

12 **Cooperative Compliance in Action: A UK/Dutch Comparison** 260
Dennis de Widt and Lynne Oats

List of Contributors

Lotta Björklund Larsen

Lotta Björklund Larsen is Associate Professor in social anthropology at the Department of Thematic studies: Technology and social change at Linköping University. She researches on tax compliance and avoidance applying a qualitative perspective and ethnographic methods paying special attention to societal changes. Her recent publications include *A Fair Share of Tax: A Fiscal Anthropology of Contemporary Sweden*. 2018 London: Palgrave Macmillan and *Shaping Taxpayers. Values in action at the Swedish Tax Agency*. 2017. Oxford – New York: Berghahn Books.

Riad Cheikh

Riad Cheikh is a 4th year PhD student at the J.E Cairnes School of Business and Economics, National University of Ireland (NUI), Galway, Ireland. He was awarded a Bachelor in Management from Ecole des Hautes Etudes Commerciales (HEC), Algeria in 2008, and a Master in Finance from University of Dundee, Scotland. His area of interest is tax compliance; and more specifically he is interested in the role of tax morale in enhancing the tax compliance behaviour of taxpayers.

Daniele de Carolis

Daniele de Carolis received his PhD from the School of International Studies of the University of Trento in March 2010. He also holds an LLB from the University of Milan and an LLM in International and European Law from the University of Aberdeen. Currently employed at the Legal Department of the Italian Revenue Agency, he is carrying out the post-doctoral research project "Improving and Developing the Dispute Resolution Procedure under the European Arbitration Convention on Transfer Pricing" at the International Max Planck Research School on Successful Dispute Resolution in International Law.

Dennis de Widt

Dennis de Widt is a Lecturer in Accounting & Finance at Cardiff Business School, which he joined in August 2017. After graduating from Leiden University, the Netherlands, he worked as a Junior Researcher at the Centre for Public Sector Reform at Leiden University. He moved to the UK in 2011 to conduct his PhD at Queen Mary College, University of London, conducting a European comparative study of the impact of intergovernmental financial structures on local government debt. Subsequently, he worked as a Postdoctoral Researcher at the University of Exeter Business School where his EU funded research focused on tax compliance initiatives for large businesses. Dennis continues to be involved as an Associate Research Fellow with the ESRC/HMRC/HMT funded Tax Administration Research Centre (TARC) at the University of Exeter Business School. Dennis' research in the areas of public sector finances and accounting is characterised by a strong interdisciplinary, and often international comparative approach.

Ken Devos

Dr Ken Devos is an Associate Professor in the Faculty of Business and Law at Swinburne University, Australia. Ken has worked in academia since 1998 after 11 years at the Australian Taxation Office. He completed his PhD in taxation at Monash University, has published in both Australian and overseas tax journals and presented numerous conference papers on taxation issues. Ken is a member of the Australasian Tax Teachers Association and CPA Australia. He has presented seminars on behalf of CPA Australia and is one of the authors in the CPA Tax Program. Ken is also a member of the Taxation Law and Policy Research Institute and is represented on the editorial board of the New Zealand Journal of Taxation Law and Policy. Ken's areas of teaching include taxation law and business taxation at an undergraduate level and workplace taxation at a post graduate level. His research and supervision interests include taxpayer compliance behaviour, tax policy and reform, tax simplification, and administration. Ken received an external research grant from Taxpayers Australia and was awarded a Faculty Prize for the best research poster in relation to his doctoral research.

Hanna Filipczyk

Hanna Filipczyk is a post-doctoral researcher; a collaborator of the Centre of Fiscal Studies at the Nicolaus Copernicus University in Toruń, Poland; a member of the Committee for Codification of the General Tax Law; and a tax advisor at Enodo Advisors. Hanna is a law and philosophy graduate from the Nicolaus Copernicus University in Toruń. She completed Postgraduate Studies on Negotiation, Mediation and Other Alternative Dispute Resolution Methods at the Law Faculty of the University of Warsaw, and holds a PhD in law from the Nicolaus Copernicus University in Toruń. Hanna specialises in the general aspects of tax liabilities, tax proceedings, tax and fiscal control, and proceedings before the administrative courts in tax matters (tax litigation).

Marco Greggi

Marco Greggi is a Full Professor of Tax Law and International Tax Law at the University of Ferrara, Department of Law. He was admitted to the Italian Bar, is a Member of the scientific board of the Review *Novità Fiscali* (Lugano, Switzerland) and of the Editorial board of *European Tax Studies* (Bologna, Italy), he is external advisor to the Tax Court of Appeal of Bologna (Italy). He has been an invited guest and speaker at a number of seminars and conferences across the world, including Australia, Russia, Hong Kong, Brazil, Iran, Korea, Liechtenstein, Switzerland, Israel and many others.

Hans Gribnau

Hans Gribnau is a Professor of Tax Law at the Fiscal Institute and the Centre for Company Law of Tilburg University and at Leiden University. In 2007 he received the Jan Giele-award for his 'substantial contribution to just taxation in the Netherlands'. In 2013 he was visiting professor at Antwerp University. He is currently the chair of the Dutch Spinoza association ('Vereniging Het Spinozahuis'). He is member of the jury of the VBDO-Tax Transparency Award. He teaches methodology of tax law, procedural tax law and research skills. His current research interests lie in the quality of tax regulation, the regulatory use of tax law, governance and tax ethics.

Felienne Hermans

Felienne Hermans is an assistant professor at Delft University of Technology. Her team at the Spreadsheet Lab works on making spreadsheets better by designing tools to test and improve them. One of Felienne's biggest passions in life is to share her enthusiasm for programming with others. Therefore she co-organises the yearly "Joy of Coding" conference in the Netherlands and teaches robotics at a community centre each Saturday. Her research interest focuses on applying software engineering methods outside of traditional textual programming.

Ave-Geidi Jallai

Ave-Geidi is a PhD researcher in the Department of Tax Law, Tilburg Law School. The topic of Ave's PhD research is 'Corporate Social Responsibility and Tax Avoidance - Does One Exclude the Other?' In her PhD project she analyses the challenges of globalisation on the use of law in the context of international business taxation. She is focusing on multinational corporations (MNCs) that claim to be socially responsible companies. In her research she studies theories and practices on tax avoidance, corporate governance, and corporate social responsibility (CSR), in order to develop a framework for socially responsible tax planning (as a soft law instrument).

Reinout Kok

Reinout Kok is professor of tax law at the Erasmus School of Law at the Erasmus University in Rotterdam. He specializes in the taxation of multinational enterprises.

Michelle Maher

Michelle is a Post-doctoral Researcher at the Irish Centre for Social Gerontology, National University of Ireland, Galway. Michelle completed a PhD in October 2016 on the politics of pensions in Ireland. Working within a power orientated theoretical framework that linked actors and ideas with an institutional analysis, an evaluation of half a century of pension policy was conducted. The hypothesis located a 'knowledge elite' within the institutional structures of pension policy-making, giving them privileged influence over policy. She is a member of the Pension Policy Research Group at Trinity College Dublin, the European Network for Research on Supplementary Pensions at the University of Munster, Germany and an affiliate researcher at the Pension Policy Center in Washington DC. Her research interests lie in the field of political sociology and include the Irish and international pension systems, pension policy, gender inequality, power in state – society relations and elite power.

Emer Mulligan

Dr Emer Mulligan is a lecturer in taxation and finance and former Head of the J.E. Cairnes School of Business & Economics at the National University of Ireland Galway. She is a Fulbright/CRH scholar, and has published in international peer reviewed journals including *Accounting, Organisations and Society*, *Critical Perspectives on Accounting* and *Advances in Taxation*. She is an International Fellow at the University of Exeter's Tax Administration Research Centre, a member of the Editorial Boards of the *Journal of Tax Administration*, and *Advances In Taxation*. Emer currently leads a research project entitled *European Pension Policies and Intergenerational Fiscal Sustainability, Fairness, and Consolidation*, which is part of an EU H2020 funded project. Prior to joining academia, Emer was a tax manager at PWC, Dublin, Ireland.

Lynne Oats

Lynne Oats is Professor of Taxation and Accounting, University of Exeter Business School, Co-Director of the Tax Administration Research Centre, UK. Lynne's research interests centre on taxation as a social and institutional practice, embracing historical and contemporary tax policy both nationally and internationally. She has a particular interest in new initiatives in relations between large corporate taxpayers, tax advisers and tax authorities and is part of an EU funded research consortium, FairTax. Lynne plays an active role in the tax academic community and has recently been appointed as a Commissioner on the Charity Tax Commission. Lynne is Managing Editor of *Journal of Tax Administration*, Assistant Editor (Accounting) of *British Tax Review*, and has published widely in the accounting and taxation fields. She is co-author of Taxation Policy and Practice, Principles of International Taxation and Accounting Principles for Tax Purposes. Lynne's 2012 edited book Taxation: A Fieldwork Research Handbook contains contributions from tax scholars from across the globe.

Niken Evi Suryani

Niken Evi Suryani is PhD Candidate at the Department of Business Law and Taxation, Faculty of Business and Economics, Monash University, Australia. She was awarded a Bachelor in Accounting from State College of Accounting, Indonesia, and a Master in Accounting from University of Indonesia. Her thesis is entitled 'General Anti-Avoidance Rule (GAAR): An Option to Tackle Aggressive Tax Planning in Indonesia'.

Breda Sweeney

Breda Sweeney in Personal Professor in the Discipline of Accountancy & Finance at the J.E. Cairnes School of Business and Economics, NUI Galway. She is a Fellow of Chartered Accountants Ireland, having professionally trained in PricewaterhouseCoopers in Dublin and Sydney. She is currently a member of Governing Authority in NUI Galway and Head of Discipline of Accountancy & Finance. Breda's research is in the field of performance management. Specifically, she has focused on the role of management control systems in enabling innovation and organisational ambidexterity and in managing organisational tensions. She has also examined the responses of individuals to pressures induced by management control systems. Her research studies have investigated these issues in a number of different contexts including audit firms, medical device companies and green energy construction companies. She has published widely in these areas in international accounting and business journals.

Menno van Werkhoven

Menno is doing part-time PhD research at Erasmus School of Law, department of Tax Law supported by the Delft University of Technology, on the topic of Tax Technology and its use within MNEs. In addition Menno performs the function of Director of Sales and Strategic Alliances at TaxModel in Den Bosch, the Netherlands, a company focussed on providing Tax Technology focussed solutions.

Dinali Wijeratne

Dinali Wijeratne is a Post-doctoral Researcher at the Irish Centre for Social Gerontology, National University of Ireland, Galway. She holds PhD in Economics from National University of Ireland, Galway, a Bachelor of Commerce from Kelaniya University, and an MBA from Colombo University, Sri Lanka. She is a member of the Association for Accounting Technicians (MAAT), and is a finalist (ACA) of the Institute of Chartered Accountants of Sri Lanka. Prior to taking up PhD studies at NUI Galway, she was a senior lecturer in the Department of Commerce and Financial Management in Kelaniya University, Sri Lanka. She is a member of the Irish Economic Association (IEA), Pension Policy Research Group (PPRG) at Trinity College Dublin, The European Network for Research on Supplementary Pensions (ENRSP) and working group member of the EU COST Action on Gender and Health Implications of Extended Working Life Policies.

Recep Yucedogru

Recep Yucedogru is Assistant Professor at Bulent Ecevit University, Turkey. He holds an MA in Fiscal Law, BA in Public Finance, and was awarded with his PhD in 2016 from the University of Nottingham on the topic of 'Understanding tax morale and tax compliance of owner-managers of small companies'. Recep's research is in the field of tax compliance. Specifically, he has focused on the role of tax morale on tax compliance behaviour. He has also examined influence of Religiosity on tax compliance behaviour of both corporate and individual taxpayers.

1 Contemporary Issues in Taxation Research: An Overview

Emer Mulligan and Lynne Oats

The chapters in this collection are based on papers presented at the 24th Annual Conference of the Tax Research Network (TRN) held at Hull University in September 2015, and the 25th Annual Conference of the TRN, held at Roehampton University in September 2016. The conferences were sponsored by the Chartered Institute of Taxation and the Centre for Business Performance of the Institute of Chartered Accountants in England and Wales.

The TRN is an interdisciplinary group of academics and practitioners from the UK and elsewhere with a shared commitment to pursuing and furthering academic research in taxation. The TRN held its first conference in 1991 and since then has gone from strength to strength, attracting scholars from all over the world and now incorporating a special workshop for early career academics as part of the commitment to capacity building.

Recent developments in the EU and elsewhere, continue to raise the profile of tax issues significantly, and in the case of the UK this has brought to the surface concerns about underinvestment in tax as an area of academic research. This volume serves as another reminder that tax research is, in fact, alive and well, if unfortunately, often lacking in visibility. The diversity of the topics covered in the ensuing chapters, including contributions by some early stage researchers and doctoral students is testament to a vibrant community of scholarship with wide ranging interests and approaches to research.

The chapters provide valuable insights into the rich diversity of contemporary tax research. They draw on a variety of perspectives including law, anthropology, social and public policy. Contributions come from a rich mix of scholars ranging from doctoral students through to more experienced tax researchers and cover a range of themes including taxpayer compliance, tax administration for large businesses, tax avoidance and tax policy. Contributions from a number of doctoral students are particularly welcome. This volume provides insights and inspiration for aspiring and experienced tax researchers and policy professionals alike.

Whilst this volume presents research and asks interesting questions across a broad range of tax matters, and the chapters are not thematically presented, a number of overlaps and connections between chapters are noteworthy:

- Two chapters (*Björklund Larsen, de Widt & Oats*) address Cooperative Compliance initiatives as introduced in various countries by tax authorities in an effort to improve how they deal with large businesses.
- The factors which influence individual tax compliance behaviour are considered both theoretically, focussing on the role of social norms (*Cheikh et al.*) and empirically focussing on the effect of religion (*Yucedogru*).
- Perhaps unsurprisingly, in the context of the ongoing challenge of dealing with international tax avoidance and evasion, two chapters (*Greggi* and *de Carolis*) look at the interface of EU law with domestic tax rules, focussing on anti-avoidance/anti abuse legislation in particular, and both authors examine the Italian case, with *de Carolis* also referencing the UK situation.
- Staying with the theme of anti-avoidance legislation, *Evi Suryani* and *Devos* explore the potential for introducing GAAR in Indonesia.
- Interestingly, the remaining chapters consider the interface and integration of tax with other areas of policy and practice, such as CSR (*Jallai* and *Gribnau*), alternative dispute resolution methods, (*Filipczyk*), technology in the working lives of tax executives (*van Werkhoven et al.*), and social policy (*Wijeratne et al.*). Such studies go some way perhaps to further lifting the lid of the black box of taxation.

The following overview gives a flavour of the content of each of the ensuing chapters.

Lotta Björklund Larsen examines a Cooperative Compliance initiative introduced by the Swedish Tax Agency in 2011 – an enhanced collaboration project – which notwithstanding being re-launched in 2014, was subsequently put 'on hold'. Whilst similar projects have been introduced in various countries with a view to improving how tax authorities engage with and manage large corporates, with some claiming success, this paper provides interesting insights and perspectives on the Swedish experience. The study presented here applies an ethnographic approach, and following in-depth data collection and analysis, suggests eight concepts that made this attempt at Swedish collaboration/cooperation between large taxpayers and the tax agency problematic.

Ave-Geidi Jallai and Hans Gribnau adopt an interdisciplinary approach, to explore the possibility of integrating tax with corporate social responsibility, by combining insights from corporate law, taxation, and applied business ethics. Drawing on both shareholder and stakeholder theories of corporations, they argue that corporate directors enjoy sufficient discretion for making socially responsible decisions, with both theories allowing managers a choice to act with an interest beyond shareholder value maximisation, thereby avoiding corporate social irresponsibility.

Hanna Filipczyk highlights the difficulties of integrating alternative dispute resolution methods into the Polish tax procedure, focussing on the "Directional Assumptions of the New Tax Ordinance" adopted by its government in 2015. The author explains policy problems dealt with along the way to adopting the proposal, discusses normative objections that have been raised by stakeholders against the proposal, and points to possible practical difficulties which can hamper its implementation and operation. This chapter arguably offers the reader an opportunity to critically reflect on their own attitudes towards "negotiating taxes", when confronted with objections coming from the tradition of legal formalism, and on prospects for cross-fertilisation of differing legal cultures.

Recep Yucedogru presents a study which examines the effect of religion, Islam in this case, on tax compliance decisions. A qualitative research approach was adopted by the author, who conducted interviews with SME owner-managers in Turkey. Findings shed light on critical issues for Muslim taxpayers including effects of their Islamic stance on tax compliance; rightful due concerns of tax evasion behaviour; comparison of Zakat with taxes; and the intervention of Islamic scholars on the tax compliance decisions of Muslims.

Menno van Werkhoven, Reinout Kok and Felienne Hermans present findings from their study on how IT is used in practice by tax professionals – non-IT technical specialists. This study is set against a context of the increasing role of technology in the lives of professionals. The focus is on the perspectives of tax professionals employed by multinationals. Evidence is presented from semi-structured interviews on educational background and experience with IT, daily usage of IT programs, and issues with IT experienced by these professionals. Educational requirements from an IT perspective are also discussed.

Riad Cheikh, Emer Mulligan and Breda Sweeney address the importance of the role of social norms in tax compliance decision making at the individual level. They argue that tax authorities are required to go beyond the traditional approach of ensuring tax compliance through enforcement and deterrence systems. In the absence of a consensus regarding the precise definition of social norms, or how to operationalise these norms in tax compliance studies, this chapter examines the definition and underlying dimensions of social norms by presenting a review of the relevant literature on the theory of social norms and on ethical behaviour (specifically moral intensity). By drawing together these different strands of literature, the authors unpack the dimensions of social norms and their role in tax compliance decision making and identify the need for further research in this area.

Dinali Wijeratne, Emer Mulligan and *Michelle Maher,* in light of increasing pressure on pension systems across the globe, take a timely look at pension systems, focussing on how taxation and social policy are interlinked. Drawing on the trajectory of pension reform in Ireland, insights are provided on the gendered impact of the current pensions system and current drivers of reform, which include sustainability, coverage, the European Union, as well as concerns over security of income. The emerging trend of governments moving towards encouraging individual responsibility for income security in old age via private saving is highlighted. The authors set the stage here for future research in this area, to include evaluating the appropriateness, role, and effectiveness of tax reliefs as used in the pensions context.

Daniele de Carolis posits how the metaphor of 'reverberation' can effectively be used to explain the impact of the EU notion of abuse of law on the Italian tax legal system and the horizontal interaction of this latter system with other Member States' legislations. Specifically, the author attempts a comparison between Italian and English anti-abuse provisions to demonstrate an example of possible horizontal interaction between the two national systems.

Marco Greggi, in the context of the struggle against international tax avoidance and evasion, examines the EU Directive against Tax Avoidance (ATAD-1), comparing the solutions adopted by the EU in the Directive with the domestic provisions already in force in some member states, including Italy and the UK. Such domestic provisions include General Anti-Abuse Rules and Diverted profits Tax. Whilst this comparative analysis points to uncertainty around compatibility of DPT with OECD recommendations and EU law, the national GAARs looked at appear to already be compliant with the new European standards. In the latter case, however, the author argues the influence of EU law will be essential in terms of interpretation of the rules, and the widening or narrowing of its scope, together with the need to counterbalance the power of the tax administration with the protection of the fundamental rights of the taxpayer, rights that some administrations are reluctant to grant while making use of GAARs.

Niken Evi Suryani and *Ken Devos* address the issue of whether a General Anti-Avoidance Rule (GAAR) should be introduced in tackling aggressive tax planning in Indonesia. Prior studies have concluded that the Specific Anti-Avoidance Rules (SAARs) in Indonesia have been inadequate in dealing with inappropriate tax-related practices. The authors employed a qualitative research methodology carrying out interviews with key informants from the Indonesian tax authority, Tax Court judges, taxpayers, and tax advisors, and argue their evidence supports the introduction of GAAR in Indonesia.

Dennis de Widt and *Lynne Oats* also address Cooperative Compliance (CC) initiatives and in this chapter provide a UK/Dutch comparison. Whilst there is no universal cooperative compliance model, they identify common features across different cooperative compliance initiatives introduced in various countries, in the areas of risk assessment procedures, real-time working, and the spirit of mutual understanding. An historical perspective on the development of these initiatives across various countries and the role of institutional players such as the OECD and IFA in this trajectory is provided and this comparative study is set and analysed in this context. Interesting questions are raised here about looking at CC as risk-based regulation. At a time when large corporates are increasingly under public scrutiny, the role, viability and benefits of CC initiatives needs further consideration.

Whilst the chapters demonstrate methodological diversity, the increasing use of qualitative methodologies, including interviews in particular, is notable. As with previous volumes the geographical spread of the work presented here continues to underscore how the TRN brings together tax scholars from around the world: Italy, The Netherlands, Sweden, Ireland, Poland, Indonesia, Turkey, Algeria and the UK.

We hope that these chapters will serve as inspiration for future research work. We must continue to celebrate, and make visible, the rich and diverse perspectives that can be brought to bear on tax issues, particularly in light of growing public interest in tax matters.

Finally, we would like to acknowledge and thank the contributors of these chapters for their commitment to this volume and for the patience they have shown in its preparation and publication.

Emer Mulligan and Lynne Oats

2 Sweden: Failure of a Cooperative Compliance Project?

Lotta Björklund Larsen

Abstract

This chapter outlines the Swedish cooperative compliance project *Fördjupad samverkan* - FS (enhanced collaboration) - introduced in 2011, and the modified initiative re-launched as *Fördjupad dialog* - FD (enhanced dialogue) - in 2014. It describes how the Swedish Tax Agency proposed the initiative that incorporated international success stories from similar projects; however, in the Swedish version and context it met with strong resistance and is now on hold awaiting proposed changes in the law. The study is performed from a qualitative research perspective, drawing on interpretive taxation methods in analysing relevant information.

Following a chronological trajectory implementing the cooperative compliance projects, issues are teased out that impact tax compliance among large corporations, tax advisers, the Swedish Tax Agency and other stakeholders in Swedish society. These issues make up eight aspects that require attention when implementing cooperative compliance initiatives that work for all stakeholders. Such aspects seldom stand alone, but are drawn upon in various combinations, thus making criticism possible in the Swedish case.

Keywords: Cooperative compliance; taxation in practice; Sweden; qualitative tax research methods; tax compliance; regulation of tax

Introduction

This chapter describes one Swedish initiative to engage proactively with large corporate taxpayers in so-called 'cooperative compliance' projects. FS (*Fördjupad Samverkan*) was initiated by SKV (*Skatteverket* or the Swedish Tax Agency) and transformed into FD (*Fördjupad dialog*) which for various reasons has been put almost entirely on hold. The focus of this chapter is on the launch of FS and what can be learned from the process regarding the implementation of cooperative compliance initiatives. It identifies key concepts that made this initiative problematic in Sweden, and it argues that these concepts are important to consider when successfully implementing a cooperative compliance initiative. FS/FD is a highly contested and a very political issue in the tax arena in Swedish society. This should be kept in mind when hearing differing opinions. These opinions are often supported by legal arguments (cf. Hambre, forthcoming), especially from those who are against such initiatives, but as will be shown in this chapter, there are many other types of concern.

The emphasis of this chapter is on the empirical content. It consists of four separate sections, and is organised as follows:

The first section describes the material and the analytical perspective on which this chapter is based.

Second follows a chronological outline of events: the start and development of FS, what prompted the change into FD, followed by its demise. Throughout this story, surges of opinions, arguments and proposed ways of working, as well as issues, have made this way of working problematic in Sweden. The unfolding and order of events had an impact on how FS was received and thus on its apparent failure.

The third section illustrates the ways of working of the few corporations that came into existence both from the corporations' point of view as well as from those of SKV and other stakeholders.

The chapter concludes by suggesting eight concepts that may have made the Swedish collaboration/cooperation between large taxpayers and the tax agency problematic. These concepts will be related to other research on tax compliance among large corporations elsewhere.

Names and genders of interviewees are anonymised in the chapter. For pedagogical reasons, issues that contribute to the concepts at stake for cooperative compliance initiatives are emphasised.

Method and Material

This project approaches cooperative compliance initiatives from a qualitative research perspective, more specifically drawing on interpretive taxation methods in analysing relevant information. Interpretive taxation methods mean that I approach taxation as an organisational, institutional, social and cultural phenomenon (Boden et al., 2010; Oats, 2012). This qualitative and holistic approach is well suited to addressing and understanding the complex unfolding of events and manifold issues that made FS/FD unsuccessful in Sweden, in contrast to many other places where cooperative compliance projects are working. More specifically, the research is conducted with an ethnographic focus in order to understand the views and actions of all stakeholders.

Applying an ethnographic focus means studying an issue from the point of view of the subjects who are participating. Various methods, often jointly, can be used but at the core is an ethnographic analysis often based on participant observation. The original aim was to participate in meetings between corporations and SKV; but due to the sensitive nature of FS/FD, this was not deemed possible. This analysis relies instead on an ethnographic reading of documents (Riles, 2011; Björklund Larsen, 2015) and on ethnographic interviews (Davies, 1999). An ethnography of taxation practices has been described in detail elsewhere (Boll, 2012, 2014; Björklund Larsen 2017); however it is important to underline the following points when performing interpretative research with an ethnographic gaze on such a contested issue.

The documents collected have been read and interpreted with the aim of understanding the views the authors propose (Björklund Larsen, 2015, p.80), and an apprehension for their analytical concerns (Riles, 2006). Many of the documents are authored by legal scholars and thus propose reasoning within the realm of the law, yet quite a few of these simultaneously voice a specific – often negative – opinion on FS/FD. Media materials are written with another focus (e.g. news-worthiness and sometimes staging confrontations), while the SKV intranet articles inform (on) its employees' views, yet often conclude according to SKV strategies (supporting FS/FD).

The interviews were more or less formal, mainly taking place as conversations (cf. Spradley, 1979, p.58) in a casual and explorative tone (Fangen, 2005; Kvale 1997, p.94). I tried to stimulate the discussion (Wästerfors, 2004, p.20) using an increasingly intuitive knowledge for follow-up questions (cf. Flyvbjerg, 2001, p.21 citing Dreyfus & Dreyfus, 1986; Kvale, 1997, p.102). I have posed questions, but also discussed issues at length trying to probe into this delicate and manifold matter. Some of the interviewees have been contacted several times.

The materials used for this chapter are therefore interviews with various stakeholders: with employees working with this issue at SKV, at the Confederation of Swedish Enterprise, and with financial officers/managers at corporations that participated or had declined to participate in FS/FD.

There was unfortunately only one participating corporation that agreed to be interviewed – mainly due to the fact that the initiative slowly stalled to a halt during the fieldwork. The documents come from a variety of sources: academic articles, newspaper articles, reports, correspondence made public, legal [court] decisions and a selection of SKV's intranet articles. Some materials have been provided by SKV, and others by the Confederation of Swedish Enterprises, but most have been collected by the researcher where the criterion was that it addressed FS or FD.

Table 2.1: Material

Material	Quantity
Interviews: Swedish Tax Agency employees Anna, Bertil, Carl, Daniel, Eva, Fredrik	6
Group interview: Swedish Tax Agency contact persons (5 participants)	1
Interviews: Non-participating corporations Gustav, Helen, Ivar and Jane	3
Interview: Participating corporation Kristian	1
Interview: Other stakeholders Lars, Marianne, Niklas, Ola	4
Media material	18
Articles, reports and presentations	22
SKV intranet articles	14

Note: Names and genders of interviewees are anonymised.

It was evident from the start that both FS and its successor FD were highly contested projects and thus a political issue in the tax arena in Swedish society. Although an ethnographic approach means taking all participant positions and views seriously, stakeholder agendas have to be kept in mind when interpreting the different material. These 'positionings' can take place at all levels: arguing for the good of society; taking a stance inside organisations; being the result of inter-organisational politics and/or competitions; and even illustrating personal relations among stakeholders. It is thus essential to note who draws which issues into the limelight and who voices which opinions. I make this caveat not to demean or agree with any stakeholder position; the aim here is to account for all issues that had an impact on how this particular cooperative compliance initiative played out in Sweden.

Researchers risk being used as a megaphone for stakeholder positions. As will be shown, this is not simply a story of FS/FD proponents among initiators and tax collectors (at SKV) on one hand, and opponents among corporations, taxpayers and their interest organisations (a noteworthy example is the Confederation of Swedish Enterprises) on the other. The Swedish cooperative compliance project presents a more complex, and in my view, more interesting mix of arguments from various perspectives which can help us shed more light on why certain cooperative compliance projects are successful and others less so.

The chronological outline of events addresses opinions, intentions and proposed ways of working. These opinions are often supported by legal argument, especially from those who are against such initiatives, but as will be argued in the following, there are many other types of concerns.

Background: The Transition from FS to FD

Reasons to Create FS

Fördjupad Samverkan, FS – literally meaning 'enhanced collaboration'[1] – is at SKV referred to as 'cooperative compliance'[2] following the contemporary international OECD (Organisation for Economic Cooperation and Development) and IFA (International Fiscal Association) discourse[3]. FS was launched in 2011 and was an initiative that has been in the making since at least 2008[4]. There exist various accounts of how it came about; these stories do overlap

---

1 Samverkan can be translated in several ways. To cooperate is 'to work jointly towards the same end' or to 'assist someone or comply with their requests' whereas to collaborate is 'to work jointly on an activity or project' or 'to cooperate traitorously with an enemy' (Oxford English Dictionary (OED)). I will in the following refer to collaborate when discussing FS and cooperate when discussing FD, noting the slightly larger distance in the latter way of working together.

2 Intranet article 4.3.2011.

3 Proposed by OECD's Forum on Tax Administration, these initiatives were initially referred to as 'Enhanced Relationships' when proposed in 2008 (OECD, 2008). The name was chosen to distinguish this way of working from the traditional obligation based relationship. Due to changing compliance risk evaluations by tax agencies, tax control frameworks developed by MNEs as well as a critique that an enhanced relationship could imply improper facets and unequal treatment in practice, it was proposed to change the term to cooperative compliance. The latter was deemed to emphasise the goal of compliance: paying the right tax at the right time (OECD, 2013).

4 There were many different views on when the FS initiative started. Most interviewees recall the start to be 2010, yet 2008b is mentioned in one interview (14.4.2015). The diverse recollections are probably influenced by where and at what level you work in at SKV. The active start however took place in 2010 when two employees returned from a trip where they had been inspired by the Dutch working with 'Horizontal Monitoring'.

but in different ways have an impact on how FS was received by stakeholders:

- FS came about as part of overall strategy change at SKV.
- FS was the result of developing a classification model of risky taxpayers (corporations).
- FS fitted well with ideas about finding ways to increase efficiency.
- FS was a response to the international development of new compliance strategies.

SKV changed strategies during the 2000s (Wittberg, 2005). These are described in the publication *Right from the Start*, where it was argued that SKV would, from then onwards, work proactively with the aim of collecting the correct, not necessarily the maximum, tax from all taxpayers and in this way increase trust. These strategies[5] were based on international research and followed a trend of working together with taxpayers to ensure that information, taxes and fees were to the largest extent correct and as timely as possible. Additionally, trust in the tax collector depended on the attitude it has towards taxpayers (Wittberg, 2005, p.6). Trust and compliance were described as reinforcing each other; trust would increase if all taxpayers were deemed to comply.

While this work went on, SKV also ran a large project where the aim was to identify massive tax planning on the fringes of licit behaviour among larger corporations.[6] The project aimed to classify corporations based on risk evaluations, especially focusing on corporations active in tax planning schemes. Inspired by the UK's Her Majesty's Revenue and Customs' (HMRC) and the Australian Taxation Office's (ATO) work with classifications of risky taxpayers, Swedish corporations were to be divided into three different groups of taxpayers where audits and control measures were applied according to 'riskiness'. It was a challenging project as SKV auditors at the time often described the relationship with corporations as a cat and mouse game; SKV and corporations were seen as opponents. These older strategies did not provide tools for SKV auditors either to develop or ameliorate the relationship with corporate taxpayers and the project was therefore abandoned.

In the constant demand to find more efficient and cost-saving ways of working, FS was argued to be just such a solution both for corporations and for SKV. Participating in FS would provide a quicker response time for questions posed; there would be less uncertainty in tax positions as questionable

---

5   Interview 14.1.2016.
6   Interview 14.1.2016. It was the so-called SPA, *skatteplaneringsaktiva*, project.

tax issues would be resolved before reporting; and there would be fewer issues to be decided in court. At SKV this way of working with corporations was argued to release more resources, which could be concentrated on fighting taxpayers deemed much more risky. In short it was seen as a modern and more efficient way of building relationships between large corporations and SKV. Yet the administration held internal critiques who voiced the opinion that SKV outsourced control to those who were supposed to be controlled. They questioned the efficiency aspect more broadly; what might be gained in the short term by being cost-effective and shorten response time for questionable tax issues, would be lost in the longer term with corporations' decreased compliance.

Finally, FS was a response to the international trend of new compliance strategies – working proactively with taxpayers to ensure that information, taxes and fees were to the largest extent correct as early as possible in the taxation process. More explicitly the OECD's Forum on Tax Administration had for some years advocated so-called 'Enhanced Relationship' projects to take place among its member states' tax administrations. The 2007 financial crisis and the calls for diverse regulations that came about in its aftermath underlined the need for more control of corporations – which also came to include a tax perspective. The OECD and other organisations such as IFA and Fiscalis (an EU programme where national tax administrations exchange information and expertise) held conferences where this way of working was discussed. A number of reports describing such projects and national experiences were authored (IFA, 2012; OECD, 2008, 2010, 2013, 2014). Member states' tax administrations were encouraged to start such initiatives and report on their *experiences*. SKV was of course also interested and visited, for example, the Netherlands and Ireland to learn from respective national tax administrations work with Enhanced Relationship. Most FS inspiration is said to come from the internationally acclaimed and 'well marketed' Dutch experience of 'Horizontal Monitoring'[7]. As Bertil, an SKV employee, said: "All of a sudden ;everybody; organised conferences on this new topic". Even among tax administrations there is a certain level of competition and no one wants to be seen to be left behind.

These ideas contributed to forming the FS project and are also reasons for why it was, in many stakeholders' opinions, too hastily launched. On all four accounts this cooperative compliance initiative was a sign of the times.

---

7   Representatives from the Dutch Tax Authority also visited SKV in 2010 and presented their views on cooperative compliance and what was described as their success with it.

Introducing and applying this working method was seen as being at the cutting edge of compliance issues; it was a beacon of modernity that was hard to avoid for a modern and successful tax administration (cf. Ekonomistyrningsverket, 2012; Skatteverket, 2012).

SKV's mixed messages about FS

The years 2010–11 were quite hectic for *Storföretagsregionen*, the Department of Large Corporations at SKV, as it prepared for the launch of FS. A group of employees authored a report on how FS would work, planned for the media launch, and conducted information meetings with a selected number of Sweden's largest corporations as a preparation to inviting them to participate. Information about the project was communicated on several occasions on SKV's intranet.

The broader business community was introduced to FS in early March 2011 in an article in *Dagens industri*, Sweden's pink business journal, signed by SKV's Director General and by the manager for the Department for Large Corporations.[8] In the article, they describe the background for developing FS being the result of SKV's increased focus on multinational corporations' risk taking and their internal control procedures in the aftermath of the financial crisis. It was argued that the management of such corporations had difficulties foreseeing tax risks that could potentially result in drawn-out legal processes and costly tax reassessments. FS was argued to be a new way of working; it was formalised cooperation where large corporations would get a specified contact at SKV. Yet, the details of FS cooperation were not yet teased out as SKV would be perceptive to the wishes of participating corporations. A few large corporations would be invited to participate at the end of 2011, a group that would be enlarged to eventually encompass all larger multinationals.[9] The intention of FS was thus a long-term commitment and both parties would sign a declaration of intent. These declarations would however not be legally binding.

The article describes ways of working within FS. SKV would be committed to appointing a specific contact person and to openly declaring its judgement of a corporation's tax risk, as well as proposing remedies to decrease tax risks. In addition, SKV would also use its knowledge and competence to ensure that the corporations' internal routines and control systems regarding tax issues were adequate. Participating corporations would on the other

---

8   Interview 7.3.2011.

9   How the large multinationals working in Sweden would be identified is a question in itself. Perhaps it is those with head offices in Sweden?

hand be expected to be open about their own judgement of taxation risks as well as to put difficult tax issues on the table at an early stage for discussion. In FS, SKV and the corporation would together make an inventory of internal procedures and control systems in order to make sure that correct information is delivered to SKV.

The article concluded that both SKV and participating corporations would benefit from FS. The corporation would lower taxation risks, costs and administrative burdens. The corporation could, through collaboration, prevent audits or other control measures that could lead to tax reassessments or drawn-out legal processes. FS would make sure that divergent opinions on tax issues became apparent at an early stage. For SKV it is beneficial to prevent errors instead of auditing and correcting them *a posteriori*. While cooperating with corporations in FS, SKV could be more efficient and use its control resources elsewhere.

At the same time as the publication of the article, SKV invited Sweden's largest corporations and the larger tax advisor firms to four information meetings about FS in Sweden's three largest cities[10]. In those well-attended meetings, where perhaps a total of 100 corporations participated, SKV outlined arguments for FS and how it was meant to work. SKV's presentation[11] described the new initiative as a development of the existing *Dialogen* (dialogue) project. Dialogen is a way for corporations to pose questions to SKV either by email or by phone. The advantages with Dialogen are said to be several: the corporations obtain SKV's view on issues from a tax perspective prior to making doubtful transactions; and the possibility of quickly solving unclear issues. Corporations seemed pleased with Dialogen and it has made taxation issues less insecure and more predictable with the result that there was growing trust in relations between SKV and corporations. But in the presentations it was argued that a greater number of questions with increased complexity had been posed within Dialogen and that many corporations responded with follow-up questions through this forum. SKV concluded that other measures were needed.

FS was thus introduced into the meetings based on these experiences. The arguments were basically the same as in the article, although the benefits for participating corporations were further specified. Participating corporations were said to be able to:

- secure their tax position
- increase efficiency in their handling of taxes and fees

---

10 One was held in Göteborg, one in Malmö and two in Stockholm.
11 Presentation 'Dialog och fördjupad samverkan', March 2011.

- be subject to fewer audits and other *a posteriori* controls
- have a specific contact person and thus just one 'entry' to SKV
- decrease compliance costs
- increase goodwill

The benefit for SKV would be to:

- reduce the risk of tax errors for a participating corporation
- reduce costs of handling taxes and fees from corporations
- increase resources handling taxpayers deemed posing larger risks of making tax errors
- have a positive effect on societal tax compliance (at large)

Before describing the practical details, SKV noted that participation in FS required:

- a will to participate
- trust
- openness

Following the four meetings, SKV's project leader felt that the response was quite positive although apprehensive.[12]

After the media launch and the debate that followed (see below) SKV published a report,[13] which described the context and background for this initiative, outlined the benefits of FS for both corporations and SKV[14] and issued a draft of how the collaboration would work in practice (Skatteverket, 2011).

In contrast to the article, the report is more explicit on SKV's strategies and how SKV intends to work with large corporations. Working with them does not always mean cooperating but also taking proper action with them. FS is described as a way of identifying that the correct measures would be taken towards the right corporations. For example, the report states that the aim is to decrease aggressive tax planning among all taxpayers. In addition to the earlier stated arguments of decreased tax risks and tax errors, FS would make possible an increased flow of information, transparency and thus trust between SKV and the participating corporations.

---

12 Interview 19.3.2015.
13 Dnr 480-698289-10/1211, published 31.3.2011., that is, three weeks after the article that started the media debate.
14 The report refers to SFR (*Storföretagsregionen*), but as it is part of SKV I will continue to use this term instead of SFR as the report states as having agency. SFR cannot act on its own account.

The report argued that large corporations[15], often referred to as MNEs, are of particular interest to SKV as they have considerable impact on the functionality of the tax system and their ways of working are often an inspiration for smaller corporations. Large corporations' fiscal contribution is important as they pay corporate tax and VAT. In addition, they have many employees and thus transfer large amounts of money consisting of social fees and preliminary individual income taxes. Corporations also face very real and complex issues over their international activities. It is thus difficult for them to foresee tax consequences. Based on these insights, SKV proposed two ways to address them – on one hand, to legally enforce a duty to provide information according to the so-called 'disclosure rules'; and on the other, to engage in voluntary cooperative compliance initiatives like FS. Such increased information exchanges between SKV and corporations, as well as between tax administrations across borders, would follow the OECD's recommendations.

SKV also recognized in this report that there are varied attitudes among corporations towards taxation and that they have different ways of tackling them. These attitudes and ways of working were incorporated in SKV's strategic classification model at the time, consisting of three categories of corporate taxpayers. The aim of the model was to intensify the control work where it is deemed most plausible to find taxpayers that engage in evasive tax planning and intentional errors. Group A consists of those who participate in FS and are thus willing to collaborate. Group B consists of corporations that do not want to collaborate or and are seen to pursue aggressive tax planning, *skatteupplägg*.[16] The B group of corporations would be subject to individual judgement and risk analysis. The remaining corporations, including A and B, would be grouped into C and thus subject to collective auditing. Corporations that do not participate would be treated as previously, yet the message in the report is somewhat contradictory as it could be read that if you do not collaborate, you would end up in group B (Skatteverket, 2011, p.7).

The implementation of FS would start with an invitation from SKV to a chosen corporation's board of directors or its top management. After initial meetings where expectations and preconditions would be discussed, discussions would continue to agree on how and in what timescale the corporation's tax handling and the minimization of risk would be addressed. The participating corporation and SKV would write and sign a declaration of intent. Although these declarations are not legally binding, the report argues

---

15   Report 480-698289-10 (Skatteverket 2011).
16   Note that it is not talked about here as aggressive tax planning.

that such a written statement underscores the will and commitment[17] for both parties. Any of them can at any time end such declaration of intent.

The declaration of intent would be the starting point for the practical work between the corporation's tax department and SKV's designated contact person(s). Cooperation can vary depending on the declaration of intent, but it is said that SKV would always supply help, and support the corporations' aim to declare and pay the right tax and fees. Therefore, the practical work outlined can mostly be described as future expectations from SKV's point of view[18].

SKV's report concludes that the FS concept was thoroughly looked into by SKV's legal department and that a definite clearance of the details would be completed before the actual launch. It was stated that FS is not contrary to the principle of equality or against uniform application of the law. All laws and tax rules apply to everybody and SKV, like other public authorities, adjusts its handling and measures depending on the subjects it serves, in this case large corporations. Thus, a need-based service can actually be a prerequisite for equal treatment, as different taxpayers are deemed to have different needs.

As a final point, SKV regarded a corporation's willingness to participate in FS/FD as a way of minimizing tax compliance risks. It was argued that to be a subject of audit or even worse, to be caught cheating with taxes, is bad for a corporation's trademark.[19]

The public debate for and against FS

Following these events, and especially SKV's article published in *Dagens industri,* a quite hectic and high-pitched media debate ensued in the same newspaper. SKV obviously defended FS, whereas representatives of the Confederation of Swedish Enterprises and several law professors argued against it or at least recommended putting the initiative on hold awaiting legal decisions. The arguments against the initiative were mainly from a legal perspective, yet I argue that the resistance displays underlying emotional currents that for various reasons deny closer relations between SKV and large corporations.

---

17   Report 480-698289-10 (Skatteverket 2011).

18   This will not be addressed here as the suggested cooperation in practice came to naught and was reformulated.

19   Interview 14.4.2015.

In the following excerpts from the media debate and from a few seminars where FS was discussed, issues deemed of importance for the development of FS into FD are emphasised.

'Should SKV be a buddy'[20] asked a heading rhetorically. In this first responding article, written by Professor of Law Robert Påhlsson, he questioned how well FS fitted with contemporary Swedish law, in particular concerning the issue of equal treatment before the law. Påhlsson situated FS as one among many of SKV's changing strategies over the years – the tension between control on the one hand and information to taxpayers on the other. The FS initiative was argued to be two sides of the same coin. An interesting viewpoint in this article is the articulation of underlying sentiments among stakeholders that hides behind the rational legal arguments proposed by opponents of FS. Påhlsson writes (author's translation):

> *I choose to interpret SKV's initiative seriously and not at all as an insidious or conspiratorial way to undermine economic discretion or entrepreneurship. Although there is always a risk when roles coincide; when an institution that should control and make difficult decisions also aims to be a buddy.*

The response from SKV came four days later with an article under the heading 'SKV does not aim to cheat corporations'.[21] In the article, the Director General and the head of Department for Large Corporations recognised Påhlsson's legal apprehensions, yet argued for the need to change ways of working at governmental bureaucracies in general. "Laws and taxation rules apply to all, yet bureaucracies have to adapt their service and administration to the users, in our case taxpayers, diverse needs". FS was described to be just one of many adaptations that SKV had undertaken in its change of strategies and ways of working, e.g.: information in different languages; information directed towards newly registered corporations; and e-services. Countering the argument of unequal treatment of taxpayers, SKV argued that on the contrary different services are a necessity so that the law can be applied equitably.

The FS proposal can thus also be seen in a wider context of SKV's ambition to change how the Swedish tax system should work in practice; that it should not only rest on the application of black letter law but be governed by the spirit of the law. The incumbent Director General, Ingemar Hansson, took the opportunity to expound this view three days later in yet another

---

20 Påhlsson 11.3.2011.
21 ansson & Landén 15.3.2011.

article, this time when he commented on the resignation by the chairman of one of Sweden's largest pension funds due to his tax planning scheme.[22]

Hansson argued that this case was just one example of changing the tax moral in Swedish society. Taxpayers in general are today less forgiving towards tax planning; to pay tax is to show a concern for the society in which the taxpayer works and operates. Tax policy ought therefore to be part of a corporation's ethical guidelines and thus of overall Corporate Social Responsibility (CSR). The Director General compared taxation to environmental issues, where many corporations have larger ambitions than just following the letter of the law; to be seen as not paying the right tax could diminish trust in a corporation and in its brand name. Participation in initiatives such as FS would therefore be a way for corporations to show societal responsibility and also minimise the risks that uncertainty in taxation issues pose.

The negative response to this proposal came promptly the next day.[23] In yet another article a representative of the Confederation for Swedish Enterprises argued that it is public law which should govern any rulings by bureaucracies as well as relations between bureaucracies and taxpayers. Nothing else. If there are doubts regarding interpretation it is up to the courts to decide. Therefore SKV's employees should not consult with taxpayers on issues of ethics and morals. If the law has flaws, it should be up to democratically elected politicians to change it.

Public debate then moved on from newspaper articles to live debates. The Confederation for Swedish Enterprises organised a seminar to discuss FS entitled: "SKV's invitation to large corporations – an offer you can't refuse" that took place end of May,[24] just two months after the launch of FS. It was a half-day event at its headquarters[25] and the list of speakers featured legal advisors, tax advisors, SKV's manager for the Department for Large Corporations as well as the head of SKV's legal department, the Confederation's tax experts, politicians and academics.

---

22 Hansson 18.5.2011. The Chairman of AMF (which is a pension fund jointly owned by the confederation of unions, LO, and employers, Confederation of Swedish Enterprises), Bertil Villard, had through his private company used a so-called Peru scheme. The revelation of this scheme made for his resignation from AMF. The Peru scheme was based on a bilateral tax agreement from the 1960s between Peru and Sweden that made it possible to transfer profits from a Swedish company to a Peruvian one. Profits transferred to Peru were only taxed at 4.1 per cent. In a decision by *Högsta Förvaltningsdomstolen*, Supreme Administrative Court, in March 2012, such profit transfers were ruled illegal. If the activity generating the profit had taken place in Sweden, taxation on such profits would take place there.

23 Nyquist 19.5.2011.

24 Interview 27.5.2011.

25 The event was entitled *Skatteverket inbjuder storföretagen – 'an offer you can't refuse'?*

Dagens industri commented on this seminar the following day in an editorial discussing the so-called softer aspects of the FS.[26] The editorial argued that cooperative compliance initiatives have to rest on a foundation of trust and that there ought to be more advantages than drawbacks in such cooperation (following the prerequisites for cooperative compliance initiatives). This seems, it was said, to be lacking for both SKV's and the Confederation of Swedish Enterprise's in the proposed FS. Referring to the OECD recommendation to consider the cultural, administrative and legal environment when putting such initiatives to work (OECD, 2010), it appeared there were a number of provisions applied in the Swedish context to this way of working. First, Sweden's legal constitution provides the right of public access to almost all documents, a fact that differs from many other OECD countries that have cooperative compliance initiatives. Second, commercial awareness, for example, at the Dutch tax administration[27] (seen as implementing a successful cooperative compliance project) is greater than at SKV. It has to be noted that this fact could be changed if FS took place and tax auditors learnt more about tax operations in large corporations. Finally, SKV needs to take an increasingly impartial role if it is to judge what ought to be subject to tax and what not. This impartiality seems difficult to connect with SKV's contemporary role as a judge of what the 'right tax' is.

The editorial suspected that SKV's intention with FS was to collect information about new tax planning schemes while offering a certification stamp with moral overtones for participating large corporations. SKV's motto of "providing one's fair share" does not apply to corporations, it was argued. The overarching aim for a corporation is to run a profitable business and to keep costs down, one of which is corporate tax. Compliance emphasis should be on personal income tax as this, in financial terms, provides a much larger source of income for the Swedish state than corporate tax.[28] The editorial's concluding message was for Swedish institutions to keep their traditional roles: laws are passed by the *riksdag*, parliament; courts should decide when taxpayers and tax collector do not agree; and SKV should fulfil its mission of collecting tax. Full stop. In summing up the editorial did quote a tax advisor who voiced the following advice for a better tax system:

---

26 Editorial, Dagens industri 28.5.2011.

27 The Dutch tax administration paid much attention to broadening its employees' skills while introducing horizontal monitoring. The focus was on the commercial structure of businesses beyond the tax function, and the commercial 'way of thinking' in general, but also on softer skills, such as how to interact with taxpayers in a friendlier, less hierarchical manner. They aimed to create a 'shift in mindset' which seems to have largely paid off, as proposed in interviews with Dennis de Widt 2015 and 2016 (oral communication).

28 Income tax provides for about 2/3 of all Swedish tax revenue.

Speed up the response time for advance rulings at skatterättsnämnden (a board organised under SKV but whose members are nominated by the government); reinforce the Ministry of Finance's tax department so that new laws can be set in motion; and continue with existing cooperative schemes that work (such as Dialogen) between SKV and corporate taxpayers.

The next public incident was the receipt of a letter addressed to SKV.[29] It was drafted by the Confederation of Swedish Enterprise and signed by tax managers, chief financial officers and other senior managers from 25 of Sweden's largest corporations.[30] Although the content is a compromise and the text is quite bland,[31] as the signers had different views on the initiative,[32] one cannot minimise the importance of this letter. It stated that although the corporations were pleased with services like Dialogen, which was said to increase trust in their relations with SKV, they had numerous concerns with the collaboration suggested in FS. Corporations were already required to report on many and diverse types of risk and also had an obligation to provide an increasingly large amount of information to SKV. The administrative burden had thus increased, although the result was that they also had good control over tax risks and were very transparent regarding those. If engaging with FS, the benefits of it had to correspond to the increased administrative burden AND legal risks, especially concerning the secrecy of information. In addition, the letter argued that the tax law environment in Sweden does not provide proper prerequisites for FS (here the reference was to the OECD report) and Swedish law limits this type of cooperation.

The letter ended with declining to even be invited to participate in FS – the letter's very purpose. Sweden's 25 largest corporations did not want to be part of FS and did not even want to have to consider it. Although it is not explicitly mentioned in the letter, it is noteworthy to recall SKV's previous work with the classification scheme for large corporations.

This letter ended the public debate and attention in the media petered out. During the autumn of 2011 and into 2012, SKV continued its work on how to pursue FS. Invitations were sent out but the corporations that had signed the letter were of course not considered; instead 12 other corporations were welcomed to an information meeting. These corporations had either showed interest or were among the largest remaining on SKV's original list.

---

29 The letter was written on the Confederation's letterhead and dated 6.7.2011.
30 Among the signatories were Atlas Copco, Electrolux, H&M, IKEA, Investor, Volvo.
31 Interview 24.3.2015.
32 Interview 24.3.2015.

Eight of these were willing to participate[33] and collaboration started in 2012. Most of the participants are said to be government owned corporations or cooperatives, with a few exceptions. Today however, there is just one collaboration active and this is for some very specific reasons (see below).

The Confederation of Swedish Enterprise had thus spearheaded the critique towards the cooperative compliance initiatives in Sweden and it was followed up with the report *Fördjupad samverkan/horizonal monitoring i svensk offentligrättslig miljö* (FS in the Swedish public legal environment), presented at yet another public seminar in 2012.

Robert Påhlsson, the law professor who early on participated in the public debate, had been commissioned by the confederation to investigate the legal status of FS. In the report, he compared the Dutch experience of Horizontal Monitoring with the plans for the Swedish variety. In essence he considered it a replica, yet there were noteworthy differences; especially FS was deemed more individualised yet also more contained. The report stated three main concerns (Påhlsson, 2012a):

- First, any participating corporation was asked to share information and inform on dubious tax issues beyond a corporation's legal obligations.
- Second, there was the issue of equal treatment before the law. Being selected to participate in FS meant a special, positive treatment of tax issues that could not be substantiated compared to other corporate taxpayers.
- Third, FS is not adapted to the principle of legality that governs Swedish administrative law. For example, agreements could be made behind closed doors and historical errors in previous tax returns would not be corrected within FS cooperation, something otherwise required. SKV could thus turn a blind eye for wrongdoing if not too evident.

Påhlsson concluded that SKV's proposed way of working with FS was not according to Swedish public governance tradition, as it did not follow the basic legal requirements within Swedish administrative law.[34] FS should therefore be redesigned and SKV ought to await the regulation of such cooperative initiatives into Swedish public law before continuing to develop and work with them.

---

33 Said in an interview to be zero, yet eight were reported to the Riksdag (Proposition 2013/14:1:8).

34 For the legal implications, see Påhlsson 2012a, 2012b, and on FD Hambre forthcoming.

The nail in the coffin for FS came when one person[35] challenged it, demanding information about participating corporations, referring to the principle of public access to official records, *offentlighetsprincipen*. He argued that this type of collaboration was more like counselling than having a specific relation to specific tax cases (which are excluded from public access). SKV denied this request and the case went to the Administrative Court of Appeal who ruled SKV to be correct (February 2013). The case was then taken to the Supreme Administrative Court, *Högsta förvaltningsdomstolen*, which ruled that SKV had to provide information about participating corporations. The information that can be publicly disclosed did not stop there; it was also ruled that details about issues handled were not secret if these did not refer to specific tax cases.[36] Given this ruling, one corporation did decide to withdraw (July 2013)[37]. "still cooperate on smaller issues with SKV, yet given these circumstances it is not good" said Helen, CFO at corporation B, who continued: "We would like to work in this manner, with a handshake as we do in many other countries we operate in but in this country it is quite messy."

Transforming FS to FD

All these events made SKV take the critique to heart and the initiative was redesigned. Instead of FS, FD[38] (*Fördjupad dialog*) was introduced with new guidelines published in March 2014. The FD guidelines were considerably shortened compared to those describing FS and cooperation ambitions were much lower key. The change of name displays the lesser ambition; it is now a dialogue instead of a collaboration, emphasising communication instead of working together. These guidelines describe two FD aims: to make corporations' provision of taxes and fees to be 'right from the start' and to address the need for increased and continuous communication between corporations and SKV.

Both parties can ask to start such cooperation but SKV decides if it will take place. It is underlined that both parties should see benefits with FD compared to the other ways SKV offers support to corporations. According to the guidelines for FD, a (big) change is that SKV cannot, within FD, demand material or information or make any other type of control such as

---

35 This person is referred to as a journalist by one person interviewed, as a corporate representative by another.
36 Interview 30.11.2015.
37 Interview 28.4.2015.
38 Interview 10.3.2014.

those discussed as a way of working within FS.[39] Instead SKV may account for its risk assessment of the corporation through questions, and help and support the corporation in its internal work so it can provide the right tax information at the right time. SKV also promises to help reduce the uncertainty of which taxes should be paid by giving precise and quick replies to questions.

The guidelines also state that the aim with FD is not to change faulty historical decisions but to direct future work. The corporation participates in FD on its own initiative, providing information about issues that might impact the possibility of fulfilling its tax-legal responsibility, which includes asking questions on how to ameliorate its internal tax systems and routines. All questions and answers within FD should be documented, but although the answers ought to be relevant, they are not legally binding. There are also other, more specific questions that are part of other regulations (e.g. about transfer pricing) but those cannot be addressed within FD. Finally, it is stated that SKV's contact person can only be appointed for four years at most. Both parties can end the cooperation at any time.

Yet the criticisms against such cooperation continued and no additional corporations have signed up since the launch of FD. As an illustration, the Confederation of Swedish Enterprise again commissioned law professors, in this case Ulf Bernitz and Jane Reichel, to make a similar examination of FD as had been made with FS.[40] Their report, published in June 2015, renews the critical stance towards cooperative compliance initiatives in Sweden (Bernitz & Reichel 2015).

The report concludes that SKV's new ways of working are different from the generally accepted public management model in Sweden. As the information exchanged between participating corporations and SKV is not subject to tax confidentiality (as ruled by the Supreme Administrative Court), this way of working ends up in an 'informal grey-zone', not previously encountered in Swedish administrative law. It is suggested that FS cannot be categorised by the Swedish administrative authority in the usual triangulation of activities, between the actual administration of issues, case handling,

---

[39] Guidelines for FS were never finalized, but there is a report (Skatteverket, 2014) describing the way of working. It was never specified that SKV would have the right to demand information from the corporation, yet the FS way of working meant that "SKV had to acquire a broad knowledge about the corporation and its conditions" (p.10) and that the cooperation would be based on "openness and trust where both parties would contribute with knowledge and information".

[40] Their report also addressed SKV's cooperation with FAR/SRS, an initiative that according to information at a meeting with SKV on 23.1.2015 has been phased out.

and the exercise of public authority towards subjects. The implication is that formal warranties of legal certainty are lacking. The proposed ways of working within FD would mean SKV departing from the traditional and ordinary roles of public authorities as stated in administrative law (Bernitz & Reichel, 2015). Noteworthy is the provocative usage of 'informal' and 'grey-zone'; wordings that are usually associated with tax avoidance and evasion.

The report thus also points out a number of other implications of FD that are not supported by the Swedish tradition of how public administrations work; it identified this method of cooperation as 'foreign'.

As Daniel, one of SKV's contact persons pointed out:

> *FS worked well for a while until the tax confidentiality issue surged. SKV had not done its homework properly[41] and especially had failed to clear the issue of what type of taxpayer information could be treated as confidential. We did not get the legal back-up that we should have had. In hindsight it would have been better if we had run a pilot on the project.*

Ways of working

This section describes the various stakeholders' views on how FS/FD works in practice. There are a handful of existing agreements in the FD cooperation arrangements (as of 2015),[42] yet some of those are dormant in practice. Both corporation Y and corporation Z have agreements in place and a (short) history of participation. They have not agreed to be interviewed so their views on the cooperation derive solely from SKV's contact persons. The only currently active agreement SKV has is with corporation X, a large Swedish nationally owned company going through very specific structural change. The information about this sole cooperation is based on interviews with corporation X's tax manager Kristian and with former or current contact persons at SKV.

What is the infrastructure/network for cooperation?

Z is a cooperatively owned corporation. Its core business activity has a very long-term focus, which is why it wanted to participate in FS. Z wanted SKV to take the initiative on the issues to be discussed. The original plan was to go through all types of taxes, one after another. There have consistently been three or four open issues and in total perhaps seven or eight have been

---

41 Interview 14.1.2016.

42 There are in all five different agreements signed, yet in reality there is only one really active cooperation, that with corporation X.

discussed, handled and closed. The issues were usually shared at a general level and specific details were seldom addressed. Z have agreed to almost all of SKV's proposals for solutions. For example, following a presentation from a specialist from the IT department, the accounting system was up for discussion. Another issue was the cooperative's shipping facility to which there are some very specific tax issues connected.

SKV and corporation Z decided from the start to have two proper meetings a year; one held before the summer vacation and the other before the annual closing of the accounts. Usually the attendees were SKV's one or two contact persons and one or two employees from Z. At special presentations, such as when the accounting system was under discussion, other people attended. According to SKV's contact person, Carl, it was beneficial to discuss the corporation's situation in general terms, as you are then able to recognise issues that might pose problems in the future. You do not always know beforehand what issues can be problematic. What is done in practice is often different from what is proposed in policies and guidelines.

With the change from FS to FD, SKV is not allowed to propose issues for discussion and there are no longer any overarching issues. Cooperation with FD has thus ceased and Z has instead chosen to pose its very specific questions through Dialogen, although these must now be stated in general terms, as information generated this way is not protected by the secrecy clause.

Y is another corporation with whom this contact person has been involved. This cooperation has been very different and been pursued at a different pace. Through its CFO, it has Y posed some very specific questions regarding, for example, transfer pricing and the restructuring of businesses. Y said it wanted to signal some specific challenges it has and get them sorted out. Such questions are now part of Dialogen so that SKV can provide Y with a written answer.

About four to six such questions have been on the table, and on each issue five or six people have been involved during the 18 months the co-operation has been in place. For example, Carl might have asked if the Tax Control Framework for corporation Y had been discussed. There were different opinions on the outcome and after the corporation has already stated their position in the annual return, SKV might have a different opinion. Such an issue would then have to go to court and of course would take more time. "As far as I am concerned, the cooperation has worked well in both cases, even if we have had different opinions on certain specific taxation issues. This is the way it should work," says Carl.

The only really active participant in the FD initiative is corporation X. It is government owned and faces unique and new tax questions given the extraordinary circumstances that will prevail for the coming 25–30 years. Kristian, Tax Manager at X, indicated that these are the two reasons for its participation in FD. Ownership does not have anything to do with these issues, he says, but being owned by the government makes for special attention to tax issues. "We cannot engage in any tax-planning schemes or activities," he said, "even though we operate in a highly competitive global environment."

The issues they discuss within FD are everything, from large questions concerning huge amounts of money, to petty deductions. According to Daniel, SKV's contact person, 'X is a perfect fit' for FD. He has been involved in the development of FS/FD since its very beginning. X constantly faces new taxation issues that need to be addressed fairly quickly. If the FD cooperation had not existed it would have been a much larger workload for SKV. "It is really a win-win situation", he says.

The corporation and SKV meet four times a year for about a day or two each time. Participants are Kristian and his assistant and Daniel from SKV. Prior to the meeting they agree an agenda. Sometimes specialists, such as tax advisors or technical experts from the corporation's side, attend and provide input when a specific issue is discussed. Apart from the face-to-face meetings they are in contact on average once a week. Daniel showed me the print-out of his diary. On average he has in 2015 made an entry weekly, each contact time consisting of one to two lines of entry. The entire print-out was four pages long. He uses about a quarter of his working time as a contact person for X. The questions are mostly quite simple and his answers are both oral and written. If the questions are more difficult, they become part of Dialogen and then someone else will reply, often engaging with SKV's legal department. It is noteworthy that in the era of electronic messaging, SKV is still not allowed to reply on email due to tax confidentiality.

Daniel finds it strange that this type of cooperation is, through court decisions, regarded as counselling and that the information provided is not considered subject to tax confidentiality, as it more resembles (tax) rulings in advance (*förhandsbesked*). Corporation X took a sceptic stance when the initiative was originally proposed, yet Kristian felt they had nothing to lose given the earlier questions put to SKV. It had previously taken SKV 26 months to respond to the five unique but characteristic questions for this corporation's specific situation and even so the responses given were not adequate enough to be translated into practice. "What did we have to lose?" asked Kristian "We had to try FD out."

For X, new tax issues continually spring up, given the extraordinary circumstances and it has a very long-term commitment to the local community where it operates. There is a lot of 'new' knowledge needed for interpreting existing tax laws. The overarching questions for X are regarding who will pay for what: the corporation, other corporations, the municipality, the state or private individuals? An appropriate question is whether the costs imposed are tax deductible. The result is that in the end it is Swedish society, in fact all other taxpayers, that pay. It is appropriate to ask what this does to tax compliance at large in society, but it is not a direct subject for this chapter and ought to be addressed elsewhere.

The accumulation of new knowledge regarding these taxation questions, both at corporation X and at SKV, is the most important issue for the corporation. If possible, Kristian would like to keep Daniel as the contact person for much longer than the stipulated four years. "The only good thing about changing the initiative from FS to FD was that now we can keep Daniel for six years. He served for two years under FS and with FD we could start all over again". Otherwise the change to FD means longer response times for questions posed by the corporation, as Daniel as the contact person cannot personally sign responses to questions under FD.

This way of working has thus been very advantageous for the corporation for several reasons, says Kristian and concludes:

> FD resolves issues much quicker. X had decided not to deduct costs before being certain that they were allowed to do so. Due to the special circumstances the corporation faces, there were many costs that had never occurred previously; costs that could perhaps be deducted from the tax owed.

FD has given them access to more specialists, and thus knowledge, at SKV. "We have a much larger cooperation range" says Kristian and adds that he spends much of his working time trying to figure out how new issues should be addressed. SKV has now more knowledge about X, which is deemed positive and in turn has made opportunities for other ways of working together.[43]

X has not been subject to any audit control since 2008. This is a very positive result as an audit control requires and takes up a lot of resources.

---

43 For example, SKV visited in order to check that the identification of workers at construction sites worked properly.

These audits previously took place every two or three years. However, not all issues can be resolved within FD. Currently, there is one issue that the corporation has decided to bring to court against SKV; they have agreed to disagree. Both parties are fine with this; that there are certain issues that have to be resolved outside the cooperation (or in the traditional way), says Kristian. "Without FD I would have dreaded the challenge we have."

Why is this approach chosen?

The architecture of FD can be seen as a response to the strong criticism FS received. But as the activity level within FD has dwindled and it is admittedly an unsuccessful cooperative compliance project, it is appropriate to ask why the project is not closed. SKV seems hesitant and one contact person with a dormant cooperation voiced the opinion that perhaps SKV's Director General would close projects at his up-coming visit to a regional office. Yet it is still alive although perhaps not kicking. Three reasons for its survival can be proposed.

First, it functions relatively well for X, where both parties see large efficiency synergies (as described above).

Second, there is a certain amount of both national and international prestige. SKV was too quick to launch FS and even most of its proponents agree that SKV should have been more careful in introducing the initiative. Perhaps the Confederation of Swedish Enterprise and other stakeholders in the Swedish tax arena should have been invited prior to its launch and participated in the drafting of how FS should work. Legal issues should also have been more properly investigated before the launch. However, dismantling the project could be seen as losing face in both the national and international tax arenas. In Sweden, SKV would have to demur on both an organisational and personal stakeholder level; internationally SKV would be seen as unable to keep pace with the progression of other OECD countries. The Dutch tax administration has for example 'marketed' its project successfully at conferences and in the OECD, EU and IOTA (Inter-European Organization of Tax Administration) contexts. Even among tax organisations there is a certain competition, and no one wants to be seen to be left behind. The Swedish well-esteemed tax agency has to show that it is also on this bandwagon.

Third, it is difficult to close down a way of working that is seen as the future; one that corresponds to agency strategies and which is working in most other OECD countries. 'When I get the question why [we should work with] FD I usually counter with "Why not? We cannot continue to just do audit controls. It is the future to work proactively. But the obstacle is the Swedish principle of public access"[44] said Daniel.[45]

The proponents of FD hope and work for legal changes addressing the secrecy issue. According to one interviewee there is probably some lobbying going on aiming to change the law in favour of protecting more information using the tax secrecy clause. The issue is currently at SKV (November 2016) after a failed proposal to the Riksdag to make changes in the law as to what is protected in public data registers.[46] The result of failed FS/FD is that many corporations have reverted to posing questions through Dialogen. Such questions are anonymous which means that SKV cannot connect issues with actual tax returns. "The only winners are the tax advisors," claimed Eva.[47]

What type of information is subject, or not, to tax confidentiality is an issue that has concerned much of SKV's proactive work during the last decade. Having to return to the seemingly old-fashioned ways of tax audits as the only means of control would be very unfortunate, counterproductive and costly, say proponents of the changed law. This issue thus encompasses information collected not only from FD but also from other ways of working with taxpayers.

How are stakeholders engaged?

As described earlier, FS would start with an invitation by SKV to a chosen corporation's board of directors or its top management. After initial meetings where expectations and preconditions would be discussed, the conversations would continue by agreeing on how and in which timescale the corporation's tax handling and the minimisation of risk would be addressed. The participating corporation and SKV would write and sign a declaration of intent. Although these declarations are not legally binding, the report argues that such a written statement underscores the will and commitment[48] for both parties. Any of them can at any time end such a declaration.

The declaration of intent would be the start of the more practical work between the corporation's tax department and SKV's designated contact person. The cooperation can appear different depending on the declaration of intent, but SKV would always supply help, and support the corporation's

---

44 *Offentlighetsprincipen.*
45 Interview 14.1.2016.
46 Dataregisterlagen. According to interview 30.11.2015.
47 Interview 30.11.2015.
48 Report 480-698289-10 (Skatteverket 2011).

aim to declare and pay the correct tax and fees. The practical work is mostly described as expectations.[49]

FD is more modest in its description about the engagement; the existing cooperation started with FS. In the current guidelines (Skatteverket, 2014), it is stated that either a corporation or SKV can make the proposal to start a cooperation (FD) but it is solely SKV that decides on the start, after joint consultation. A corporation can at any stage ask to end FD; if SKV proposes an end to such an agreement it has to be followed by a reason. The corporation would then have three weeks to respond to the reason. It is solely SKV that decides on the ending.

How do stakeholders resist?

Gustav, CFO at corporation A, was one of the 25 signatories of the now infamous letter. He had declined an invitation to participate and said that corporation A had felt early on that this type of collaboration was not for them; at least not from the start. The relationship they have with SKV is described as good, although it is difficult when it comes to the legal aspects of tax (*skatterättslig*). SKV then changes societal roles and becomes a counterparty. The legal aspects of the different roles SKV has to play are said to prevent corporations from participating and require attention.

It is not uncommon that court decisions are challenged with a changed result in many instances. As Jane, one of corporation C's tax managers, said, "about 30% of SKV's decisions are reversed if taken to court. This is a large proportion and SKV needs to be more perceptive about [how to respond to] issues before taking them to court". This statement has to be seen in the context of SKV's changed strategies. FS was seen as yet another example where the legal consequences had not been properly investigated. As she said, "FS could even conflict with constitutional law".

C's other tax manager, Ivar, had a similar reasoning; they were reluctant to engage in FS as he visualised SKV making decisions without legal support. SKV strategies are increasingly based on values, not on law. What is the 'right tax' that SKV should focus on? He argued that "it is not only SKV that can decide what the correct tax is".

Corporation C did not want to risk being challenged in court by SKV if their views on a specific issue should differ. Through FS, SKV would have acquired much previously unknown information about C. As SKV is seen as

---

[49] This will not be addressed here as the suggested cooperation in practice came to naught and was reformulated.

having the upper hand in making legal decisions that are not always based on the law, cooperating within FS posed just too much uncertainty for C. Therefore this corporation did not even want to risk being challenged in court by SKV, should their views on a specific issue differ. In C's argument, not everybody is equal before the law in Sweden. SKV has the upper hand.

Trust is built on getting adequate answers to our questions, explained Jane, meaning that SKV often has a good view on what is right and reasonable when it comes to specific questions. There are always new commercial sectors and new techniques for which tax aspects need to be addressed. These statements contradict their previous arguments. Corporation C seems to want to steer away any communication it has with SKV unless directly stipulated by law; if C's taxation practices are challenged it should be through working ways they know, e.g. control audits. "It is not only SKV that should have the goodies without listening to our concerns," concluded Jane.

Ivar said that he actually missed the audits; not for their own sake but as he sees it, it is the only way to thwart non-compliance among competitors. "Does SKV not have the resources [to perform audits anymore]" he asked rhetorically. In addition he found working within FS time-consuming and questioned what all the knowledge amassed at SKV would be used for. All issues combined, he concluded that FS had not anything for corporation C. Trust in SKV, described as a prerequisite for an enhanced relationship ways of working, was just not there.

B is a multi-international corporation. "We work with cooperative compliance initiatives in many countries", says its tax manager, Helen; "with a handshake. We started collaborating within FS, but when the information that was up for discussion was not secret and could be made public, we ended the collaboration." The problem according to her is that SKV is afraid of creating their own precedents; it wants everything to be decided by courts.

The arguments against participating in FS offered by the few corporations that participated in these interviews could be easily seen as contradictory. On the one hand, corporation C proposes that SKV often has a good view on what is right, and is reasonable when it comes to specific questions; on the other hand SKV is seen as making decisions without the support of the law. Corporation B works with a handshake in many countries, yet it complains that SKV does not confirm oral advice in writing.

Overall, reluctance towards FS seems to be a lack of trust in SKV's decision-making process. Would SKV's decisions hold up in court? This is supported by the legal uncertainties within this way of working. This pronounced itself clearly when the court decision on information disclosed in FS/FD was seen as counselling and would therefore not be confidential but available to the public. This was also the reason for why SKV's cooperation with Z and Y has petered out. There is just too much at risk when information can be disclosed to competitors or to anyone else.

How do different stakeholders perceive the collaboration/cooperation?

At SKV there are both proponents and sceptics of FS/FD. Their opinions were voiced in numerous intranet articles about FS, especially published around its launch and following the development of FS into FD. *Intranätet* is the internal news feed for employees, it is not public, but is a good insight into discussions taking place inside SKV. *Intranätet* news stories are written in a fairly informal manner with the aim of informing staff about work performed, anticipated changes in work at SKV, and comments about media events where SKV figures. The text is often adorned with pictures of employees at work or in meetings, or with official portraits of persons figuring in the article.

Chronologically, the articles addressing the cooperative compliance initiatives start out by depicting the working activities of the FS project, describing how it is transferred to 'production' and the ensuing launch. It is a newsfeed both describing the development of FS, and providing counterarguments as well as corrections to criticisms posed in public media. One article depicts a meeting between SKV and employees from the Dutch tax agency working with Horizontal Monitoring; it is referred to as the cooperation project. Another comments on some of the criticism voiced by the Confederation of Swedish Enterprise in particular. A third article mentions the letter described earlier, stating that "a number of Swedish corporations do not want to cooperate".[50] Six months later it is reported that 13 corporations are engaged in discussions about FS and at least three of these show great interest in this type of cooperation although in very different ways.[51] This particular article is somewhat triumphant in the way it conveys the message, ending with "I am sure that our region is ready for this challenge". Positive news about FS was also reported by a local SKV employee who was a contact person to one participating corporation. The article describes issues that have already been handled and the practical work within FS.[52] Another

---

50 Interview 13.9.2011.
51 Interview 3.7.2012.
52 Interview 4.11.2013.

article commented on Påhlsson's very critical report on FS (2012a) and noted *Storföretagregionens* manager's response in the media to errors in the report.[53] It corrected the false view that had been voiced in public media that within FS that SKV could offer tax exemption retrospectively, which is contrary to the principle of equal treatment.[54]

Yet views among SKV employees on the FS/FD cooperation are divided.[55] "I could not see this aggressive resistance coming," said one of the project leaders. "What we aim to do is to correct tax errors; errors that are often interpreted as cheating. This was not at all the intention with FS."

There seems to be fairly widespread reluctance, although not publicly stated, towards the initiative. Although those working directly with FS/FD are positive, they also confirm the existing hesitation in interviews. There are several reasons. One concern is regarding what role SKV will have when it acts both as an arbiter and a consultant. Another concern poses the question of what will be the changing societal role of a tax agency which is engaged in cooperation like FD with taxpayers; what will this do to the trust in SKV and to tax compliance in general?[56]

A third opinion questioned the competence of auditors at SKV. Such doubts were, for example, voiced in an article entitled *Mys med storföretagen*, 'Embrace the large corporations'. The reporting employee participated in an internal training session on communication skills and, as he was involved in FS, he chose this subject as one of his presentation tasks on the course. In the ensuing discussions, one of the course leaders related to the project in terms of 'snuggling'. This somewhat humorous remark was said to reflect a fairly widespread view among SKV employees that the bureaucracy risked being subject to ridicule in such collaborations. Cooperative compliance initiatives provide a way for corporations to deceive SKV. However, the article is loyal to FS in its conclusion. It was argued that the possibility to deceive is much greater in regular audit controls and corporations that aim 'to deceive us' will not even engage in FS.

---

53 Interview 18.4.2013.
54 'Principen om likabehandling' (Skatteverket 2011:12) does not exist in the Swedish Courts' glossary.
55 These opinions have been voiced in numerous discussions with other SKV employees and are not part of the formal interviews.
56 Explorative interview with a SKV analyst 2013.

Concepts to consider for a (failed) cooperative compliance project

The Swedish case shows hard resistance from some actors against cooperative compliance initiatives. The initial debate offered a plethora of arguments for and against the project in general, and more specifically against the proposed Swedish variety, first regarding FS, which was later transformed into FD. There are many things to learn at various levels from the apparent failure of the Swedish experience with such initiatives.

This chapter has so far described SKV's internal work preparing and launching the initiative. It has followed the unfolding of the media debate concerning FS and introduced the main stakeholders and reported on how the few that engaged in cooperation FD, worked out in practice. There have been other events, organised both by academics[57] and by the Confederation of Swedish Enterprise. These, however, neither change the casting of who played the major roles in the failure of the Swedish experience, nor what issues were important, nor the arguments used for and against it/them (if FS/FD is considered two sides of the same coin). The initiative has also been discussed in several articles in *Skattenytt*, a leading Swedish journal for tax-legal scholars (cf. Kristoffersson, 2014; Påhlsson, 2012b; Sörensson, 2011). The merits of the resistance strategy will not be debated here; instead in the following discussion I will hone in on concepts that need to be addressed for the successful – or poor – implementation of cooperative compliance initiatives, through learning from the Swedish experience.

There are thus a number of arguments and issues that have been raised in articles, reports and other documents, and also in interviews and discussions with various stakeholders. Sometimes these arguments appear alone, but most often they are supported by selected legal decisions and/or arguments; hard-core facts that are seldom disputable. The arguments are used in different set-ups which support the importance of observing the eight concepts I propose below in learning from the Swedish case. The empirical content of these concepts thus overlap by definition.

These concepts are important to consider if implementing a successful cooperative compliance initiative.
- confidential information – tax confidentiality
- legal culture

---

57 e.g. a one-day seminar 14.6.2014, at Gävle Högskola organized by Professors of Law Eleonor Kristoffersson and Börje Leidhammar (Kristoffersson 2014).

- unfairness (competition and legal equality)
- societal roles and trust
- ways of working
- competence
- benefits for all involved
- project launch.

A more thorough discussion engaging with existing research on such initiatives and the proposed concepts' universal applicability will be discussed elsewhere. It is however suggested that these issues boil down to matters of trust, or rather distrust, in the relationship between SKV and large corporations. And perhaps it is the lack of trust in the first place, the very essence of relationships within cooperative compliance ways of working (OECD, 2008, 2013), that rendered the Swedish case a failure?

Legal considerations

What has emerged as the most problematic issue within cooperative compliance initiative such as FS or FD is the legal status of documents regarding secrecy within the Swedish legal system.

Sweden poses a somewhat particular case concerning access to public records. Since 1766, with the first Freedom of the Press Act, it is stated that secrecy constitutes a restriction of public access to official documents (Hambre, 2015, p.122); "public access is the main rule and secrecy is the exception" (ibid., p.129). Yet there are instances when secrecy is needed for the protection of individuals and organisations. Taxation is one of these issues. Accordingly only decisions taken at SKV and documented in official documents are made public (ibid., p.152);[58] for example decisions regarding annual tax returns. The key issue here is thus the transformation of any document into an official document under the Freedom of the Press Act. Note that documents encompass almost any matter that can provide information: written, pictorial, maps, drawing, recordings, films, etc.

Of all legal issues it is the confidentiality argument that is the most pertinent and has been most discussed in the debate and used by critics of FS. The first case was not initially aimed at FS, but was a test of what type of information exchanged between the tax administration and taxpayers was protected by the confidentiality clause.[59] The case was tried in various courts.[60] Judges

---
58 Please see Hambre 2015, chap.3 for a full discussion on the legal reasoning.
59 Interview 14.1.2016.
60 e.g. decision Kammarrätten i Stockholm. Mål nr 554-13.

in the first instance, *Kammarrrätten,* were not unanimous, as one of the judges considered such information of concern to an individual's tax affairs. From this view the issue should be seen as part of SKV's taxation work and therefore be encompassed by absolute secrecy. The court ruled that it was up to SKV to decide if there are other concerns preventing this information from being made public. This decision was raised in 2013 in the Supreme Administrative Court,[61] *Högsta förvaltningsdomstolen,* which ruled that the documents produced within the auspices of FS could not be considered part of what should be protected by secrecy. This way of working, regardless of SKV's intention to make annual statements more correct, is instead seen as counselling. Information about who participates in FS and what the discussions address can thus be disclosed if requested.

The legal objections regarding tax confidentiality are those that stand against the continuation of FD in Sweden. There are thorough discussions of the legal intricacies (e.g. Bernitz & Reichel, 2015; Hambre, 2015; Kristoffersson, 2014; Påhlsson, 2012a), but the main objections have been emphasised above. Yet there are ways to work around the secrecy. Corporation X described how they now pose questions through Dialogen in more general terms and perhaps supplement these questions with more informal discussions on the phone. From the opposite perspective, it is valid to ask if cooperative compliance is not intended for a legal system like the Swedish one, which is built on the transparency of most taxation details.

But I argue that there are also other reasons, just as strong and important for opponents of FS/FD. Individually, these reasons have perhaps not as much clout, but they underlie the trajectory that cooperative compliance projects have taken in Sweden. Tax confidentiality is the most pertinent issue right now, but there is more to the legal discussions and decisions on specific cases.

The experience from FS/FD also shows how different actors choose to relate to tax law. As Lars, a legal expert at the Confederation of Swedish Enterprise, argued:

> We all ought to follow the law and it is above everything. The state makes certain claims on us and we all need to follow them. Then there are those who want to do more, like sorting waste. Some are exceptionally proper [in their treatment of waste] but it is not what the law says. When society changes, like it has done with sorting waste, then we have to change the laws. Like the tax law.

---

61 HFD 2013 ref 48.

According to his view, SKV should not require more information or more work of taxpayers than what has been stated by law and enforced during decades. To get a cooperative compliance initiative to work successfully, the proper way to go is, first, to work for legal changes through parliament, and then implement these ways of workings.

The secrecy issue has been attempted to be addressed at several instances and is currently (November 2016) back at SKV's legal department. Otherwise, according to one contact person, SKV has to reconsider its entire communication strategies; these do not seem sustainable given the above court decisions. Yet, at SKV the view is that there is of course the application of tax law but in meeting the taxpayer there is much room for manoeuvre, which SKV uses to fulfil the governmental requirement of being more serviceable as well as treating taxpayers with respect and understanding, etc.[62] SKV thus proposed a change of law making more information exchanged between taxpayers and SKV to be treated as confidential. It was suggested that such information should be included in *beskattningsdatabasen* (Skatteverket, 2015, p.39), the database that contains taxation information that is not public. It was included in a larger proposal of changes regarding public storage of data.[63] The proposed change was criticised by various societal institutions; for example, the Confederation for Swedish Enterprise (Svenskt näringsliv, 2015) argued that the proposed change was a slippery slope for making almost any tax-related issue confidential. The proposal was denied following widespread criticism.

Unequal treatment and unfair competition

Information exchanged in FS/FD is thus seen as a counselling practice and is not considered part of tax confidentiality under current laws. This is crucial for what is kept public and what is private. But the reason given for the issue brought to court was that one taxpayer had asked for such information, arguing that other taxpayers who engaged in FS had had more advantageous decisions regarding VAT levels. The results were that the former had lost customers. Not only is the issue of fair competition at stake; these court decisions bring us to the issue of unequal treatment of taxpayers.

---

62 Interview 30.11.2015.

63 What information can be publicly stored about citizens and how such data should be handled was recently subject to a large public review (SOU, 2015). There are many laws that govern this area, which covers many diverse societal sectors, and its legal status was deemed complex and diffuse. The proposal was taken back after criticism from various public actors and a new proposed change is being prepared by SKV's legal department and will eventually be presented to the Swedish riksdag.

The implication of this critique is that not all taxpayers would be treated equally before the law, which goes against the constitution and also against values held in Swedish society. A related issue against FS/FD is *gräddfil*, a VIP lane for certain taxpayers.[64] Participants in FS/FD would get different – better – treatment that is not consistent with Swedish administrative law or practice. The issue of equality before the law arose, which is also appalling from the perspective of free competition, commented interviewee Marianne.[65] Corporations cannot compete on equal terms if they are subject to different legal treatment. A parallel initiative comparative to FS (and also initiated by SKV) was cooperation with the organisation for authorised tax advisors, FAR/SRS. In this initiative, corporations using the services of FAR/SRS tax advisors would be exempt from certain types of audit. It was argued that this way of working would primarily benefit larger corporations.[66] The FS/FD initiatives provide another case for criticism of favouring larger corporations in Swedish society.

The counter-argument from SKV is that different taxpayers have to be met in different ways. FS/FD would just continue the long tradition SKV has developed; for example, by providing different types of information material for various categories of taxpayers (in different languages, written in easily accessible language, etc.) and arranging information meetings for various types of taxpayers, e.g. small and medium-sized enterprises and the self-employed. This is an adaptation of SKV's insight that taxpayers *are different* and therefore have various needs. Not everybody has the capability to adequately pose tax-related questions for example.

That FS/FD made it possible to make agreements behind closed doors is one of the main problems according to Niklas. Many decisions would be made in smaller meetings with a potential risk of accusations of cronyism and what has been referred to as 'sweetheart deals' (*vänskapskorruption*). It was argued that professional integrity might be challenged when contacts are frequent and although all stakeholders agree that Sweden does not have a culture of monetary reimbursement corruption, there can be an issue of revolving doors between opposing tax institutions in society. It was also mentioned that SKV does not pay well and a contact person can build up a relationship with the corporation s/he handles. Could a corporation be, more or less intentionally, treated more leniently in the tax audit handling if

---

64 Interview 14.1.2016.
65 The membership clause was later changed to having a certification from FAR/SRS. See note 33.
66 Interview 16.3.2015.

a better-paid job in the corporate sector was available? Although the contact person would be changed every four years, it does not resolve the concern about sweetheart deals.

Inequality and unfairness are thus issues that are accentuated by these three criticisms.

Societal roles

> Compared to many other nations, we in Sweden have well-defined roles between the authorities and the private sector.[67] I think many other countries would love to have similar relations. The Netherlands, for example, where the first attempts at Horizontal Monitoring were made, has a culture of negotiation. They are an old trading nation and a corporation negotiates with the tax administration as to how much tax should be paid. One gets to know one another by giving and taking. Denmark [the Danish Tax Authority] has also tried this with three different corporations, each with diverse results. They apparently thought there was too much room for arbitrary decisions.

said Lars, the tax expert at the Confederation of Swedish Enterprises.

It was not only the CSE who took a somewhat conservative view of different actors' roles and responsibilities in the tax arena in Swedish society. As described above, SKV employees also stated diverse concerns with SKV's role in society as both arbiter and adversary in such cooperations and were concerned about the possibility of being cheated when audit controls were exceeded. FS is a variety of the OECD's proposed modern ways of working through co-production, thus resulting in slight changes to stakeholders' traditional roles.

SKV should 'not be a buddy' as Påhlsson stated in a media article. SKV and the taxpayer should instead retain their more separate and explicit roles on taxation issues. "We have different roles in society; diverse interests, tasks, capabilities and responsibilities. We cannot blend roles and responsibilities in a big cuddle box"[68] said Niklas. Roles teased out over centuries by different societal institutions are important.

There are two issues at stake here. First, there were several taxpayers who spoke about the necessity to get 'the right person' at SKV. The right person is a knowledgeable employee; someone who is knowledgeable both about the issue at stake (e.g. VAT issues) but also about the corporation in question. Is the real issue here the need to have these issues written out in policies and guidelines?

---

67   Interview 16.3.2015.
68   Interview 24.3.2015.

Second, it is doubtful that anyone participating in this debate wishes for a return to the times when SKV controlled and collected tax without much nuance in its practices. But is the implication also to retain the old-fashioned role of corporations as profit-making entities which sole purpose is to maximise profit and continue to hold down costs, of which one is taxes? Or should they continue to take on a more responsible role in society, as several tax managers said their corporations do? There has been a change over the last ten years in tax planning activities. Society around us is changing and so is the view on what is sustainable and fair taxation.

SKV thus awaits a legal solution so it can address the trust issue – or rather the lack of it. As the FD project leader said:

> This project addresses trust issues between SKV and large corporations. The project is there, but the tax confidentiality issue stands in the way. There are corporations who actually think positively about such cooperation however it is difficult in these circumstances to invite other corporations to FD.

Unclear ways of working

The ways of working both within FS and FD are deemed unclear. SKV has efficiency goals to live up to and has to show results from the internal projects it undertakes. It was argued that it might then be easy to go after the low-hanging fruit and miss the more elaborate tax planning schemes. For example, any audit only has so much allocated time, and SKV has to both collect the money and show that it has spent the time on the right issue; all according to the agenda of New Public Management. Lars argued that it was better for SKV to retain working with audits instead of these modern, so-called efficiency-creating cooperations. "We would prefer that they perform more of the old-fashioned audits to catch the real crooks."

That cooperative compliance works well regarding different stakeholders in other countries can also be explained by 'legal cultures' (Sörensson, 2011). He does not provide an exact definition of what legal culture is, but I interpret it to encompass established praxis from interpretation of the law governing the relationship between all stakeholders. To what extent are taxpayers responsible for assessing the amount of taxes it should pay and the information it should provide? What is the national administrative tradition concerning these issues? In Sweden, where taxpayers already provide large amounts of information and where openness, proportionality and objectivity (three of the five issues stated in the OECD requirements for Enhanced Relationships) are regulated by law, Sörensson (2011) questions whether perhaps FS will be too much of an administrative burden. Reporting information in real time will require an increased workload that is not offset by fewer audit controls.

How much extra workload would the cooperative compliance initiative put on corporations? "Would we do the work of SKV?" asked several of the non-participating corporations. Does SKV aim to make corporations to do the work themselves; does SKV outsource audit control? This stance suggests a view on tax compliance that if they just continue talking and keeping the discussion alive, things will be all right.[69] The implication for corporations is that it is nice to travel in the priority lane, as you are then considered one of the good guys. Yet this provides for much criticism from non-participants; once admitted to the priority lane you could engage in all sorts of schemes that would have risked being detected in regular audit controls.

Yet participation in FS did not exclude the corporation from being part of the Common Risk Evaluation[70] carried out at SKV. Thus any corporation could still be subject to audit, which however can be questioned, based on X's favourable experience of not being subject to audit during participation in FS and then in FD. There is of course no proven causality; however X's previous experience was undergoing an audit with a few years in between. Yet as Carl stated this is the whole purpose with FD: "We know the corporations better and thus know better when to audit them".

Competence

The FS initiative was deemed naive from a legal, practical and policy perspective, noted all critical stakeholders. The reasoning went along the lines of how can one of SKV's tax auditors help and/or teach a big corporation to ameliorate its extremely complex accounting system with regards to reporting and paying the 'right tax'? SKV employees are helpful and friendly and this goes well with private citizens, or taxpayers. When it comes to the more detailed, in-depth knowledge about complicated tax matters the issue is different. "SKV's auditors fresh from university do not have the knowledge needed," proposed Marianne. This criticism seems somewhat unfounded. The contact persons at SKV are selected for their experience and communication capabilities; Carl suggested on the contrary that 'his' corporation had adopted several of SKV's proposals. The contact person is also the *contact*; it is not s/he who decides but instead forwards questions to specialists within SKV. What was missing in this simplified critique was not that SKV would solve all complicated tax issues but rather would help to identify those

---

69 Interview 16.3.2015.
70 *Allmänna riskvärderingen.*

issues that make taxation in Sweden unnecessarily cumbersome. For example, helping corporations to be timely in the manifold reporting deadlines or identify why certain errors are made repeatedly.

Opponents to FS/FD also argued that these initiatives were a way for SKV's relatively underpaid and inexperienced tax auditors to learn more about actual taxation practices; the same criticism is also expressed as a reason for why SKV should not involve themselves in cooperative compliance initiatives! This is also where the largest corporations are able to negotiate advantages compared to the smaller ones that do not possess the same knowledge/clout – thus again a competitive issue.

Benefits for all involved

"We just do not see the benefits of being involved in a cooperative compliance initiative" was a common view among representatives for non-participating corporations.

Perhaps the Swedish cooperative compliance initiative did not address problems perceived by the corporations? Similarly, the Dutch version was created as a response to complaints by corporations; about the level of service and the numbers of decisive responses to questions posed by corporations (de Leeuw, 2010; Sörensson, 2011). In Denmark the Tax Governance project seems to work well at resolving issues as they occur (Boll, forthcoming; Elkjaer et al., 2013). In the Swedish case, it was SKV that was proactive and SKV was seen to be the main beneficiary of such cooperation: learning more about contemporary tax planning, transferring certain of its workload to the corporations, and thus increasing the taxation workload for corporations. For the corporations it was an initial investment of time and resources for which it was difficult to envision the 'pay-back'. X received many benefits from this cooperation and Kristian, its tax manager, is thus very favourable towards FD.

Launch of project

It is important to launch a cooperative compliance initiative carefully. Projects gone astray have often many different reasons and so did this one. FS was introduced as a means of killing several birds with one stone, yet perhaps the birds just flew away?

In hindsight there seems to be consensus that the introduction of FS went too quickly and was somewhat sloppily executed.[71] SKV was keen, like

---

71 Stated in a number of interviews by SKV employees.

other internal revenue bodies, to implement cooperative compliance ways of working. The legal issues should have been more thoroughly investigated by SKV's legal department and perhaps even been tried in court as now it is the legal issues that stand in its way. As Anna said, "we did not get the proper attention we ought to have had from the legal department"; others suggested that the Department for Large Corporations had not been paying enough attention to the legal checks although the report describing FS stated that it had been checked by SKV's legal department.[72] Perhaps SKV ought to have acted a little more cautiously, starting with a pilot project inviting very few corporations?

There should perhaps have been a working group that involved various stakeholders to tease out the initiative. There were several opinions voiced that SKV should perhaps have invited the Confederation of Swedish Enterprise and tax advisors to discuss the initiatives so that the ideas might have been supported by stakeholders.

Perhaps the communication should have been more streamlined? Another mistake was that when SKV launched FS it had not detailed the precise ways of working. The proposed guidelines stated that ways of working would be decided in cooperation with participating corporations. In the initial launch several issues were poorly described, such as that SKV promised that participating corporations would be excluded from audits and the like. This SKV can never do[73] and this criticism was well founded. The rush to launch can also be illustrated by three SKV documents where arguments did not align with each other: a media article, an internal report, and an SKV presentation for corporations at four information meetings. The contradictions in these three documents made FS an easy target for adversaries of the very idea of more cooperation between corporate taxpayers and SKV in Sweden.

After the first seminar for corporations held by SKV, quite a few of them raised concerns. The Confederation of Swedish Enterprises has regular meetings with SKV, but also regular meetings with what they refer to as *Storföretagsgruppen,* the group for large corporations. "Do we dare to say no?" asked members of this group. SKV has all the power but if we say no collectively, we will not even be able to respond to the question[74] that would automatically avoid us being put in the group of risky taxpayers. There were many mixed opinions among those signing the letter, received

---

72 Skatteverket 2015.
73 Interview 12.10.2015.
74 Representatives for some corporations said that it was the Confederation of Swedish Enterprises who suggested the drafting of a collective letter.

on 6 July 2011 by SKV. The opinions ranged from those seeing the initiative as inappropriate, to those who were very, very sceptical. The writing of this letter mirrored the diverse opinions. SKV tried to correct the numerous criticisms voiced against FS with the re-launch of FD but the damage was already done. "We just do not see the difference between FS and FD," said Ivar, yet as we know there are several.

Conclusion

This chapter outlines the Swedish cooperative compliance project *Fördjupad samverkan* – FS (enhanced collaboration) – introduced in 2011 and the modified initiative re-launched as *Fördjupad dialog* – FD (enhanced dialogue) – in 2014. I have described how SKV proposed an initiative that carried with it international success stories from similar projects, but in the Swedish version and context met with strong resistance and is now almost put on hold awaiting proposed changes in the law. This chronological trajectory teases out issues that impact on tax compliance among large corporations but perhaps also among ordinary taxpayers in Swedish society.[75]

The chapter suggests eight concepts from the Swedish case for consideration for successful implementation of a cooperative compliance initiative. These concepts seldom stand alone, but are drawn upon in various combinations making criticism possible. A cooperative compliance initiative has to be in accordance with existing laws and, in the Swedish case, in particular with regards to confidential information. Fair market competition and legal equality has to be ensured. Stakeholders' societal roles cannot be drastically changed. Ways of working have to be carefully explained. The initiative has to be based on relevant competence among both participating tax authority and taxpayer. Clear benefits for both taxpayers and tax administration have to be evident and recognised. Finally such an initiative must be well planned and carefully launched. Many of these follow the prerequisites for those who advocate cooperative compliance projects e.g. OECD and the Institute for Austrian and International Tax Law at Wirtschaftsuniversität, Vienna.

There have been many reasons stated against FS/FD that could also be viewed as reasons for it. Having an assigned contact person at SKV could make sweetheart deals possible; yet corporations simultaneously expressed their need to have someone who 'knows' them. SKV was accused of bringing badly prepared legal cases to court; but on the other hand it could be a sign

---

[75] The distrust from corporations is not necessarily to SKV's disadvantage. There are many citizens who distrust the large corporations. This is not however a question for this project.

that SKV is not as high-handed as its opponents want to present it. SKV's employees were said to lack commercial awareness yet there was criticism of the claim that the introduction of FS/FD would make them learn more about 'taxation in practice'. These few examples indicate that there is more at play here than just rational arguments for or against the initiative.

Was it perhaps that the entire issue of working along cooperative compliance lines in Sweden was illegal? The question can be asked as the initiative is on hold awaiting changes in the law. Following this unfolding of events, there were continuous and various combinations of legal issues arguing against FS and then against FD. Yet as has been shown, the opponents articulated one issue after another to counter the proposed corrections and such counter-arguments could in turn be said to display signs of deeper distrust. However, I doubt that the explanation for the Swedish failure is as simple as one of the general (mis)trust that governs relations between large corporations and SKV. The trust issue needs to be explored in detail, for example, if governance of the relationship between large corporations and SKV is structured in such a way that changes to it could lead to greater distrust. The result would then be the opposite of what cooperative compliance initiatives were supposed to address. The Swedish case provides rich material to engage with earlier research on cooperative compliance initiatives and more explicitly issues that impact on tax compliance. The insights proposed in this chapter thus raise several issues to be further developed into a more conceptual and theoretical framework in order for us to draw any conclusions as to whether cooperative compliance actually increases tax compliance.

Acknowledgements

A version of this chapter has been published as *FairTax Working Paper Series No 07*. I am grateful for comments and suggestions from the audience following my presentation at Tax Research Network 25th Annual Conference in Roehampton. I am also indebted to comments given by Karen Boll, Benedicte Brøgger, Dennis de Widt, Hans Gribnau, Anna-Maria Hambre, Emer Mulligan and Lynne Oats as well from participants of a workshop with SKV's strategy group on cooperative compliance, the regional managers of *Storföretagsgruppen* (the group for large corporations), and of tax experts at the Confederation of Swedish Enterprises. Any remaining faults are my own.

References

Bernitz, U. & Reichel, J. (2015). Effektivitet eller legalitet? En bedömning av Skatteverkets nya samarbetsformer. Stockholm, Svenskt näringsliv.

Björklund Larsen, L. (2015). 'Common Sense' at the Swedish Tax Agency. Transactional Boundaries Separating Taxable and Tax-Free Income. *Critical Perspectives on Accounting*, 31, 75-89.

Björklund Larsen, L. (2017). *Shaping Taxpayers. Values in action at the Swedish Tax Agency*. Oxford: Berghahn Books.

Boden, R., Killian S., Mulligan E., Oats L., & Edgley, C.R.P. (2010). Backstage in Legal Theatre: A Foucauldian Interpretation of 'Rationes Decidendi' on the Question of Taxable Business Profits. *Critical Perspectives on Accounting*, 21(7), 560–572.

Boll, K. (2012). Ethnography and Tax Compliance. In Oats, L. (Ed.), *Taxation: A Fieldwork Research Handbook* (p.50-58). Abingdon: Routledge.

Boll, K. (2014). Shady car dealings and taxing work practices: An ethnography of a tax audit process. *Accounting, Organizations and Society*, 39,(1), 1–19.

Boll, K. (forthcoming). *National practices of Cooperative Compliance – Denmark*. FairTax Working Paper.

Davies, C.A. (1999). *Reflexive Ethnography: A Guide to Researching Selves and Others*. New York, Routledge.

de Leeuw, E. (2010). Large corporation Monitoring Programme in the Netherlands, *IOTA Tax Tribune*, nr. 27.

Editorial. (2011, May, 28). Skatteverkets erbjudande förtjänar ett nej tack. *Dagens industri*.

Ekonomistyrningsverket. (2012). *Medborgares Syn På Myndigheter*. YouGov. Stockholm.

Elkjær, J.K., Pedersen, M.K. & Andersen, R.B. (2013). Erfaringer Og Perspektiver I Samarbejdet Mellem SKAT Og de Store Virksomheder – TAX Governance. *Revision & Regnskabsvæsen*, 82(7), 84-91.

Fangen, K. (2005*). Deltagande observation*. Malmö, Liber

Flyvbjerg, B. (2001). *Making Social Science Matter: Why Social Inquiry Fails and How it Can Succeed Again*. Cambridge, Cambridge University Press

Hambre, A-M. (2015). Tax confidentiality: a comparative study and impact assessment of global interest. Dissertation, Örebro University.

Hambre, A-M. (forthcoming). Fördjupad dialog. En studie av Skatteverkets arbetsform fördjupad dialog ur ett svenskt offentligrättsligt perspektiv.

Hansson, I. & Landén, A. (2011). Skatteverket vill inte lura företag. *Dagens industri*, March, 15.

Hansson, I. (2011). Företagets inställning till skatter är en styrelsefråga. *Dagens industri*, May, 18.

IFA (International Fiscal Association). (2012). *IFA Initiative on the Enhanced Relationship Key Issues Report*. Version 3.3 31 August 2012. IFA.

Kristoffersson, E. (2014). Från fördjupad samverkan till fördjupad dialog. Konferens om Skatteverkets nya riktlinje i Gävle den 12 juni 2014. *Skattenytt*, 953-957.

Kvale, S. (1997). *Den Kvalitativa Forskningsintervjun*. Lund: Studentlitteratur.

Nyquist, K. (2011). Skatteverket ska prata lag inte moral. *Dagens industri*, May, 19.

Oats, L. (2012). *Taxation: A Fieldwork Research Handbook*. Oxon: Routledge.

OECD (Organisation for Economic Cooperation and Development). (2008). *Monitoring Taxpayers' Compliance: A Practical Guide Based on Revenue Body Experience*. Paris, OECD Centre for Tax Policy and Administration.

OECD (Organisation for Economic Cooperation and Development). (2010). *Overview: Evaluating the Effectiveness of Compliance Risk Treatment Strategies*. Paris, OECD Centre for Tax Policy and Administration.

OECD (Organisation for Economic Cooperation and Development). (2013). *Co-Operative Compliance: A Framework. From Enhanced Relationship to Co-Operative Compliance*. Paris, OECD Centre for Tax Policy and Administration.

OECD (Organisation for Economic Cooperation and Development). (2014). *Measures of Tax Compliance Outcomes: A Practical Guide*. Paris, OECD Centre for Tax Policy and Administration.

Påhlsson, R. (2011). Ska Skatteverket bli en kompis? *Dagens industri*, March, 11.

Påhlsson, R. (2012a). Fördjupad samverkan/horizonal monitoring i svensk offentligrättslig miljö. Stockholm, Svenskt näringsliv.

Påhlsson, R. (2012b). SKV:s projekt fördjupad samverkan i svensk offentligrättslig miljö. *Skattenytt*, 831-849.

Riles, A. (2006). *Documents: Artifacts of Modern Knowledge*. Ann Arbor: University of Michigan Press.

Riles, A. (2011). *Collateral Knowledge: Legal Reasoning in the Global Financial Markets*. Chicago: University of Chicago Press.

Skatteverket. (2011). *Fördjupad samverkan mellan Skatteverket och Sveriges största koncerner*. Dnr 480-698289-10/1211 1(13). Solna, Skatteverket.

Skatteverket. (2012. Medborgarnas synpunkter på skattesystemet, skattefusket och Skatteverkets kontroll. Solna, Skatteverket.

Skatteverket. (2014). *Riktlinje för fördjupad dialog*. Dnr 131-409414-13/111. Solna, Skatteverket.

Skatteverket. (2015). *Beskattningsdatabasen, bouppteckning och äktenskapsregister.* Promemoria, bilaga till Dnr 131 89000-15/113. Solna, Skatteverket.

SOU - Statens offentliga utredningar. (2015*). Myndighetsdatalag.* Stockholm: Statens Offentliga Utredningar, report 39.

Spradley, J P. (1979). Interviewing an Informant. In J.P. Spradley (Ed.) *The Ethnographic Interview* (pp.55–68). Fort Worth: Harcourt Brace Jovanovich College Publishers.

Svenskt näringsliv, (2015). Remissvar. Skatteverkets promemoria Beskattningsdatabasen, bouppteckning och äktenskapsregister, bilaga till dnr 131 89000-15/113.

Sörensson, C. (2011). Något om Skatteverkets förslag till fördjupad samverkan med storföretagen. *Skattenytt*, 625-633.

Wittberg, L. (2005). *Right from the Start.* Solna, Skatteverket.

Wästerfors, D. (2004). *Berättelser om mutor: det korruptas betydelse bland svenska affärsmän i öst-och centraleuropa.* [Stories about Bribes: The Meaning of Corruption among Swedish Businessmen in Eastern Central Europe]. Stehag: Symposion.

3 Aggressive Tax Planning and Corporate Social Irresponsibility: Managerial discretion in the light of corporate governance[1]

Ave-Geidi Jallai and Hans Gribnau

Abstract

The purpose of this contribution is to explore the possibility of integrating tax with corporate social responsibility (CSR). Some corporate directors seem to argue that they do not have a choice with regard to tax planning, implying that a responsible tax planning strategy is not an option. This contribution shows such argument to be wrong. First, the issue of management accountability and choice will be dealt with in the context of corporate governance systems in order to find out what kinds of obligations corporate governance entail for managers. It will be shown that corporate directors enjoy sufficient discretion for making socially responsible decisions. To this end, two existing theoretical frameworks will be analysed, according to which corporate decisions should prioritise either shareholders' or stakeholders' interests. Both theories allow managers a choice to act with a wider interest than purely shareholder value maximisation. Furthermore, it will be argued that managerial discretion to take CSR into account does not oblige managers to aspire to some kind of ideal social responsibility but rather to stay away from corporate social irresponsibility (CSI). Therefore, corporate managers in different corporate governance regimes have sufficient room for aligning their tax planning strategies with societal expectations and avoiding aggressive tax planning.

Thus, this paper aims to make two contributions to academic theory. First, it is shown that both shareholder- and stakeholder-oriented corporate governance regimes allow for managerial discretion to take CSR on board in tax matters. Second, the concept of corporate social irresponsibility is introduced to enhance a more balanced debate about multinationals' tax planning practices.

---

1   The authors wish to thank Ronald Russo and Ger van der Sangen for their comments on a previous draft of this paper.

> As for methodology, this contribution explores managerial discretion within various corporate governance systems and relates this to CSR and tax planning. Thus, this interdisciplinary research comprises three different perspectives: corporate law, taxation, and applied business ethics.

Introduction

This contribution explores possibilities to integrate tax with corporate social responsibility (CSR). Recent scandals such as the so-called 'Panama Papers' and 'LuxLeaks' have shown that there is something wrong with international tax planning. In this respect, multinational corporations attract much media attention (see e.g. Miliband, 2015; Birrell, 2014; TJN, 2014; Conway, 2015; Setzler, 2014; ICIJ LuxLeaks; ICIJ Panama Papers). The general public seems to expect multinationals to change to less aggressive tax strategies – deployed to achieve higher net profits. However, during the UK Public Accounts Committee hearing, Google's Matt Brittin[2] claimed that (aggressive) tax planning "is not a matter of personal choice" (UK/PAC HMRC, 2012, Q. 485, p. Ev 40). This is a surprising statement that makes one wonder, for if corporate management does not face choices with regard to tax planning then what determines corporate decision-making? Which corporate laws determine or limit managers' choices? This contribution answers this question and elaborates on corporate managerial discretion with regard to international tax planning and corporations' social responsibilities.

International tax planning has become a societal issue. The shift of tax burden to individuals and SMEs has created the feeling of inequality, especially in the aftermath of economic crisis. People have started to pay more (negative) attention to large international companies that earn immense profits but have the possibility to achieve a very low effective tax rate. Therefore, according to the public, businesses are not free to do as they wish to increase their income, market share or alike (Jallai, 2017). In this contribution, we do not focus on the question whether companies or states[3] are to blame for the existing tax planning practices. We focus on the question whether corporate governance leave multinationals elbow-room with regard to the degree of tax planning. Thus, we approach the topic of tax planning from a corporate perspective. Is aggressive tax planning – paying (almost) nil corporate income tax by keeping with the letter of the law while completely under-

---

2   Vice President for Sales and Operations, Northern and Central Europe Google.

3   States are also important players on the international tax market, competing with one another by using taxation to create a favourable investment climate to attract business.

mining the spirit of the law – for multinational corporations indeed an obligation and not a matter of "personal choice"?[4] Based on different corporate governance traditions we explore whether corporate managers have a choice with regard to tax planning and if so then what needs to be taken on board.

In this paper, we relate the issue of choice to CSR, which is often conceptualised as a matter of voluntary choice. CSR assumes that (managers of) multinational companies enjoy some kind of discretion. We will argue that CSR could be seen as a tool for good tax governance. The fact that taxes are of utmost importance to sustain our society, places them at the heart of the idea of CSR. This contribution proposes that tax should be an integral part of a company's CSR strategy. In light of this, we will discuss to what extent and what kind of responsibilities companies have towards society. Moreover, if corporations do want to improve their tax governance under the auspices of CSR, do corporate governance rules allow for it and under which conditions? We argue that corporations should stay away from tax planning practices that would qualify as corporate social irresponsibility (CSI).

Corporate governance (CG) "concerns the manner in which corporations are regulated and managed" (Du Plessis et. al. 2015, p.XXV). Corporate tax governance is a complicated affair for corporations themselves are complex organisations. In every-day business-making, corporations have to consider much more than just tax. Moreover, in their decision-making processes corporate boards need to consider many (conflicting) interests. For instance, from a business perspective, tax is also seen as a cost and costs should be kept low. Low costs satisfy shareholders (at least in the short-term) (Erle 2008, p.205). However, the general public expects companies not to use all the existing legal possibilities to minimise their tax liability (Avi-Yonah, 2014; Gribnau and Jallai, 2016). Aggressive tax planning thus may imply reputational risks. Here, businesses may face a conflict. On the one hand, corporations should enhance, maybe even maximise, shareholder value and satisfy shareholders' demands; on the other hand, companies should contribute their fair share to society in the form of taxes.

Of course, this assumes that corporate responsibility presupposes different choices the board can make. Thus, the question is, what kinds of interests should corporate boards consider while deciding on tax planning strategies?

---

[4] Here we use the term 'letter of the law' as shorthand with regard to tax planning that exploits the technicalities or differences between tax systems by making use of 'a bewildering variety of techniques (e.g. multiple deductions of the same loss, double-dip leases, mismatch arrangements, loss-making financial assets artificially allocated to high-tax jurisdictions)'; (Piantavigna 2017, p.52).

Should they prioritise shareholders' economic interests and choose therefore as aggressive tax planning as possible? Or should the board be willing to pay more (than the minimum in accordance with the letter of the law), if that is necessary in order to meet (ethical) responsibilities towards society at large? In this sense, members of society are a company's stakeholders, whose interests can be advanced by tax payments spent on infrastructure for transport and communications, social security, education, healthcare, environmental protection and other public goods. However, corporate governance systems might seem to force managers to exclusively focus on shareholder value at the expense of stakeholders' interests (see e.g. Schön, 2008) – or so Google's Matt Brittin seems to suggest. Does corporate governance therefore (in)directly oblige multinationals to engage in aggressive tax planning and limit their possibility to engage in CSR? And with regard to CSR, how does one translate a company's voluntary responsibility into taxation? Does CSR demand managers to use their discretion like an ideal(ised) citizen, paying a *fair share* in taxes, or sufficiently to meet a certain threshold – i.e., not to act in an irresponsible way?

Based on the described situation and conflicts, the main research question of this contribution reads as follows: how can managers of a (multinational) corporation translate the commitment to CSR into a responsible tax planning strategy within the limits set by corporate governance? First, the issue of management accountability and choice will be dealt with. What is corporate governance and what kinds of obligations does it set for the managers? Do they enjoy discretion? As it will be argued, there are two existing theoretical frameworks, according to which corporate decisions should prioritise either shareholders' or stakeholders' interests. We will investigate these theories and find out whether managers have a choice to act in the wider interest than purely shareholder value maximisation. Furthermore, we will research what different corporate governance models and their underlying theories require in this situation. Based on that, we investigate whether corporations have conflicting responsibilities towards shareholders and other stakeholders in their tax planning. And if so, which one prevails?

As for methodology, this contribution explores managerial discretion within various corporate governance systems and relates this to CSR and tax planning. Thus, this interdisciplinary research comprises three different perspectives: corporate law, taxation, and applied business ethics. Corporate governance and business ethics are used to better understand the managers' responsibilities towards shareholders and stakeholders in the context of tax planning. Moreover, international tax planning is placed in an area between corporate social responsibility and corporate social *ir*responsibility.

3: Aggressive Tax Planning and Corporate Social Irresponsibility

This contribution is subject to several limitations. First, it focuses only on multinational enterprises; wealthy individuals and their tax planning practices are not the focus of this contribution. Second, this research does not provide an extensive analysis on CG theories. Thus, our starting point is the statement of Matt Brittin who seems to prioritise shareholders' interests exclusively; on the other side, we explore the opposite view – stakeholder theory, which strongly reacted to the one-sidedness of the shareholder value theory. Therefore, we focus only on a very specific aspect of corporate governance: the question whether corporate managers have the possibility of influencing tax planning under CSR.

Corporate governance and the duty of the managers

Do corporate managers have a choice? In order to answer this question, we need to find out what the legal responsibilities of managers are in the first place. Therefore, we turn to corporate governance regimes, in order to understand what is legally expected from corporate managers. Thus, in this section we give a brief overview of what corporate governance is and what is the main legal responsibility that managers have, according to corporate governance rules.

Corporate governance is about the governance of corporate entities and their activities. It refers to the way power is distributed within a corporation and the decision-making process with regard to the use of this power. Corporate governance is generally understood as sets of rules and principles for how a (large) company is regulated and managed (Du Plessis et. al. 2015, p.XXV). Corporate governance originates with the birth of corporations. In *An Inquiry into the Nature and Causes of the Wealth of Nations* of 1776, Smith even then writes:

> *The directors of such companies, however, being the managers rather of other people's money than of their own, it cannot well be expected, that they should watch over it with the same anxious vigilance with which the partners in a private copartnery frequently watch over their own .... Negligence and profusion, therefore, must always prevail, more or less, in the management of the affairs of such a company.* (Smith 1776, p.741).

Smith thus points to the need for the supervision of managers because of the (legal) separation of ownership in capital from the control over that capital – i.e. the management of a business. In the same vein, nowadays there is an underlying assumption in most of the corporate governance literature that corporate managers "operate with self-serving motivation" (Buchholtz et. al. 2008, p.329).[5] Thus, corporate governance should set certain rules and principles for company management in order to decrease possible negative externalities that might rise from such self-interested behaviour of managers. In the other words, corporate governance should prevent managers, who do not run the business with their own capital, abuse their power at the expense of the capital owners'– shareholders' – interests. The most complex tension in the corporate governance debate that has not been solved yet is how to balance "the profit-making objective of corporations and company officers against broader social responsibilities owed to the wider community" (Du Plessis et. al. 2015, p.XXV). The focus of this contribution is, however, on managers' discretion: would managers abuse their managerial position at the expense of shareholders' interests when they promote the interests of (other) stakeholders in the company? In order to answer this question, we need to better understand what corporate governance is.

The concept of corporate governance can have varying definitions. Many theoretical definitions of corporate governance reflect the concern for the supposedly self-serving motivation of managers related to the separation of ownership and control. For instance, Shleifer and Vishny define corporate governance as "the ways in which suppliers of finance to corporations assure themselves of getting a return on their investment" (Shleifer and Vishny, 1997). However, there is need for control of those who have to realise this return on investment. La Porta, Lopez-de-Silanes, Shleifer and Vishny define corporate governance as "a set of mechanisms through which outside investors protect themselves against expropriation by the insiders" (La Porta et. al., 2000, p.4). Friese, Link and Mayer aptly summarise the common general elements as "the sum of all mechanisms of control and supervision that are aimed at ensuring the successful operation of a business in a corporate form and in this respect to remedy the effects of the separation of ownership and management" (Friese et. al. 2008, p.364).

If we look at the attempts of commissions and regulatory authorities to define CG we also see different definitions. For instance, according to the UK Cadbury Commission, corporate governance is "the system by which

---

5 Nowadays the managers' self-serving motivation is conceptualized as agency theory, according to which one person (agent) has to make decisions on behalf of (or that affects the) another person (principal). Corporate governance rules should offer a safety net in case there occur conflicts between agents and principals. Agents are usually corporate managers and principals are stakeholders, while shareholders are often considered as the most important group of stakeholders. See more on agency theory: Eisenhardt 1989; Desai & Dharmapala 2008, p.14 who point at the centrality of the agency problem to the intersection of corporate governance and taxation.

companies are directed and controlled" (Cadbury 1992, para. 2.5). The direction of the companies should be controlled to protect investors. According to the Dutch Corporate Governance Code, corporate governance is about good governance and supervision of listed companies; it regulates relations between directors, auditors and shareholders.[6] So corporate governance concerns mechanisms to supervise the behaviour of different actors. According to its preamble, the Dutch point of departure is that the corporation is "a long-term alliance between the various parties involved in the company." The Dutch Code refers to different actors – the stakeholders. Such stakeholders are, according to this Code, "the groups and individuals who, directly or indirectly, influence – or are influenced by – the attainment of the company's objects: i.e. employees, shareholders and other lenders, suppliers, customers, the public sector and civil society." The Code states that "the management board and the supervisory board have overall responsibility for weighing up these interests, generally with a view to ensuring the continuity of the enterprise, while the company endeavours to create long-term shareholder value."[7] Furthermore, according to the OECD "corporate governance involves a set of relationships between a company's management, its board, its shareholders and other stakeholders. Corporate governance also provides the structure through which the objectives of the company are set, and the means of attaining those objectives and monitoring performance are determined" (OECD 2015b, p.9). The OECD further notes that "the purpose of corporate governance is to help build an environment of trust, transparency and accountability necessary for fostering long-term investment, financial stability and business integrity, thereby supporting stronger growth and more inclusive societies" (OECD 2015b, p.7).

These examples show that there are differences in definitions and therefore also to a certain extent in the principles of corporate governance. Such various definitions indicate different starting points – supervision mechanisms protecting first and foremost shareholder interests on the one hand, or taking also explicitly into account stakeholder interests on the other hand. Both positions are hotly debated. We will discuss these different starting points further in this article.

---

6   "Corporate governance gaat over goed bestuur van beursgenoteerde bedrijven en het toezicht daarop. Het regelt verhoudingen tussen bestuurders, commissarissen en aandeelhouders. De overheid heeft wetten opgesteld voor goed en eerlijk bestuur van bedrijven. Ook is er een gedragscode: de Corporate Governance Code." <https://www.rijksoverheid.nl/onderwerpen/corporate-governance> accessed 14.07.2016.

7   Preamble point 7.

In this contribution, we approach the corporate governance debate from the perspective of tax planning. An important distinction is made between the shareholder perspective and the stakeholder perspective on corporate governance. Some authors argue that the differences between these two conflicting views have become smaller (Stout, 2012, p.26). To a certain extent this can be agreed with, especially considering that there are many globalised multinationals operating in an international setting. This convergence notwithstanding, tax matters provide nuances, which still make it a difficult debate. This is because taxes are not only an expense, but also have a moral aspect which apparently confuses companies (see e.g. Gribnau, 2015; Gribnau and Jallai, 2016). Taxes, therefore, have a societal and an economic dimension; they are important contributions to a sustainable society while they can also be seen as a cost element for a company. This provides us with questions such as, for example, whether managers should view tax planning from the perspective of the shareholders or from the ethical perspective, which demand to take companies' societal obligations into account?

Corporate governance theories are largely based on theories of companies, and on the question to whom should a corporation be responsible and accountable – shareholders or stakeholders. Among economists, there has long existed an understanding that corporations should generally be run so as to maximise its owners' – shareholder – value (Berle and Means, 1968; Friedman, 2002, p.133). This view directly relates to the central focus of this contribution: do multinationals and their managers have any choice in tax planning, and therefore, ethically responsible tax governance, and, if so, how should they choose whether they should satisfy their shareholders or society at large, or maybe both?

Whose interests should a corporation serve – shareholders or stakeholders?

Amongst corporate law scholars, there have long existed two prevailing theories when talking about the essence of a corporation: shareholder theory and stakeholder theory. These two theories reflect upon to whom corporations should be responsible and accountable. To a certain extent convergence has developed between these theories.[8] Consequently, there is less disagreement

---

8 The alleged convergence between the two systems has probably much to do with globalisation and growth of international business making. It is, however, not entirely clear what this convergence exactly entails. In 2002, shortly after the Enron scandal, leading US CG scholars Hansmann and Kraakman argued that there is an international convergence towards the 'standard' model of corporate governance – the shareholder model since it is the

nowadays in regard to the board's discretion to also serve wider stakeholders' interests as well as shareholders. However, managers like Google's Matt Brittin seem not be aware of this convergence, especially in the context of tax planning. They seem to stick to an out-dated conception of the shareholder primacy. In order to convince these kinds of managers, we address the question of managerial discretion by presenting the two theories in a traditional, rather black-and-white way, though without leaving out nuances evidencing some convergence.

The shareholder theory marks "the importance of the primacy of the shareholder interest and the enhancement of the shareholder value" (Farrar, 2005, p.5). The stakeholder theory, on the other hand, presumes that "corporations exist to serve a number of different interests and not just shareholders" (Farrar, 2005, p.5). Stakeholders are individuals (or a group of individuals) who have "a commitment to a corporation that stems from the fact that they work for it, supply it, purchase from it, live near it, or are affected in some way by its activities" (Mayer, 2013, p.32). Naturally, also shareholders are (internal) stakeholders but since shareholders are stakeholders who invest money in a company and are thereby also 'the owners', they are different from the rest of the stakeholders.

These two theories represent also two theoretical models of corporate governance: the 'market-oriented' Anglo-Saxon model and the 'network-oriented' Rhineland model of corporate governance (see e.g. Wymeersch, 2002, p.231; Campbell and Vick, 2007, pp.250-252). These models illustrate two diverging regulatory and business culture approaches towards stakeholders and shareholders in company management (Habisch, 2005, pp.367-370). In the Anglo-Saxon countries, such as the UK and US, directors of a company have a fiduciary duty towards its shareholders. In the Rhineland model countries in Europe, such as Germany and the Netherlands, managers have no judicial obligation to exclusively maximise shareholder value (see also Reinhardt et. al., 2008, p.11; Neri-Castracane, 2015, p.13). In German corporate law, which

---

best / strongest to work, according to the authors (Hansmann and Kraakman, 2002, pp.56-58, 76). On the other hand, there are scholars who criticise theories of convergence because corporate governance is very much attached to national systems and therefore there is no possibility for one general international system (Farrar, 2005, pp.11-13.) In this vein Mallin (2007) notes that "while recognizing that 'one size does not fit all' in terms of corporate governance, institutional investors are increasingly converging on the basics of good corporate governance, encompassing such areas as basic shareholder right, independence of directors, and presence of key board committees." For further discussion in the context of tax planning these two systems still offer various insights to consider; especially when we aim to place tax planning in the context of CSR. Then the question of whose interests managers should consider – shareholders or society at large – is raised again.

is a representative of the Rhineland model, the concept of the plurality of interests exists: "corporations are expected to abide by commonly accepted legal and ethical norms, and directors are required to take account of the interests of the parties in addition to those of shareholders" – stakeholders, thus (Mayer, 2013, p.40).[9] European companies therefore also have to take into account the interests of employees and creditors (Lambooy, 2010, p.56). For a contrasting example, Sweden has a corporate governance system that lies in between these two 'extremes'; directors have the possibility to "interpret the company's interests as extending beyond those of the shareholders" but they are not obliged to do so (Mayer, 2013, p.41).

Donaldson argues that the differences between American/UK (shareholder) and European (stakeholder) models of the corporation and corporate governance can be summarised by "contrasting the extent to which the respective institutions of the United States and Europe either embed or fail to embed the interests of the community in the governance of the corporation" (Donaldson, 2008, pp.545-546). He further adds that in the US the focus lies more on "issues of individual liberty and economic freedom," while in Europe the central point of interest is focusing more on "class difference and community solidarity" (Donaldson, 2008, p.546).

For the context of this contribution, the differences between the two models raise the question whether both these systems of corporate governance leave elbow-room for managerial decision making. In order to answer that question, we focus explicitly on corporation managers' responsibilities towards shareholders and other stakeholders, and examine whether these theories have conflicting and common elements in this regard.

Shareholder value maximisation

One school of thought that supports the view that corporations should be run to increase shareholders' value originates from the writings of Milton Friedman (see e.g. Friedman, 1970). This neo-classical economic (or neo-liberal; Weyzig, 2009) perspective is often presented as the absolute opposite to the idea of possible social responsibilities of businesses. It is also referred to

---

9 In the same vein: Schön, 2013, p.1098; Muchlinsky, 2007, pp.341-342: "the classical Anglo-American model of the single board corporation may not give adequate voice to the interests of stakeholders other than shareholders. By contrast, the German dual board model has been supplemented by a mandatory allocation of seats on the supervisory board for workers representatives under the co-determination laws (Mitbestimmung)." The participation of stakeholders in the decision-making process is one of the premises (besides transparency and accountability), which are common to both corporate governance and CSR (Lambooy, 2010, pp.49-104).

as "Shareholder Value Theory" (SVT) or "Fiduciary Capitalism." This theoretical approach supports the idea that the only responsibility of business is making profits. Moreover, the supreme goal according to this theory is "increasing the economic value of the company for its shareholders" (Melé, 2008, p.55). Based on that, all other social activities that corporate boards could think about, would only be acceptable in case obliged by law or in case they add to maximisation of shareholder value (Melé, 2008, p.55).

Milton Friedman, the famous proponent of this essentially economic approach, argued in 1970 that the only one responsibility of business towards the society will generally be the maximisation of profits to the shareholders, "while conforming to the basic rules of the society, both those embodied in law and those embodied in ethical custom" (Friedman, 1970, pp.32-33). This broad view on the basic rules of society is often not taken into account when Friedman is quoted. Namely, in contradiction to the received view, Friedman is not opposing any social responsibilities of a company, he is supporting a thin theory of CSR (Schwartz, 2011, p.56). To his mind, it is justified that managers of a corporation that is a major employer in a small community devote resources to providing amenities to that community or to improving its government, because it is in the long-term interest of that corporation (Parkinson, 2006, p.9). But for him it is a matter of generating goodwill rather than social responsibility (Friedman, 1970, pp.122-126). He labels this as acting from self-interest. Note, that self-interest thus may include a commitment to certain social and ethical values – for example, in response to public pressure. According to Schwartz, Friedman's position could be summarised as a responsibility "to make as much money as possible" (e.g. maximise profits) while complying with the "rules of the game" or "basic rules of the society" in which the firm is operating (Schwartz, 2011, p.52). Such rules of society include obeying the "law," conforming to "ethical custom" (e.g. business norms where you do business), and acting "without deception or fraud" (Schwartz, 2011, p.52).

There are, nevertheless, some unclear elements in Friedman's theory for the purposes of this contribution. For one thing, Friedman has not clearly defined what he means by "ethical custom". Schwartz believes that "presumably this consists of what would be considered acceptable behaviour by the corporate community in the place in which the firm is doing business" (Schwartz, 2011, p.55). However, it could well be the wider society rather than the corporate community for Friedman considers "ethical custom" as part of the basic rules of society. Moreover, as also shown above, according to Friedman companies should not engage in deception or fraud, even if by doing so they are maximising profits while abiding by the law (Friedman, 1970, pp.32-33; Schwartz, 2011, p.55). Deception in this context may include "the ethical obligation to act honestly, with sufficient transparency in one's actions such that they can be effectively evaluated by others" (Schwartz, 2011, p.55). Interpreted in this way, Friedman again would leave room for ethical obligations beyond (mere) compliance with the legal system (Clark and Grantham, 2012, p.32). To conclude, according to Friedman managers may engage in practices that take into account the interests of stakeholders, though not solely of stakeholders, in order to advance the long-term interests of the firm. Moreover, managers have elbow-room to respect widely held social and ethical values, which are part of the rules of the game, in the long term interest of that corporation.

The idea of shareholder value maximisation in general focuses on the predominance of property relations (see e.g. Sternberg, 2000; Melé, 2008, p.58). This means that shareholders, as the owners of their investment (capital) should be protected against unreasonable spending. Managers are agents whose function is to maximise shareholders' value (Keinert, 2008, p.60; Logsdon and Yuthas, 1997). Such a view is generally backed by a high level of distrust vis-à-vis managers because of their self-serving motivation (Keinert, 2008, p.60). Friedman's theory considers the shareholder value maximisation as "the supreme reference for corporate decision-making" (Garriga and Melé, 2004, p.54). However, what this theory initially does not consider is the fact that shareholders are highly mobile. They have the possibility to pull back their investment at any time (see e.g. Chang, 2010, pp.17-21). The role of shareholders has changed through the time and has been affected by globalisation. If previously we could identify shareholders as the owners of a corporation of which they owned shares, then nowadays it is more complicated and we should consider shareholder as the owners of the shares rather than the corporation. Focusing on multinationals, we see that "shareholders no longer personally identify with the corporation they own" (Molz, 1995, p.791). Therefore, as Molz argues, "most owners today only identify their ownership in the corporation as an investment" (Molz, 1995, p.791; see also Mayer, 2013, p.34.). Such shareholders today expect that "the corporation should generate a steady stream of increasing quarterly profits and higher stock prices" (Molz, 1995, p.791). If such expectation is met, "the investors are satisfied and unlikely to question the decision making in the firm." Based on that, Molz argues that "this preoccupation with short-term financial performance overwhelms corporate considerations for broader social issues in the decision making process" (Molz, 1995, p.791, referring to Drucker, 1986).

The issue that we face here is, however, that the high mobility of shareholders allows them to step out any time they wish; other stakeholders usually cannot do that. Therefore, focusing only on the (short-term) shareholder value is not in the interests of the company nor the economy neither society at large (see also Chang, 2010, p.19). Moreover, shareholders' short-term interest might be bad for the company's long-term interests. Nevertheless, we do recognize that due to the same mobility factor of shareholders, managers might often be under pressure to satisfy their needs in order not to lose the investment. This can, however, create negative externalities for the rest of stakeholders or society at large. Nonetheless, fear that shareholders might leave is not equal to lack of elbow-room in decision-making.

As explained above, shareholder value maximisation has long been the basis of Anglo-Saxon corporate governance models (Melé, 2008, p.60). One of the common elements in the SVT supporters' argumentation is 'freedom'; it seems to be the keyword of this theory. Depending on the economic and political power one supports, this could be considered an argument for supporting this theory. Another strength of this model, according to supporters of the SVT, is that it contributes to an efficient economic system. They maintain, in the wording of Melé, that the best conditions for wealth creation are "conducting business for self-interest, presenting profits as the supreme goal, and operating under conditions of free and competitive markets within a minimalist policy" (Melé, 2008, p.60). Some authors have also added that the conditions of the free-market economy help to create social benefit if negative externalities and trade-offs would not exist (see e.g. Jensen, 2000, pp.35-78). If companies are free to make their own decisions, the whole economy will benefit in the end. Therefore, the free market economy supports the creation of a strong and developed economy whereas "the tax system permits a part of the wealth generated to be shared by society through governmental mediation" (Melé, 2008, p.60). This naturally provides an interesting question from the perspective of taxation – would this argument fail if companies avoid paying taxes? As we will briefly explain below, tax is an obligation towards society that many aggressive tax planners fail to meet.

Despite the arguments which favour economic growth and development, shareholder value theory has also gained a lot of criticism. The free market economy and focus on shareholder value maximisation would be efficient for the economy where negative externalities do not exist. However, they do exist. Therefore, some authors have criticized the SVT. For instance, Arrow has argued that the market involves asymmetric information and that causes negative externalities for some parties and the rest of the world

(Arrow, 1985, pp.130-142; Arrow, 1973). This, in turn, "destroys the invisible hand of Adam Smith and the connection between the micro and macro levels, and therefore the efficiency of markets" (Melé, 2008, p.61). Therefore, this SVT approach might not be as beneficial for economic development as some tend to believe. In addition, the fact that the shareholder value maximization approach is frequently connected with short-termism, supports the arguments that it might not be efficient for the economy as a whole. Short-term profit making rather than long-term corporate value maximisation is namely believed to be rather negative way of running a business (see e.g. Melé, 2008, p.61).

Furthermore, Melé has argued that besides "self-interest and concern for profits" a successful firm requires more: "trust, a sense of loyalty, and good relationships with all stakeholders and, as a consequence, an enduring cooperation among those who are involved in or are independent with the firm" (Melé, 2008, p.61; see also Hosmer, 1995; Kay, 1993; Kotter and Heskett, 1992). Nowadays, pure shareholder value maximisation that precluded any socially responsible behaviour has to some authors been proven wrong in itself because shareholder wealth would most likely decrease if companies act in socially irresponsibly ways (Keinert, 2008, p.65). Garriga and Melé argue that nowadays "it is quite readily accepted that shareholder value maximisation is not incompatible with satisfying certain interests of people with a stake in the firm (stakeholders)" (Garriga and Melé, 2004, p.54).

Based on the fact that extreme shareholder value maximisation theory is incompatible with efficient economy and social welfare, Jensen has proposed the so-called enlightened value maximisation theory (see Jensen, 2000, pp.49-50). He implies that it is more important to focus on a long-term value-creating vision and organisational strategy as a whole instead of focusing on pure value maximisation as a sole corporate strategy (Jensen, 2010, p.38). Jensen argues that the basic principle of enlightened value maximisation is "we cannot maximize the long-term market value of an organization if we ignore or mistreat any important constituency" (Jensen, 2010, p.38). Therefore, he continues, corporations need to keep good relations with stakeholders. Pichet has elaborated on Jensen's theory and argued for an 'enlightened shareholder theory', according to which managers "must defend the firm's long-term social interests" (Pichet, 2011). Furthermore, Pichet adds that in terms of 'enlightened shareholder theory', corporate board composition practices should be changed so that it includes "different kinds of expertise" and that it is "capable of integrating and understanding a company's culture" (Pichet, 2011). Thus, we witness that even the most critical view on social responsibilities of companies has gained more moral flesh on the profit bones. Proponents of shareholder value maximisation theory explicitly stress the importance of good relations with stakeholders: taking into account the interests of stakeholders and the wider society may advance the company's interests. This leads us to the opposite theory, the stakeholder theory that will be discussed next.

Stakeholder theory

As CSR requires managers to take into account the interests of members of society, which are seen as company's stakeholders, the concept of 'stakeholder' needs further clarification. Shareholder value theory has, as shown above, often been considered being too one-sided and narrow. It has also gained a lot of justified criticism. Therefore, scholars have proposed alternative approaches. Many authors have argued that corporations should be responsible to a larger group of stakeholders than just shareholders (see e.g. Freeman, 1984; Friedman and Miles, 2006; Donaldson and Preston, 1995; Melé, 2008, p.64). Thus, the interests to be served by managers include those of the shareholders (who are internal stakeholders) as well as the (other) stakeholders. This is advocated by the stakeholder theory, taking stakeholders rather than shareholders as its point of departure.

What is a stakeholder? Freeman's classic definition is often quoted. "A stakeholder in an organization is (by definition) any group or individual who can affect or is affected by the achievement of the organization's objectives" (Freeman et. al., 2010, p.207, quoting Freeman, 1984; see also Friedman and Miles, 2006, pp.25-27). Stakeholder theory scholars describe a corporation by placing stakeholders in the middle of it: "The firm is a system of stakeholders operating within the larger system of the host society that provides the necessary legal and market infrastructure for the firm activities. The purpose of the firm is to create wealth or value for its stakeholders by converting their stakes into goods and services" (Clarkson, 1995, p.105). The basic idea is that value creation is the result of interaction among groups which have a stake in the activities that make up business. "Business is about how customers, suppliers, employees, financiers (stockholders, bondholders, banks), communities, and managers interact and to create value" (Freeman et. al., 2010, p.24). In these relationships the principles of reciprocity and responsibility are at play; for instance, "the local community grants the firm the right to build facilities and, in turn, it benefits from the tax base and economic and social contributions of the firm" (Freeman et. al., 2010, p.25).

For Freeman and others, stakeholder theory is not an antipode to shareholder theory but "instead a larger view about corporations that encompasses shareholder theory" (Freeman et. al., 2010, p.206). They argue that the introduction of stakeholder theory entails an "invitation to a conversation that forces managers and the public to examine together two questions 'what is the purpose of a corporation?' and 'to whom are managers responsible?'" To this he adds that these two questions "have both ethics and business thoroughly embedded in them" (Freeman et. al., 2010, p.206). This is clearly a non-positivist view.

Initially the stakeholder theory was introduced as 'a managerial theory' for better strategic management. According to Hansmann and Kraakman, "at the core of this view was the belief that professional corporate managers could serve as disinterested technocratic fiduciaries who would guide business corporations to perform in ways that would serve the general public interest" (Hansmann and Kraakman, 2002, p.60). Nevertheless, they continue arguing, "while managerial firms may be in some ways more efficiently responsive to non-shareholder interests than are firms that are more dedicated to serving their shareholder, the price paid in inefficiency for operations and excessive investment in low-value projects is now considered too great" (Hansmann and Kraakman, 2002, p.60). This point of view reveals one of the most important criticisms that shareholder theory supporters have towards the stakeholder theory – it is considered to be economically inefficient. However, the stakeholder theory has also been considered to be "a normative theory which requires management to have a moral duty to protect the corporation as a whole and, connected with this aim, the legitimate interests of all stakeholders" (Melé, 2008, p.63). Whether protecting the corporate interests as a whole is always economically inefficient is up for a debate.

Stakeholder theory, as any other theory, has its proponents and opponents who have pointed out some strengths and weaknesses. For instance, in comparison with the shareholder theory, stakeholder theory is considered to be more ethical, just and "more respectful of human dignity and rights" (Melé, 2008, p.66). Therefore, stakeholder theory is strongly related with the concept of CSR where corporations have wider responsibilities than purely towards shareholders (Freeman et. al., 2010, pp.21-23). According to Freeman and others ideas and concepts like CSR, corporate citizenship and corporate governance "share a common aim in the attempt to broaden the obligations of firms to include more than financial obligations." Thus, the literature in this field deals with "questions of the broader purpose of the firm and how it can deliver on those goals" (Freeman et. al., 2010, p.235). In their view, "the stakeholder idea can and should be used as a foundational unit of analysis for the ongoing conversation around CSR" (Freeman et. al., 2010, p.236).

Several authors believe that one of the strengths of the stakeholder theory is that it has replaced the conceptual vagueness of CSR because it is addressing concrete interests and practices and it focuses on the specific responsibilities to specific groups that are affected by business activity (see e.g. Blair, 1995; Clarkson, 1995; Melé, 2008, p.66). It is somewhat difficult to really agree with that, because stakeholder theory in itself is also a very broad and vague theory. Moreover, stakeholders' interests are many (see Weyzig 2009, pp.418-419) and sometimes they may conflict; what should businesses do then? In light of this question, however, one of the additional strengths of stakeholder theory is that stakeholder management is not necessarily directed against shareholders; it just considers a wider group of stakeholders than shareholders only. Therefore, in corporate governance systems that attach weight to the stakeholder theory, managers do have sufficient elbow-room for decision-making (see also Schön, 2008, p.36).

Stakeholder theory is nevertheless sometimes criticised because (from the shareholder value theorists' perspective) it might pave the way for managerial opportunism (see e.g. Jensen, 2000, pp.35-78; Marcoux, 2000; Sternberg, 2000). Sternberg adds that stakeholder theory "effectively destroys business accountability ... because a business that is accountable to all, is actually accountable to none" (Sternberg, 2000, p.51). Jensen also criticises the stakeholder theory as developed by Freeman (1984) and others. He claims that any theory should provide the actors (managers in this case) guidance on how to deal with multiple "competing and inconsistent constituent interests" (Jensen, 2000, pp.44-45). Jensen argues that stakeholder theory presented by other scholars does not explain how to deal with trade-offs that managers have to deal with. Therefore, he proposes a more advanced – enlightened – stakeholder theory. Enlightened stakeholder theory requires managers to operate in a way to maximise the total long-term market value of the firm (Jensen, 2000, p.51; Jensen, 2010). Thus, the trade-offs the managers face need to consider the long-term market value of the firm as an ultimate goal. This gives managers elbow-room to assess which competing interests need to be prioritised in order to serve the long-term goals and value of the firm.

Therefore, we see where the main conflict between the two approaches arises: shareholder theory prioritises the economic interests of the company, while stakeholder theory sets society above or on the equal level with pure economic interests. However, it is not the aim of this contribution to argue in favour of one or criticise the other model. Nevertheless, for this contribution, we still need to know how far managers are allowed to go in their tax planning decisions in taking non-shareholders' interests into account – as CSR encourages. How independent are they in their decision-making and whose interest should they consider and prioritise? Moreover, does prioritising one automatically exclude considering other interests?

Shareholders, stakeholders and corporate governance

As shown above, these opposite theories have their strengths and weaknesses. The shareholder value maximisation theory, as an extreme that excluded the rest of the stakeholders, initiated a response in the form of stakeholder theory. This contribution focuses, however, on managerial elbow-room with regard to tax planning within these theories. To be more specific, in this contribution we question whether the CG regime that prioritises shareholder value maximisation allows it to practice good tax governance. Are managers allowed to consider wider interests than just shareholder value maximisation, as advocated by stakeholder theory, or is it really not 'a matter of choice'? Could managers in the shareholder model take stakeholders' interests on board or not? Therefore, we need to explore further whether companies that praise the shareholder value theory should ignore all other stakes besides shareholders'

In the Anglo-Saxon system, managers have the fiduciary duty to fulfil the financial expectations of shareholders.[10] However, the "the Delaware courts have never stated plainly that management's fiduciary responsibilities— the duties of care and loyalty — imply a general duty to maximise profits without regard to competing nonshareholder considerations" (Millon, 2011, pp.526-527). Thus, could they really be expected to plan their taxes as aggressive as possible in order to increase the returns for shareholders?

Stout has argued that "the fiduciary duty of loyalty precludes officers and directors from using their corporate positions to line their own pockets." Nevertheless, according to her, managers remain free "to pursue other, non-shareholder-related goals under the comforting mantle of the business judgment rule" (Stout, 2012, p.29). She adds that "contrary to the shareholder primacy thesis, shareholders cannot recover against directors or officers for breach of fiduciary duty simply because those directors and officers favour

---

10 See more on fiduciary duty e.g.: Lafferty et. al. 2012.

stakeholders' interests over the shareholders' own" (Stout, 2012, p.29). Stout has later also argued that it is incorrect to assume that "shareholders are principals and directors are shareholder's agents in corporations" (Stout, 2016). She claims that "corporate law treats directors not as agents of shareholders but as fiduciaries who owe legal duties not only to shareholders, but also to the corporate entity itself" (Stout, 2016). In the same vein, Schön argues that in Germany managers have discretion with regard to the choice of tax planning structures, which is protected by the business judgement rule. Only in quite extreme situations there will be a violation of their duty of care (Schön, 2013, pp.1091-1092).

The UK corporate law system recently embraced the 'enlightened shareholder value' idea (Esser and Du Plessis, 2007, pp.351-353); UK Company Law Review Steering Group, 1999, p. vi). The British Company Law Review Steering Group, established to evaluate the earlier regulation and coordinate the UK company law revision in the beginning of 2000s (see e.g. Ferran, 2005), discussed in the process of revision that there is a difference between 'enlightened shareholder value' and a 'pluralist approach'. According to the former, directors should "pursue shareholders' interests in an enlightened and inclusive way" and according to the 'pluralist' approach "co-operative and productive relationships will only be optimised where directors are permitted (or required) to balance shareholders' interests with those of others committed to the company" (UK Company Law Review Steering Group, 1999, p. vi). The latter is thus a more strongly stakeholder-oriented approach. In short, the UK has adopted the enlightened shareholder value approach in its corporate governance system (see also Du Plessis et. al., 2015, p.61). Therefore, corporate governance in the UK is not based on absolute shareholder primacy nor shortism. Moreover, awareness has shown that an even more strongly stakeholder-oriented approach should be discussed and cannot be put aside out of hand.[11] The group also pointed out that the key company law provision in the UK is the directors' fiduciary duties, according to which directors have to "honestly ('in good faith') manage the undertaking for the benefit of the company" (UK Company Law Review Steering Group, 1999, section 5.1.18 (p.39)). Hereby the Steering Group indicated that the directors should act in the long-term interests of the company.

Advancing the successful operation of the corporation demands pursuing the interests of the corporation. For instance, the courts of Delaware,

---

11 UK Company Law Review Steering Group (1999, section 5.1.42 (p.50)) for example pointed out that "as a matter of principle, the law should be changed to allow directors a discretion to sacrifice commercial advantage for ethical or public objectives."

the state in which most of the US corporations are incorporated, confirm the centrality of the company's interests. Delaware case law demands that managers should refrain from pursuing their self-interest and act in "the best interests of the company."[12] Such thinking is widespread in the Anglo-Saxon model of corporate governance under the business judgement rule, according to which the managers are obliged to act in the best interests of the company (as is the case in Germany and the Netherlands). In addition, Parkinson has analysed the UK and other Anglo-Saxon case law and found that "courts have in practice... accepted the justification of attention to wider constituents and interests as a means of enhancing long-term shareholder value" (Parkinson, 1994 as paraphrased in McBarnet, 2007, p.23).

It appears thus that in the Anglo-Saxon countries managers can – and even have to – take foremost the best care of the business interest.[13] This means that managers have discretion in pursuing the interests of the corporation and there is no major difference between the various corporate governance models in this respect. We advocate in this contribution that managers should exercise this discretion carefully but not unduly cautiously.

Managerial elbow-room and corporate social responsibility

We see that even the shareholder model, based on Anglo-Saxon regulators and courts, leaves some room for managerial decision-making when running a company. However, considering the previously discussed nuances in various corporate governance regimes – is it possible to take CSR into account?

As argued previously, different corporate governance models entail specific principles that the management board has to follow. We showed that these different principles still leave a possibility of choices within these rules. Thus, according to Delaware company law, for listed companies, the board is entitled with board supremacy and the business judgement rule, as well as the case in the Netherlands and Germany. Also Enriques et al. (2017, p.98) confirm that while in Germany, the UK and the US (as well as Brazil, France, Italy, Japan) the corporate laws "do not compel spending on social causes, they do not prohibit either." They also add that "even in the United States, where fiduciary duties to shareholders are formally perhaps the strongest, in practice directors enjoy wide latitude to further the interests of non-shareholder constituencies so long as the decision is framed in terms of promot-

---

12 See e.g. Neri-Castracane 2015, p.10, referring to *Aroson vs Lewis*, 473 A.2d 805, 812 (Del. 1984); *Kaplan vs Centex Corp.*, 284 A.2d 119, 124 (Del. 1971); *Robinson vs Pittsburgh Oil Refinery Corp.*, 126 A. 46 (Del. 1924).

13 Ibid.

ing long-term shareholder value" (Enriques et. al., 2017, pp.98-99). Moreover, even under the shareholder (long-term) value maximisation obligation the directors can (under above-mentioned business judgement rule) make socially responsible decisions "insofar as these decisions have a supposed business purpose" (Neri-Castracane, 2015, p.15, idem Sheehy and Feaver, 2014, pp.387-388).

Even though researchers have not managed to prove a systematic connection between CSR activities and financial performance as yet, the business judgement rule allows in principle for managers to consider stakeholder interests even in shareholder value maximisation-minded CG systems. Moreover, managers' elbow-room is underpinned by the fact that the managers are obliged to consider the best interest of the company. Therefore, to a certain extent managers are free to decide how aggressive or responsible the company should be in relation to the societies in which they operate. Naturally, management could have less room to manoeuvre if the majority shareholders are short-term value-seeking. Nevertheless, there are certain things that managers still can consider.

A company's management may thus engage in CSR (for listed firms, there is a formal obligation to disclose a CSR policy if they have one, and if they do not have, they still have to account for it – 'comply or explain' (see e.g. Directive 2013/34/EU)). But what is CSR? The European Commission gives a very brief definition of CRS, "the responsibility of enterprises for their impact on society" (European Commission, 2011, p.6 (section 3.1)). Companies endorsing CSR voluntarily accept obligations towards society. In this vein Carroll, a major contributor to the field of CSR, makes an analytical distinction between a firm's economic, legal, ethical and philanthropic responsibilities (Carroll, 1991; Carroll, 1999; Schwartz and Carroll, 2003; Jallai, 2017). These obligations are not mutually exclusive. Economic and legal obligations are the basis of the societal obligations that CSR companies voluntarily accept. Carroll's well-known view on CSR advocates ethical (and philanthropic) obligations on top of the obligation to comply with the law. Carroll views ethical considerations as 'beyond compliance', and businesses therefore have to go beyond what is required by the law. Indeed, one of the cornerstones of CSR is that businesses voluntarily act over and above legal requirements (Parkinson, 2006, p.5).

Managers can, thus, use their discretion to engage in CSR, which entails going beyond compliance with the legal rules. This indicates that managers are quite flexible when acting in the best interests of the company under the concept of CSR. Moreover, most multinationals already have a CSR strategy in place. This means that managers already have a certain room to manoeuvre in place. As we have argued elsewhere, to our minds, tax should not be excluded from a company's CSR strategy - and thus included in its room to manoeuvre, which may entail going beyond compliance with the law (Gribnau and Jallai, 2016).

Having argued that there is a certain room for managerial decision-making, we are still left with the question of how big that space is. As noted, the stakeholder oriented CG system strongly supports CSR, while in the shareholder oriented CG system, the board has discretion to take into account CSR-standards. Therefore, we could state that this elbow-room is the space between corporate social responsibility (CSR) and corporate social irresponsibility (CSI).

Aggressive tax planning and corporate social irresponsibility

As shown above, corporate governance allows managers discretion to take stakeholders' interests into account, and therefore engage in CRS. In this section we will argue that engaging in CSR should impact business' attitude towards tax planning. However, it is not easy to establish what a socially responsible corporate tax policy in practice is. It is easier to agree upon what companies should not do with regard to tax planning. In case of tax planning, therefore, the best interest of the company is to stay away from corporate social irresponsibility.

CSR and CSI

Why do we take this concept of 'corporate social irresponsibility' on board? To our minds, the concept of CSI is equally important as CSR – being its inseparable counterpart. Neglecting the importance of the CSI concept allows for an incomplete conceptualisation of CSR (Tench et. al., 2012, p.19).

As shown above, CSR businesses voluntarily accept the obligation to go beyond compliance with legal requirements. However, it is not very clear what is meant by acting over and above legal requirements. It does not provide clear-cut criteria and effective guidance. Does it entail that CSR companies should behave like ideal (corporate) citizens? Should they behave better than the average citizen? Moreover, what kind of behaviour does this ideal entail? Ideals are the subject of much debate and the same goes for the means (strategy) to realise ideals: consensus is often hard to reach. Thus the aspirational idea of accepting ethical obligations beyond compliance with the law is quite ambiguous. Lacking clarity, defending and prescribing behaviour beyond compliance to inspire corporate action will probably not be very convincing and effective for business practice.

Therefore, in order to help managers in their decision-making process, we might turn to the other end of CSR, so-called corporate social irresponsibility (CSI).[14] CSI seems to be a more addressable concern. It is even indispensable to remedy certain shortcomings of CSR theories. As Tench et al. argue, "without the concept of CSI, CSR is eventually empty" (Tench et. al., 2012, p.5). Armstrong has approached CSI as follows: "'Social responsibility' is difficult to define. What *should* a manager do?" He argues that it t is "easier to look at the problem in terms of what he should *not* do - i.e., at 'social irresponsibility'." A socially irresponsible act, Armstrong continues "is a decision to accept an alternative that is *thought by the decision maker to be inferior to another alternative when the effects upon all parties are considered*. Generally this involves a gain by one party at the expense of the total system" (Armstrong, 1977, p.185 original emphasis)). Thus, he argues that it might be easier to find out what companies should not do instead of dictating what they should do.

In this way, CSR becomes more clear by asking "the key question: what is not CSR?" (Tench et. al., 2012, p.8). In order to clarify what a corporation should not do, Armstrong argues that corporate managers act irresponsibly if they choose an alternative decision that has more negative externalities for other parties. Legal-but-irresponsible business is an example of the exploitation of negative externalities – negatively impacting other businesses and society at large. Such behaviour can be viewed "as anticompetitive between firms which also leads to counter-productive outcomes for social welfare" (Clark and Grantham ,2012, p.30). Moreover, such behaviour may be judged as unethical by using the Negative Golden Rule that "exhorts people NOT to do unto others what you would NOT wish done unto you" (Clark and Grantham, 2012, p.33, referring to the work of Labiano and Gensler).

Clarifying what a corporation should not do probably adds to the effectiveness of CSR. Clark and Grantham argue that clarity about what not to do may be more effective as guidance to convince businesses to take action than a prescriptive approach. Proscription by defining undesirable behaviour will be more successful because "acts which involve negative consequences

---

14 The authors would like to thank Steen Vallentin and Andreas Rasche from Copenhagen Business School (and other participants of the Workshop: 'Taxation, Corporations and the State" that took place in Copenhagen Business School, 27-28 June 2016) for introducing us to the concept of Corporate Social Irresponsibility.

are much more salient than acts resulting in positive rewards" (Clark and Grantham, 2012, p.33, referring to Janoff-Bulman et. al. 2009). Of course, CSR and CSI are logically inseparable, they exist in practice and by "eliminating or reducing CSI, CSR will significantly increase and become more effective" (Tench et. al., 2012, p.5).

Paying tax: an obligation towards society

How can one relate CSI to corporate (aggressive) tax planning? Most people will be aware of the existence of all kind of tax schemes that enable corporate (and wealthy) taxpayers to avoid taxes. They avoid paying tax legally, without engaging in (illegal) tax evasion, as they stay within the boundaries of the (letter of the) law. Of course, taxpayers may structure their affairs to achieve a favourable tax treatment within the limits set by law. Some (corporate) taxpayers, however, command the kind of resources that enable them to do this in a very sophisticated and successful manner, thus by paying hardly any (income) taxes at all they shift the tax burden to less expert taxpayers.

Taxes are financial contributions which are inherent to (corporate) membership of society and therefore part of a corporation's obligations towards society. Taxes are payments to the state for the benefit of society, rather than for the purpose of the state. In other words, the state is but an intermediary who levies taxes on behalf of society. Businesses are part and parcel of society. Members of society, citizens and business alike, reap massive benefits from society and the state. They therefore should take into account benefits others provide them. These benefits create an obligation to repay on grounds of reciprocity. As the political philosopher Rawls argues "we are not to gain from the cooperative labors of others without doing our fair share" (Rawls, 1999, p.96; see also Gribnau, 2017). This could be interpreted as an obligation of taxpayers to pay their fair share (see also Happé, 2007). This is however not an (ideal) obligation which easily translates in clear-cut rules for (corporate) tax planning.

How then should CSR firms translate their (ethical) obligations towards society that go beyond compliance with legal obligations in their tax planning strategy? After all, taxpayers engaging in tax avoidance may perfectly comply with the letter of the law while violating the spirit of the law – as the tax planning practices of many multinational corporations show. So compliance with tax rules law does not tell us anything about the amount of tax a company pays. Sure, it may entail a serious financial contribution to society but also hardly any payment at all. If so, it is clear this is probably foremost an example of corporate irresponsibility rather than of (not realising) corporate responsibility.

Aggressive tax planning as CSI

To our mind, managers of companies that claim to have a (strong) CSR strategy in place should go beyond compliance with the letter of the tax law, for tax should be an integral part of any CSR strategy (Gribnau and Jallai ,2016). They therefore should include ethical considerations in their tax decision-making framework. They evidently do not live up to their CSR commitment if they engage in aggressive tax planning and pay no or hardly any (corporate) taxes at all. CSR entails going beyond (strict) compliance with the law, so minimalist compliance with the letter of law has nothing to do with CSR. On the contrary, aggressive tax planning is a clear case of corporate irresponsibility – it involves a gain in corporate profits at the expense of (the common good of) society. Moreover, aggressive tax planning is often considered unfair, unethical or even immoral (see e.g. UK/PAC HMRC 2012, Q. 485, p.40). Therefore, managers of CSR companies should avoid this irresponsible fiscal conduct and go beyond minimalist compliance. Going beyond (minimalist) compliance with the letter of the tax law has the merit of avoiding irresponsible corporate behaviour. Thus, we propose to conceptualise aggressive tax planning in terms of corporate *ir*responsibility rather than corporate responsibility.

Tax planning is a complex topic with many nuances, varying from aggressive tax planning to legitimate tax planning responding to tax expenditures (incentives). Aggressive tax planning often fits in the area between CSI and CSR, as presented by Tench et al. (Figure 3.1). Aggressive tax planning (which should be separated from tax evasion) is usually within the legal rules – complying with the letter of the law – but it is often questionable whether it is within the spirit of the law. Therefore, it is often perceived as socially unacceptable (see e.g. Jallai, 2017). However, there are also legitimate forms of tax planning – companies may for instance lower their tax liability by making legitimate use of tax subsidies. Therefore, we see that tax planning can have many gradations, which can be put on a continuum and should be evaluated on a case-by-case basis. Nevertheless, the concept of CSI helps us to better understand the minimum standards for acceptable tax planning from the perspective of companies' obligations towards society.

Figure 3.1: The CSI and CSR Continuum

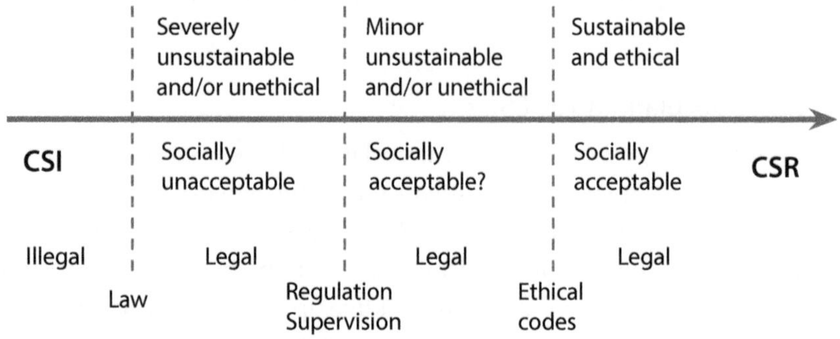

	Severely unsustainable and/or unethical	Minor unsustainable and/or unethical	Sustainable and ethical	
CSI	Socially unacceptable	Socially acceptable?	Socially acceptable	CSR
Illegal	Legal	Legal	Legal	
Law		Regulation Supervision	Ethical codes	

Source: Tench et.al., 2012, p.9.

Clark and Grantham see aggressive tax planning as a familiar example of irresponsible corporate behaviour because it exploits negative externalities. Firm costs are thus transferred "to unwilling or unwitting recipients, benefiting the firm at the expense of the total system." In their view, tax avoidance is "the gray area in which armies of accountants and lawyers help their clients to outsmart their governments and stay steps ahead of the law, such that they can avoid paying any more tax than the presently stipulated legal minimum" (Clark and Grantham, 2012, p.29). Maybe they are a bit optimistic, because taxpayers using high-tech structures designed by tax advisers often turn around the rules to their advantage, and therefore (even) around the "stipulated legal minimum".

According to Clark and Grantham this kind of tax avoidance is in stark contrast with the use of tax breaks "in the spirit of their intentions, directing investment to areas of policy priorities, that activity aligns with society's larger interests" (Clark and Grantham, 2012, p.31).[15] But companies that do not pay their fair share by engaging in creative tax compliance and exploiting loopholes generate a negative externality, they argue: "a decrease in the amount of funds available to government programs that hurts society." Additionally, Clark and Grantham see this behaviour as anticompetitive "for those businesses that pay their taxes appropriately, competition with less scrupulous firms is made more difficult since they are essentially shirking their financial responsibilities and gaining an unfair advantage, leaving an increased tax burden to others." To this we add that the tax burden is not only shifted to other businesses but also to other taxpayers. Clearly these negative externalities allow for the conclusion that such corporate taxpayers

---

[15] They 'define' tax avoidance as "the range of business behavior between tax evasion (definitely illegal) and tax seeking (very rare)."

are acting irresponsible, rather than not acting in a socially responsible way, viz. not living up to the ideal of paying a fair share. Moreover, Clark and Grantham argue that it would be a more effective communicative device, leading to more benefit for society, to specify and proactively censure these business activities "what they *are*: CSI" rather than "expose these business activities as *not* CSR" (Clark and Grantham, 2012, p.31).

Corporate tax irresponsibility

In the previous section aggressive tax planning was analysed as a typical case of corporate social irresponsibility, due to the exploitation of negative externalities, which is what makes this kind of tax planning undesirable behaviour. Clarity about the negative consequences of aggressive tax planning techniques creates more salience than prescribing multinationals to pay a fair share. This probably is a more effective approach than invoking the virtue of corporate social responsibility. However, there are two more reasons to prefer the term corporate social irresponsibility to corporate social responsibility.

First, there is no consensus in international tax theory and politics on the underlying values and objectives of international tax law. Nor is there any general agreement on the principles for the taxation of multinational companies. Of course, international tax literature reflects on principles of international taxation. According to Avi-Yonah the entire network of double tax treaties constitutes an international tax regime with common underlying principles (Avi-Yonah, 2008, p.3). These principles are the single tax principle and the benefits principle (Avi-Yonah, 2008, pp.8-13; see also other scholars advocating "principles" of international taxation, e.g. Kemmeren, 2001; Smit, 2012). However, international consensus on principles of international taxation is lacking, without which it is impossible reach agreement on principles for the taxation of multinational companies. So there are no principles of tax fairness available as yet, which flesh out the ideal of a fair share in international taxation and offer multinational companies guidance. The ideal of a fair share is therefore too vague, ambiguous and abstract to give clear guidance on the amount of (corporate) tax to be paid by multinational corporations (see also Peters, 2014, pp.297-304; De Wilde, 2015, pp.55, 313-314).

It follows that the starting point should be to aim for consensus on a bottom line, that is, stricter international tax rules to establish some minimum level of corporate taxation to make sure that multinationals have a reasonable effective tax rate. Therefore, the aim should not be to establish what paying a fair share – corporate tax responsibility – entails but what evidently should be judged to amount to *not* paying a fair share – i.e., corporate tax irresponsibility. In practice, it is far easier to agree on evident instances of injustice than on what counts as justice (Gribnau, 2015, p.244). The same goes for corporate tax responsibility and corporate tax irresponsibility, respectively. In passing, we note that the OECD's Base Erosion and Profit Shifting project and the European Commission's Anti-Tax Avoidance Package initiative are doing this, creating a minimum standard which would make it possible to put a halt to excesses of tax planning (OECD, 2013, OECD, 2015a; EU ATAP, 2016; see also Dourado, 2016, p.440).

Second, it makes little sense to talk about and demand going beyond compliance with the tax laws (and treaties) without taking into account the specific economic nature of the (legal) obligation to pay tax. For businesses, taxation is part of their cost calculation. Tax planning is therefore a way to save in expenses. Moreover, taxpayers may arrange their tax affairs as they wish. Both individuals and businesses may plan and structure their affairs to achieve a favourable tax treatment within the limits set by law. In many jurisdictions this is settled in case law (see e.g. ECJ C-255/02, para. 73). Taking tax considerations into account is perfectly legitimate for persons and enterprises alike. So trying to mitigate one's tax burden by way of tax planning is in itself perfectly legitimate. In this sense taxpayers have discretion in structuring their affairs with an eye to the tax consequences within the limits set by law. Nonetheless, minimising one's tax burden by exploiting the letter of the law (tax avoidance) may result in not paying any (corporate) income tax at all. This kind of tax avoidance, i.e., aggressive tax planning, therefore amounts to (completely) evaporating one's (financial) obligations towards society. For a CSR corporation, this clearly violates its voluntarily accepted ethical obligations that entail going beyond compliance with the law. This kind of tax planning, although it is legal, therefore clearly constitutes irresponsible corporate behaviour.

Conclusion

In this contribution, we analysed managers' discretion and responsibilities in terms of (aggressive) tax planning. The main question discussed was: do multinationals' managers have elbow-room with regard their tax planning strategy (should it be aggressive or does it not need to be), and how should they choose whether they should satisfy their shareholders' interests or the interests of their stakeholders or even society at large?

We first dealt with the issue of management accountability and discretion. We elaborated on corporate governance and on what kinds of obligations it sets for the managers. We discussed two existing theoretical frameworks in a rather traditional monochrome way, according to which corporate decisions should prioritise either shareholders or stakeholders interests. We reached the conclusion that managers do have elbow-room in corporate decision making in both corporate governance systems. We argued that a stakeholder-oriented corporate governance system leaves more room for taking CSR on board. However, it does not mean that the shareholder oriented CG system excludes all possibilities for considering stakeholder interests – it just does not permit them to gain priority over (or even balance them with) shareholders' long-term interests. This was also shown by a brief comparison of the UK and Dutch corporate regulatory regimes. We further showed that the elbow-room that managers have in both systems is in a space between corporate social responsibility and corporate social irresponsibility.

To conclude, how can managers of a (multinational) corporation translate its commitment to CSR into a responsible tax planning strategy? A CSR firm voluntarily accepts obligations towards society that go beyond (strict) compliance with legal obligations. Do these obligations demand the conduct of some ideal (corporate) citizen? Sometimes the ideal of paying a fair share of taxes is invoked, comprising a prescriptive approach. Advocating the ideal of a fair share of taxes is a way of creating "aspirations and inspiring action to overcome inertia" (Clark and Grantham, 2012, p.33). As shown above, such a prescriptive approach has its drawbacks. Invoking virtues associated with corporate tax responsibility ('paying a fair share') is less effective than clarity about aggressive tax planning and the negative externalities it that generates. Indeed, clarity about what not to do, about the undesirability of this kind of tax avoidance will be more easily convince businesses to take action and avoid aggressive tax planning. There is moreover no international consensus on ethical principles that solidifies the ideal of paying a fair share of taxes. Furthermore, this appeal to pay a fair share fails to acknowledge the right of (corporate) taxpayers to structure their affairs in a tax efficient way.

With regard to aggressive tax planning, we therefore prefer the concept of corporate irresponsibility to the concept of corporate responsibility. Managers of a (multinational) corporation should use their discretion to avoid aggressive tax planning. Again, CSR corporations voluntarily accept (ethical) obligations towards society that go beyond (strict) compliance with legal obligations. Avoiding corporate irresponsibility (CSI), i.e., avoiding minimalistic compliance with the letter of the law is the way for CSR firms to translate these obligations towards society into their tax planning strategy.

References

Armstrong, J.S. (1977). Social Irresponsibility in Management. *Journal of Business Research*, **5**(3), 185-213.

Arrow, K.J. (1973). Social Responsibility and Economic Efficiency. *Public Policy*, **21**(3), 303-317.

Arrow, K.J. (1985). *Collected Papers of Kenneth J. Arrow: Applied Economics, (Vol. 6)*. Harvard University Press.

Avi-Yonah, R.S. (2008). *International Tax as International Law: An Analysis of the International Tax Regime*. New York: Cambridge University Press.

Avi-Yonah, R.S. (2014). Just Say No: Corporate Taxation and Corporate Social Responsibility. *Law & Economics Research Paper Series, Paper No. 14-010*. Retrieved from: http://ssrn.com/abstract=2423045 (accessed 22.03.2017).

Berle, A.A. & Means, G.C. (1968). *The Modern Corporation and Private Property*. New York: Harcourt, Brace & World.

Birrell, I. (2014, January, 6). Bill Gates Preaches the Aid Gospel, But Is He Just a Hypocrite? *The Guardian*. Retrieved from http://www.theguardian.com/commentisfree/2014/jan/06/bill-gates-preaches-fighting-poverty-hypocrite-microsoft-tax (accessed 13.03.2017).

Blair, M.M. (1995). *Ownership and Control: Rethinking Corporate Governance for the Twenty-First Century*. Washington D.C.: Brookings Institution.

Buchholtz, A.K., Brown, J.A. & Shabana, K.M. (2008). Corporate Governance and Corporate Social Responsibility. In Crane, A., Matten, D., McWilliams, A., Moon, J. & Siegel, D.S. (Eds.), *The Oxford Handbook of Corporate Social Responsibility* (pp.327-345). New York: Oxford University Press.

Cadbury, A. (1992, December, 1). Report of the Committee on the Financial Aspects of Corporate Governance. London: The Committee on the Financial Aspects of Corporate Governance and Gee and Co. Ltd. Retrieved from http://www.ecgi.org/codes/documents/cadbury.pdf (accessed 14.03.2017).

Campbell, K. & Vick, D. (2007). Disclosure Law and the Market for Corporate Social Responsibility. In McBarnet, D., Voiculescu, A. & Campbell T. (Eds.), *The New Corporate Accountability: Corporate Social Responsibility and the Law* (pp.241-278). Cambridge: Cambridge University Press.

Carroll, A.B. (1991). The Pyramid of Corporate Social Responsibility: Toward the Moral Management of Organizational Stakeholders. *Business Horizons* **34**(4), 39–48.

Carroll A.B. (1999). Corporate Social Responsibility: Evolution of a Definitional Construct. *Business & Society*, **38**(3), 268–295.

Chang, H.-J. (2010). *23 Things They Don't Tell You about Capitalism*. London: Penguin.

Clark, T.S. & Grantham, K.N. (2012). What CSR is Not: Corporate Social Irresponsibility. In Tench, R., Sun, S. & Jones, B. (Eds.), *Corporate Social Irresponsibility: A Challenging Concept* (pp.23-41). Bingley: Emerald.

Clarkson, M.B.E. (1995). A Stakeholder Framework for Analyzing and Evaluating Corporate Social Performance. *Academy Management Review*, **20**(1), 92-117.

Conway, Z. (2015, May, 29). BBC Uncovers 'Aggressive' Tax Avoidance Scheme. BBC News. Retrieved from: http://www.bbc.com/news/business-32914372 (accessed 14.03.2017).

Court of Justice of the European Communities (ECJ), Case C-255/02, *Halifax plc and others v Commissioners of Customs & Excise*, [2006] ECR I-1609.

De Wilde, M.F. (2015). *Sharing the Pie': Taxing Multinationals in a Global Market*. Doctoral Dissertation, Erasmus University Rotterdam.

Desai, M.A. & Dharmapala, D. (2008). Tax and Corporate Governance: An Economic Approach. In Schön, W. (Ed.), *Tax and Corporate Governance* (pp.13-30). Berlin: Springer Verlag.

Directive 2013/34/EU of the European Parliament and of the Council of 26 June 2013 on the annual financial statements, consolidated financial statements and related reports of certain types of undertakings, amending Directive 2006/43/EC of the European Parliament and of the Council and repealing Council Directives 78/660/EEC and 83/349/EEC (Directive 2013/34/EU) as amended by Directive 2014/95/EU of the European Parliament and of the Council of 22 October 2014 amending Directive 2013/34/EU as regards disclosure of non-financial and diversity information by certain large undertakings and groups (Directive 2014/95/EU)

Donaldson, T. (2008). The Transatlantic Paradox: How Outdated Concepts Confuse the American/European Debate about Corporate Governance. In Crane, A., Matten, D., McWilliams, A., Moon, J. & Siegel, D.S. (Eds.), *The Oxford Handbook of Corporate Social Responsibility* (pp.543-551). New York: Oxford University Press.

Donaldson, T. & Preston, L.E. (1995). The Stakeholder Theory of a Corporation: Concepts Evidence, and Implications. *Academy Management Review*, **20**(1), 65-91.

Dourado, A.P. (2016). The EU Anti Tax Avoidance Package: Moving Ahead of BEPS? *INTERTAX* 44 (6/7), pp.440-446.

Du Plessis J.J., Hargovan, A., Bagaric, M. & Harris, J.R. (2015). *Principles of Contemporary Corporate Governance* (3rd ed.). Melbourne: Cambridge University Press.

Eisenhardt, K.M. (1989). Agency Theory: An Assessment and Review. *The Academy of Management Review*, **14**(1), pp.57-74.

Enriques, L., Hansmann, H., Kraakman, R. & Pargendler, M. (2017). The Basic Governance Structure: Minority Shareholders and Non-Shareholder Constituencies. In Kraakman, R. H., Armour, J., Pargendler, M., Ringe, W.-G., Rock, E., Davies, P., Enriques, L., Hansmann, H., Hertig, G., Hopt, K. & Kanda, H. (Eds.), *The Anatomy of Corporate Law: A Comparative and Functional Approach* (3rd ed.) (pp.79-108). Oxford: Oxford University Press.

Erle, B. (2008). Tax Risk Management and Board Responsibility. In Schön, W. (Ed.), *Tax and Corporate Governance* (pp.205-220). Berlin: Springer Verlag.

Esser, I. & Du Plessis, J.J. (2007). The Stakeholder Debate and Directors' Fiduciary Duties. *South African Mercantile Law Journal*, **19**(3), pp.346-363.

European Commission. (2011). Communication from the Commission to the European Parliament, the Council, the European Economic and Social Committee and the Committee of the Regions: *A Renewed EU Strategy 2011-14 for Corporate Social Responsibility* (Brussels, 25.10.2011, COM (2011)) 681 final.

European Commission. (2016). EU Anti Tax Avoidance Package. Retrieved from: http://ec.europa.eu/taxation_customs/taxation/company_tax/anti_tax_avoidance/index_en.htm (accessed 14.03.2017).

Farrar, J. (2005). *Corporate Governance: Theories, Principles, and Practice* (2nd ed.). Oxford: Oxford University Press.

Ferran, E. (2005, March). Company Law Reform in the UK: A Progress Report. *ECGI - Law Working Paper No. 27/2005*. Retrieved from: http://ssrn.com/abstract=644203 (accessed 14.03.2017).

Freeman, E.R. (1984). *Strategic Management: A Stakeholder Approach*. Boston: Pitman.

Freeman, R.E., Harrison, J.S., Wicks, A.C., Parmar, B.L. & de Colle, S. (2010). *Stakeholder Theory: The State of the Art*. Cambridge: Cambridge University Press.

Friedman, A.L. & Miles, S. (2006). *Stakeholders: Theory and Practice*. Oxford: Oxford University Press.

Friedman, F. (2002). *Capitalism and Freedom, Fortieth Anniversary Edition*. Chicago: The University of Chicago Press.

Friedman, M. (1970, September, 13). The Social Responsibility of Business is to Increase its Profits. *New York Times Magazine*.

Friese, A., Link, S. & Mayer, S. (2008). Taxation and Corporate Governance – The State of the Art. In Schön, W. (Ed.), *Tax and Corporate Governance* (pp.357-425). Berlin: Springer Verlag.

Garriga, E. & Melé, D. (2004). Corporate Social Responsibility Theories: Mapping the Territory. *Journal of Business Ethics*, **53**(1), 51-71.

Gribnau, J.L.M. (2015). Corporate Social Responsibility and Tax Planning: Not by Rules Alone. *Social & Legal Studies*, **24**(2), 225-251.

Gribnau, J.L.M. (2017). Voluntary Compliance beyond the Letter of the Law: Reciprocity and Fair Play. In Peeters, B., Gribnau, J.L.M. & Badisco, J. (Eds.), *Trust in Taxation* (pp.17-50). Cambridge: Intersentia.

Gribnau, J.L.M. & Jallai, A.-G. (2016). Good Tax Governance and Transparency: A Matter of Ethical Motivation. *Tilburg Law School Research Paper No. 06/2016.* Retrieved from: http://ssrn.com/abstract=2781205 (accessed 14.03.2017).

Habisch, A. (2005). *Corporate Social Responsibility across Europe*. Berlin / New York: Springer.

Hansmann, H. & Kraakman, R. (2002). Toward a Single Model of Corporate Law? In McCahery J.A., Moerland, P, Raaijmakers, T. & Renneboog, L. (Eds.), *Corporate Governance Regimes: Convergence and Diversity* (pp.56-82). Oxford / New York: Oxford University Press.

Happé, R. (2007). Multinationals, Enforcement Covenants and Fair Share. *INTERTAX*, **35**(10), 537-547.

Hosmer, L.T. (1995). Trust: The Connecting Link between Organizational Theory and Philosophical Ethics. *Academy Management Review,* **20**(2), 379-403.

The International Consortium of Investigative Journalism (ICIJ). *Luxembourg Leaks: Global Companies' Secrets Exposed*. Retrieved from: https://www.icij.org/project/luxembourg-leaks (accessed 14.03.2017).

The International Consortium of Investigative Journalism (ICIJ). *The Panama Papers*. Retrieved from: https://panamapapers.icij.org (accessed 14.03.2017).

Jallai, A.-G. (2017). Restoring Stakeholders' Trust in Multinationals' Tax Planning Practices with Corporate Social Responsibility (CSR). In Peeters, B., Gribnau, J.L.M. & Badisco, J. (Eds.), *Trust in Taxation* (pp.173-201). Cambridge: Intersentia.

Jensen, M.C. (2010). Value Maximization, Stakeholder Theory, and the Corporate Objective Function. *Journal of Applied Corporate Finance,* **22**(1), 32-42.

Jensen, M.C. (2000). Value Maximization, Stakeholder Theory, and the Corporate Objective Function. In Beer, M. & Nohria N. (Eds.), *Breaking the Code of Change* (pp.35-78). Harvard Business School Press.

Kay, J. (1993). *Foundations of Corporate Success: How Business Strategies Add Value.* Oxford: Oxford University Press.

Keinert, C. (2008). *Corporate Social Responsibility as an International Strategy*. Heidelberg: Physica-Verlag.

Kemmeren E.C.C.M. (2001). *Principle of Origin in Tax Conventions. A Rethinking of Models*. Dongen: Pijnenburg.

Kotter, J. & Heskett, J. (1992). *Corporate Culture and Performance*. New York: Free Press.

La Porta R., Lopez-de-Silanes, F., Shleifer, A. & Vishny, R. (2000). Investor Protection and Corporate Governance. *Journal of Financial Economics,* **58**(1), 3-27.

Lafferty, W.M., Schmidt, L.A. & Wolfe, Jr., D.J. (2012). A Brief Introduction to the Fiduciary Duties of Directors under Delaware Law. *Penn State Law Review*, **116**(3), 837-877.

Lambooy, T. (2010). *Corporate Social Responsibility*. Kluwer.

Logsdon, J.M. & Yuthas, K. (1997). Corporate Social Performance, Stakeholder Orientation, and Organizational Moral Development. *Journal of Business Ethics*, **16**(12/13), 1213-1226.

Mallin, C.A. (2007). *Corporate Governance*. Oxford: Oxford University Press.

Marcoux, A.M. (2000). Balancing Act. In DesJardins, J.R. & MacCall, J.J. (Eds.), *Contemporary Issues in Business Ethics* (4th ed.) (pp.92-100). Belmont: Wadsworth.

Mayer, C.P. (2013). *Firm Commitment: Why the Corporation Is Failing Us And How To Restore Trust In It*. Oxford: Oxford University Press.

McBarnet, D. (2007). Corporate Social Responsibility beyond Law, Through Law, for Law: the New Corporate Accountability. In McBarnet, D., Voiculescu, A. & Campbell, T. (Eds.), *The New Corporate Accountability: Corporate Social Responsibility and the Law* (pp.9-56). Cambridge: Cambridge University Press.

Melé, D. (2008). Corporate Social Responsibility Theories. In Crane, A., Matten, D., McWilliams, A., Moon, J. & Siegel, D.S. (Eds.), *The Oxford Handbook of Corporate Social Responsibility* (pp.47-82). New York: Oxford University Press.

Miliband, E. (2015, February, 6). Ed Miliband: I won't back down on tax avoidance. *The Guardian*. Retrieved from: www.theguardian.com/politics/2015/feb/06/ed-miliband-tax-avoidance-business-labour (accessed 14.03.2017).

Millon, D. (2011). Two Models of Corporate Social Responsibility. *Wake Forest Law Review*, **46**(3), 523-540.

Molz, R. (1995). The Theory of Pluralism in Corporate Governance: A Conceptual Framework and Empirical Test. *Journal of Business Ethics*, **14**(10), 789-804.

Muchlinsky, P.T. (2007). *Multinational Enterprises and the Law*. Oxford: Oxford University Press.

Neri-Castracane, G. (2015). Corporate Governance From a Comparative Perspective: Does The Business Judgment Rule Help Promote Corporate Social Responsibility? *Frontiers of Law in China*, **10**(1), 8-23.

OECD (Organisation for Economic Co-operation and Development). (2013). *Addressing Base Erosion and Profit Shifting*. Paris: OECD Publishing.

OECD (Organisation for Economic Co-operation and Development). (2015a). *Base Erosion and Profit Shifting: Final Reports*. Retrieved from: http://www.oecd.org/ctp/beps-2015-final-reports.htm (accessed 14.03.2017).

OECD (Organisation for Economic Co-operation and Development). (2015b). *G20/OECD Principles of Corporate Governance*. Paris: OECD Publishing.

Parkinson, J. (2006). Corporate Governance and the Regulation of Business Behaviour. In MacLeod, S. (Ed.), *Global Governance and the Quest for Justice - Vol II Corporate Governance* (pp.27-46). Oxford/Portland: Hart Publishing.

Parkinson, J. (1994). The Legal Context of Corporate Social Responsibility. *Business Ethics: A European Review*, 3(1), 16-22.

Peters, C. (2014). *On the Legitimacy of International Tax Law*. Amsterdam: IBFD.

Piantavigna, P. (2017). Tax Abuse and Aggressive Tax Planning in the BEPS Era: How EU Law and the OECD are Establishing a Unifying Conceptual Framework in International Tax Law, Despite Linguistic Discrepancies. *World Tax Journal*, 9(1), 47-98.

Pichet, E. (2011). Enlightened Shareholder Theory: Whose Interests Should Be Served by the Supporters of Corporate Governance? *Corporate Ownership & Control*, 8(2-3), 353-362. Retrieved from: http://ssrn.com/abstract=1262879 (accessed 14.03.2017).

Rawls, J. (1999). *A Theory of Justice* (revised ed.). Oxford: Oxford University Press.

Reinhardt, F.L., Stavins, R.N. & Vietor, R.H.K. (2008). Corporate Social Responsibility through an Economic Lens. *Review of Environmental Economics and Policy*, 2(2), 219-239.

Schön, W. (2013). Vorstandspflichten und Steuerplanung. In Krieger, G., Lutter, M. & Schmidt, K. (Eds.), *Festschrift für Michael Hoffmann-Becking zum 70. Geburtstag*. Munich: Beck.

Schön, W. (2008). Tax and Corporate Governance: A Legal Approach. In Schön, W. (Ed.), *Tax and Corporate Governance* (pp.31-61). Berlin: Springer Verlag.

Schwartz, M.S. & Carroll, A.B. (2003). Corporate Social Responsibility: A Three-Domain Approach. *Business Ethics Quarterly*, 13(4), 503-530.

Schwartz, M.S. (2011). *Corporate Social Responsibility: An Ethical Approach*. Peterborough: Broadview Press.

Setzler, B. (2014, January, 17). The Real Tax Threat to American Businesses. *US News*. Retrieved from: http://www.usnews.com/opinion/blogs/economic-intelligence/2014/01/17/americas-corporate-tax-problem-is-that-big-corporations-dont-pay-enough (accessed 14.03.2017).

Sheehy, B. & Feaver, D. (2014). Anglo-American Directors' Legal Duties and CSR: Prohibited, Permitted or Prescribed? *Dalhousie Law Journal*, 37(1), 345-396.

Shleifer, A. & Vishny, R. (1997). A Survey of Corporate Governance. *Journal of Finance*, 52(2), 737-783.

Smit, D. (2012). *EU Freedoms, Non-EU Countries and Company Taxation EUCOTAX Series on European Taxation*. Alphen aan den Rijn: Wolters Kluwer Law & Business.

Smith, A. (1776). *An Inquiry into the Nature and Causes of the Wealth of Nations of 1776*. Indianapolis: Liberty Fund.

Sternberg, E. (2000). *Just Business: Business Ethics in Action* (2nd ed.). Oxford: Oxford University Press.

Stout, L.A. (2012). New Thinking on 'Shareholder Primacy'. In Vasudev, P.M. & Watson, S. (Eds.), *Corporate Governance after the Financial Crisis* (pp.25-41). Cheltenham: Edward Elgar Publishing.

Stout, L.A. (2016). Corporate Entities: Their Ownership, Control, and Purpose. *Oxford Handbook of Law and Economics, Forthcoming, Cornell Legal Studies Research Paper No. 16-38*. Retrieved from: https://papers.ssrn.com/sol3/papers.cfm?abstract_id=2841875 (accessed 22.03.2017).

Tax Justice Network (TJN) (2014). Bill Gates: Is he just a hypocrite? Retrieved from: http://taxjustice.blogspot.nl/2014/01/bill-gates-is-he-just-hypocrite.html (accessed 26.01.2018).

Tench, R., Sun, S. & Jones, B. (2012). The Challenging Concept of Corporate Social Irresponsibility: An Introduction. In Tench, R., Sun, S. & Jones, B (Eds.), *Critical Studies on Corporate Responsibility, Governance and Sustainability*, vol. 4 (pp.3-20). Bingley: Emerald.

UK Company Law Review Steering Group. (February 1999). Modem Company Law for a Competitive Economy: The Strategic Framework (URN 99/654). *A Consultation Document*. Retrieved from http://webarchive.nationalarchives.gov.uk/20121029131934/http://www.bis.gov.uk/files/file23279.pdf (accessed 13.03.2017).

UK: House of Commons, Committee of Public Accounts, HM Revenue & Customs (PAC HMRC). (2012). *Annual Report and Accounts 2011-12. Nineteenth Report of Session 2012-13 Report, Together With Formal Minutes, Oral and Written Evidence*. London: The Stationery Office Limited. Retrieved from: http://www.publications.parliament.uk/pa/cm201213/cmselect/cmpubacc/716/716.pdf (accessed 15.03.2017).

Weyzig, F. (2009). Political and Economic Arguments for Corporate Social Responsibility: Analysis and a Proposition Regarding the CSR Agenda. *Journal of Business Ethics*, **86**(4), 417-428.

Wymeersch, E. (2002). Convergence or Divergence in Corporate Governance Patterns in Western Europe? In McCahery J.A., Moerland, P, Raaijmakers, T. & Renneboog, L. (Eds.), *Corporate Governance Regimes: Convergence and Diversity* (pp.230-247). Oxford / New York: Oxford University Press.

4 Alternative Methods for Resolving Tax Disputes in Poland: The odds of success

Hanna Filipczyk

Abstract

In October 2015, the Polish government adopted the "Directional Assumptions of the New Tax Ordinance" drafted by the Committee for Codification of the General Tax Law – a body of experts appointed by the Prime Minister of the Republic of Poland. The Assumptions now serve the basis for drafting the new Tax Ordinance, to enter into force in 2019.

The Assumptions propose to establish procedural grounds for consensual i.e. premised on an agreement between parties to the dispute, forms of tax disputes prevention and resolution – ADR *ex ante* and *ex post*.

The purpose of the paper is twofold. First, it seeks to explain the main policy problems the Committee had to solve while developing the proposal. Second, it purports to discuss normative objections that have been raised by stakeholders against the proposal and to pinpoint possible practical difficulties which can hamper its implementation and operation.

Integrating alternative dispute resolution methods into the Polish tax procedure is a difficult task. Contrary to what is commonly believed, the difficulty lies not in its alleged inconsistency with the nature of tax procedure or substantive tax law, but is linked to a host of factual determinants of how tax procedure is perceived and applied, and how tax cases are resolved.

The paper offers the reader an opportunity to critically reflect on their own attitudes towards "negotiating taxes", when confronted with objections coming from the tradition of legal formalism, and on prospects for cross-fertilisation of differing legal cultures.

Introduction

"Directional Assumptions of the New Tax Ordinance", drafted by the Committee for Codification of General Tax Law (hereinafter: the Committee) and adopted by the Polish Government in October 2015, propose to establish procedural grounds for consensual, i.e. premised on an agreement between parties to the dispute, forms of tax disputes prevention and resolution – alternative dispute resolutions methods (ADR) *ex ante* and *ex post*.

This article unfolds as follows. After providing the background information on the Committee's work and on the current status of tax ADR in Poland, the paper outlines the main policy dilemmas related to ADR that the Committee faced in the process of drafting the Assumptions and sets out the main elements of the resulting ADR proposal. Then it briefly presents the consultation process of the proposal and feedback received in this process. The core of the paper is the discussion of normative and non-normative (factual) obstacles to the implementation and successful operation of the proposal. As a final point, the paper sketches a 'to do list': a non-exhaustive catalogue of supporting activities which can aid the successful – effective, efficient and fair – implementation of the proposal[1].

Background

The Committee – consisting of tax academics, tax judges, tax advisers and tax officials – was appointed by the Prime Minister of the Republic of Poland in November 2014 and tasked with drafting a new tax ordinance – an act laying down general rules concerning tax liabilities and tax procedures replacing the Tax Ordinance currently in force[2]. It was a response to a widespread sense of dissatisfaction with the Polish tax law as it is now, and with the climate of distrustful and confrontational interaction between tax administration and taxpayers.

The Committee is independent, and the agenda of its work has not been set by the Minister of Finance. The inspiration to include alternative dispute resolutions methods in the project came from two sources.

First, it was observed by the Committee that tax disputes in Poland are not resolved efficiently. This is evidenced by the fact that the number of the

---

[1] For the purposes of the present paper, I have consulted my colleagues from the Committee on their views about chances of ADR to succeed, and favourable and unfavourable determinants of these chances. I am grateful to them for the insights which they shared with me, and which I profusely used in this paper.

[2] Tax Ordinance of 29 August 1997 [ustawa z dnia 29 sierpnia 1997 r. – Ordynacja podatkowa], consolidated text: Journal of Laws of 2015, item 613, as amended; hereinafter: Tax Ordinance.

complaints filed with the administrative courts in tax matters increased from 17,028 in 2009 to 25,663 in 2014 (i.e., by 50.71%), to decline only slightly – to 24,710 – in 2015 (*Source:* official court statistics[3]). Also, the backlog of cases in the Supreme Administrative Court (2016) continues to grow (the standard waiting time for a case to be heard has now reached 2 years). Against this backdrop, settling a case instead of litigating seems an attractive alternative. ADR can save time and money and provide the framework for simple and prompt resolution of cases to the satisfaction of disputants and without compromising the taxpayers' rights.

Second, insights from economic psychology was another motivation: the importance of procedural justice (Lind & Tyler, 1988; Tyler, 1990; Tyler, 2011), the concepts of 'responsive regulation' and 'pyramid of compliance' of Ayres and Braithwaite (1992); (see also Braithwaite, 2003; Braithwaite, 2011), and the 'slippery slope' model of Kirchler (Kirchler, 2007, esp. pp.73-96 and 182-206); Hartner et al. (2008) emphasise that the effectiveness of tax law relies on voluntary compliance and point to the necessity of enhancing the dimension of 'trust' and providing the framework for a cooperative relationship between taxpayers and the tax administration. Effectiveness and (the sense of) fairness of tax law, including procedural justice, work hand in hand – they are synergistic and not antagonistic.

The members of the Committee familiar with this research advocated integrating these insights into tax procedure. ADR seemed particularly apt for fostering subjective procedural justice. These methods, even if they do not bring about the immediate settlement of a disagreement, give those in dispute an opportunity to voice their positions, to be heard by their disputants, and to have more control over a dispute. All these are important components of subjective procedural justice – factors which contribute to the disputants' perception of the procedure as fair.

The time seems ripe for such an innovation. Introducing ADR in the administrative and tax procedures has been postulated by tax academics (Nita, 2004; Pietrasz & Siemieniako, 2011) and tax practice (PwC, 2013). While the proposal to institute tax ADR proved controversial in some quarters, the Committee was by no means the first or the only one to propose them[4].

---

[3] Available at www.nsa.gov.pl (official website of the Supreme Administrative Court).

[4] ADR are concurrently introduced in the administrative procedure, regulated by the Administrative Procedure Act of 14 June 1960 [ustawa z dnia 14 czerwca 1960 r. kodeks postępowania administracyjnego], consolidated text: Journal of Laws of 2016, item 23, as amended.

ADR in tax procedure – *status quo*

Strictly speaking, in Polish tax law as it stands now, there is no consensual procedure of general application. Consensual elements are included formally only in the advance pricing agreements procedure (APA), regulated in Section IIa of the Tax Ordinance. Some argue that such elements can also be traced in other procedures, which is a manifestation of the general trend that tax law becomes more 'responsive' (Pietrasz et al., 2013).

> *Responsive law is characterised by soft methods of conflict resolution (mediation, conciliation, arbitrage), flexibility in the application of the law to specific situations. Coercion is limited only to necessary cases. There is an increase in the significance of general clauses and general principles of law, as well as of purposive interpretation. (Brzeziński, 2011, p.36).*

This observation *de lege lata* (i.e., as regards law as it is) is far from uncontroversial. In any case, the range of 'soft', 'responsive' or 'consensual' elements in tax procedures is limited.

In practice, negotiations between tax authorities and taxpayers are occasionally undertaken despite the lack of a clear procedural basis for them, with 'standard' proceedings concluded with the issuing of a tax assessment decision (Filipczyk, 2011). Amicable settlement of tax disputes is possible in proceedings before regional administrative courts (the first-tier courts dealing with tax cases) through the mediation procedure established in 2004[5]. However, this procedure is practically irrelevant – the number of disputes resolved in it is negligible (e.g., only one in 2015; *Source:* official court statistics)[6]. A fact significant in itself, it needs to be carefully considered, and the reasons for it understood, in the current works on ADR.

Another element of the *status quo*, which is significant for the current project and its chances of success, is an inclination to formalism in the interpretation and application of tax law, as a prominent feature of the Polish legal culture. The 'formalistic' model assumes that the law application is a syllogistic (mechanical) exercise of applying legal rules to facts, that legal interpretation should ideally be constrained to linguistic arguments (hence the preference for so-called textualism), and that it is possible and necessary to keep law as a normative system hermetically closed from all extra-legal

---

5   Section III, chapter 8 (articles 115-118) of the Administrative Court Procedure Act of 30 August 2002 [ustawa z dnia 30 sierpnia 2002 r. Prawo o postępowaniu przed sądami administracyjnymi], consolidated text: Journal of Laws of 2012, item 270, as amended.

6   In years 2004-2015 the number of cases (tax and non-tax cumulatively) resolved amicably in the mediation procedure before the administrative courts amounted to, respectively: 170, 117, 66, 17, 16, 3, 2, 8, 4, 5, 4, 1 (Supreme Administrative Court, 2016, p.21).

interference (Matczak, 2007, p.15). Emblematic of legal formalism is the ideal of 'mechanical jurisprudence', famously encapsulated in the Montesquieu's *dictum* that the judges should be "no more than the mouth that pronounces the words of the law, mere passive beings, incapable of moderating either its force or rigour" (Montesquieu, 1949, Book XI, chapter VI).

As put forward by Morawski, the transition from the traditional ('subsumptive') model of adjudication to the 'argumentative' model is already under way (Morawski, 2000, pp.155-158). Yet the traditional adjudication style, premised upon the myth of the straightforward clarity of legal provisions (their direct understandability for law addressees), which makes law amenable to equally unproblematic application, is still widespread, not the least because of the judiciary's historical experiences of communism (Galligan & Matczak, 2005). In this setting it is hardly surprising that ADR are viewed with suspicion. The allegations that there exist normative obstacles to using ADR in tax cases, which will be discussed below, are rooted in the tradition of legal formalism.

Work of the Committee

The overall objective the Codification Committee has been tasked with is to design a new ordinance, which will provide a procedural framework for the effective, efficient and fair application of the substantive tax law. In order to attain this objective, the Assumptions expand a range of procedural interactions between taxpayers and tax authorities over and above the traditionally known forms of tax audits, tax rulings and tax assessment proceedings[7]. It is in this context that ADR are posited.

The above notwithstanding, at the outset of Committee's works there was no consensus on whether introducing ADR was a good idea. The majority of the membership supported the idea of integrating *some* consensual elements in the tax procedure, but ADR *ex post* were rather controversial (in the aspect of their scope of application and their effectiveness), especially with regard to settlements concerning the construal of legal rules (legal provisions). Interestingly, by the end of the initial phase of the codification project – i.e. the one finalised with the adoption of the Assumptions – ADR have reached the position of one of the main constituents of the proposal developed by the Commission. It marks the significant evolution in the attitudes of the Committee members – from reluctant approval to wholehearted

---

7   Also through entitling taxpayers to receiving tax-related information and assistance from tax officers in various forms and through various channels (in direct contacts, via email, internet communicators, etc.), and not necessarily within a formal procedure.

endorsement. The internal discussion entertained throughout the work on the Assumptions was important since doubts and reservations voiced within the Committee preceded similar ones raised subsequently by external stakeholders, and offered a chance to make the proposal more balanced and resilient to future objections.

Apart from this general dilemma, during the conception phase of the project the Committee encountered some specific problems concerning tax ADR. They related in particular to the following issues.

The scope of a settlement between tax authorities and taxpayers

Can a settlement concern only the facts of the case, or (also) the law – its interpretation and/or applicability to the disputed case? Settling a case through making an agreement on what constitutes its factual basis (background) seemed pretty innocuous from the start and quickly gained acceptance across the Committee. By contrast, serious misgivings were expressed about allowing for 'negotiating law'. Ultimately, in light of the dissenting views in the Committee and after a lively discussion, it was agreed that for the time being 'negotiating' legal issues will be neither excluded nor explicitly included in the proposal. It was decided that only one general (and unquestionable) requirement will be imposed: that an agreement must be within the boundaries of law.

The formal closure of the ADR procedure

On the one hand, it would be completely natural to assume that ADR procedure could be finalised with an agreement (settlement), which in itself would be a source of legal rights and obligations for a taxpayer and a tax authority (and would be issued instead of a tax decision). On the other hand, such a procedural mechanism would trigger a number of complications – the new type of legal act issued in the proceedings would have to be integrated into both tax and administrative court procedure. In particular, this would raise the question of the entitlement of a taxpayer to challenge a settlement before an administrative court: should such an entitlement be excluded (since *volenti non fit iniuria*) or allowed (what seems to be required by the Polish Constitution[8])?

This issue was decided in favour of the latter option. It was determined that matters should be kept simple. A tax decision will still have to be issued,

---

8   Konstytucja Rzeczypospolitej Polskiej z dnia 2 kwietnia 1997 [Constitution of the Republic of Poland of 2 April 1997], consolidated text: Journal of Laws of 1997, item 78, as amended; hereinafter: the Constitution.

based on an agreement made between a taxpayer and a tax authority and reflecting its content. In a sense, this procedural arrangement makes an agreement binding only upon the tax authority, and not on the taxpayer, who is to retain his/her right to file a complaint with the administrative court against a tax decision issued on the basis of an agreement.

The formal and substantive conditions for a settlement

It was discussed if any preconditions for entering into negotiations with the tax authority should be set forth in the law (e.g. that a case or a taxpayer were not involved in tax fraud) and if any limitations of a potential settlement should be specified (e.g. limiting it to certain areas of tax law or certain kinds of tax assessments).

There was full understanding from the very beginning that only a settlement aligned with the substantive tax law should be permitted. No other precondition or limitation has been set for either entering into negotiations or concluding them with an agreement (settlement). However, it was decided that a non-enumerative list of areas of possible settlements will be set out as well, in order to render the proposal more specific and emphasise that in these areas it is certain that a settlement can be made.

The coverage of costs of the mediation procedure

The issue concerned the distribution of costs of mediation (mostly mediator's fees and expenses): should they be covered by a tax authority (that is, by the state) or by a taxpayer only, by both in equal parts, or in a proportion agreed between them. The option of full coverage of such costs by the state was chosen in the hope that it will encourage taxpayers to use this new procedure – despite the concerns that if tax authorities are obliged to cover the costs in their entirety they will be more reluctant to initiate the mediation procedure or consent to it when it is requested by a taxpayer.

In general, the overall approach in dealing with the above issues was to keep the resulting proposal as 'conservative' as possible, without compromising the essence of the consensual resolution of the case and reducing the practicability of the proposal. The objective was to depart as little as possible from the existing legal rules and practices, with a view to enhancing the acceptability of the proposal.

Some of the dilemmas, only tentatively resolved in the Assumptions, reappear now in the drafting process. On the other hand, much to the surprise of this author, some of the issues that were highly contentious within the Committee during work on the Assumptions, are as such no longer. This is the case in particular with the above mentioned dilemma about 'negotiating law' – now it is no longer a contentious point (though curiously enough, the issue is ignored rather than resolved in favour of such possibility).

ADR proposal – main points

The main features of the proposed ADR *ex ante* and *ex post* are outlined here.

Consultation procedure

In this procedure, taxpayers will be entitled to request from a tax authority a clearance as to the tax implications of their material transactions (mergers, acquisitions, reorganisations, etc.). The parties may make arrangements and come to an agreement over the implications of a transaction, and in particular, the (often contentious) valuations issues. The procedure will be conducted at the pre- or post-filing stage.

It is considered as a measure of ADR *ex ante*, as it is purported to prevent the emergence of tax disputes. It enriches the catalogue of consultation procedures available in Polish tax law (including the most prominent one, i.e. the procedure leading to the issuance of an advance tax ruling, which is very popular but formally and practically deprived of consensual elements, as the participation of the taxpayer in this procedure is limited to filing an application in which their position is stated).

The procedure will be concluded with the issuance of a tax decision, binding for the tax administration and taxpayer. However, taxpayers will be informed in advance of the prospective content of a decision-to-be-issued and they will be entitled to withdraw the application if dissatisfied with the draft decision. Also, in the course of the proceedings, one or more meetings will be organised to make attempts to agree on how the case should be resolved. In this way the voluntary nature of the procedure, and the control of applicants over its course, will be retained.

Co-operative compliance program

Following examples of many jurisdictions (OECD, 2013; previously OECD, 2008), and in particular the example of the Dutch horizontal monitoring, it is proposed to lay down a legal basis for a cooperative compliance program in Poland. As is typical, the program will be directed at the large taxpayers segment ('strategic' taxpayers). The regulation of a tax ordinance will be rudimentary, not to overload the program and impose unnecessary formal constraints on its operation. The program will be developed in detail by the tax administration.

Settlements of disputes

Tax authorities will be entitled to enter into settlements with taxpayers over all issues which are in dispute in tax proceedings, provided that a settlement is within the boundaries of the law. Besides a competence norm for a tax authority to settle the case (formulated in general terms), the regulation will contain a non-exhaustive catalogue of areas of possible settlements. The catalogue is to comprise situations where doubts concerning facts of the case are difficult to eliminate and when further effort of evidence gathering is impracticable or cost- or time-consuming; valuation issues; cases where a relief in the payment of tax is sought by a taxpayer, and the tax authority is called upon to decide on the kind of relief to be applied and to specify its conditions (e.g., a payment in installments vs. a complete waiver of payment). Not only will the entire resolution of the case but also all secondary or partial issues arising in the course of the proceedings be open to settlement (e.g., the scope of evidentiary proceedings/hearing, or a list of points which are contentious between a tax authority and a taxpayer). A settlement will be reflected in a tax decision which taxpayers will still be entitled to challenge before an administrative court.

Third-party mediation

It is proposed as well to create the option to refer a tax dispute to mediation at any stage of the proceedings before tax authorities. This auxiliary procedure will be premised on the basic and universally accepted principles of mediation, namely: voluntary (for both parties, with a right to withdraw from the participation in the procedure at all times), impartiality and neutrality of a mediator (who will not be any way affiliated with tax administration or tax judiciary), and confidentiality. Parties will agree on a particular mediator, making the choice from the mediators list kept by the Minister of Finance. This task of the Minister of Finance (and in practice of the Ministry) is of a technical nature only. The potential scope of an agreement (settlement) reached by the parties with the participation of an intermediary (a mediator) will be the same as one of the agreement made without such participation.

In what follows, the paper focuses on the last two items on the agenda, i.e. settlements of tax disputes, either without or with a mediator – ADR *ex post*. The main reason for this choice is that they can be viewed as ADR *par excellence*, and that of all elements of the ADR proposal prepared by the

Committee, they received the most attention and criticism during consultation. However, where interesting or appropriate, the below considerations will touch upon other parts of the ADR proposal as well.

Consultation process and reception of the proposal

There were several forums where the ADR proposal was discussed (officially and unofficially). It was:

1. Discussed with tax academics[9], the Ministry of Finance and tax administration (before the adoption by the Committee);
2. Discussed with other ministries and public bodies (after the adoption by the Committee, before the adoption by the Government);
3. Subjected to the official public consultation (after the adoption by the Committee, before the adoption by the Government);
4. Presented at several events (after adoption by the Committee and both before and after the adoption by the Government), where it received feedback from academics, tax authorities, tax advisers, tax judges;
5. Commented on in the media; and finally
6. Discussed by members of the Committee in informal contacts

The proposal received mixed feedback from tax academics (the range of feedback was particularly wide in this group – spanning from sheer enthusiasm to complete rejection), rather negative from tax administration, rather positive from tax advisers, and positive from employers' and business organisations and trade unions[10]. All in all, ADR were definitely one of the parts of the Assumptions that attracted the most attention and interest. All comments and criticisms it received shed light on possible difficulties the implementation and practical employment of ADR could encounter.

It is interesting to note that amongst all proposed procedures, mediation proved to be the most controversial[11]. It seems that several factors coincided

---

9 The Committee received the opinions of nineteen tax academics, including thirteen tax law professors.

10 Konfederacja Lewiatan (The Polish Confederation Lewiatan), Pracodawcy RP (Employers of Poland), NSZZ "Solidarność" (The Independent and Self-Governing Trade Union "Solidarność"), Związek Banków Polski (The Polish Bank Association), Polska Izba Ubezpieczeń (The Polish Insurance Association), Krajowa Rada Radców Prawnych (The National Council of Legal Advisers). Oddly enough, Krajowa Rada Doradców Podatkowych (The National Council of Tax Advisers) did not comment on the proposal.

11 Cf., for instance, "[m]aybe we should first regulate the tax authority's right to conduct negotiations, and then, when we see how it works, mediation could be considered" (comment made in the consultation process; tax academic).

4: Alternative Methods for Resolving Tax Disputes in Poland   97

to produce this outcome. In mediation the consensual nature of an agreement between taxpayers and tax authorities, and their position as disputants in conflict, are the most salient. Thus, mediation brings to the fore these very elements because of which the proposed procedures give rise to misgivings. Also, one should note that the failure of mediation before administrative courts, which casts doubt on the chances of success of the procedure belonging to the same type, is proposed to be introduced in the tax proceedings[12].

The discussion of normative and non-normative obstacles to the implementation and operation of the proposed ADR undertaken in the present paper draws upon feedback received from all sources mentioned above, and additionally, from my colleagues sitting on the Committee. Wherever it can make the point clearer, the discussion is illustrated with a citation from comments or statements made by stakeholders in the consultation process of the proposal (given either in the body of the paper or in the footnotes).

Before embarking on the discussion, one final note is in order: in the consultations many technical comments and remarks have been received. The majority of them were accounted for in the final text of the Assumptions and in the actual law currently being drafted to benefit the outcome. They are not presented here, as they fall outside the interest of this paper.

Normative obstacles

In consultations the 'heavyweight' objections pointing to normative obstacles to introducing ADR in tax procedure have been put forward. They related to:

1. The principle of statutory regulation of taxation enshrined in the Constitution (*nullum tributum sine lege*) and the 'one right amount of tax' thesis;
2. The principle of legality (the rule of law);
3. The principle of equality; and
4. The current model of tax procedure (inquisitorial / non-adversarial, with a tax authority in the position to imperatively and unilaterally determine the rights and obligations of a taxpayer who is a party to the proceedings).

---

12 "Resolution of a dispute through a mediator will lengthen the proceedings in the case. (…) [T]he mediation procedure in the administrative court proceedings is hardly effective, and therefore it is difficult to suppose that in disputes between a tax authority and a taxpayer this effectiveness will be greater; additionally, the time of the resolution of the case – if the mediation fails – will in fact be longer" (comment from tax official during the consultation).

As it will be demonstrated below, these objections – which stem from the culture of legal formalism – are not theoretically valid.

The principle of statutory regulation of taxation and 'one right amount of tax'

The objection states that consensual resolution of a tax dispute conflicts with the principle of statutory regulation of taxation (the so-called 'principle of statutory exclusivity'), enshrined in Articles 217 and 84 of the Constitution[13]. It claims that settlements between taxpayers and tax administration lead to the assessment of tax liabilities in the amount differing from what "the law clearly states"[14].

One can doubt if this is entirely true that the law determines always only one way to tax – that is, that the Constitution commits us to embracing the Dworkinian thesis about the existence of 'one right answer' in all interpretative issues (Dworkin, 1977)[15] (and with regard to other problems of tax law application, also those related to the determination of the facts of the case). However, even assuming that this thesis is valid, the cited provisions of the Constitution do not imply any position about the *process* (procedure) that should be employed to come to the right answer. While they set the starting point of all analysis (and this point of departure is the law, as enacted by the Parliament – a body of legal texts) and its final point (concretisation of all constituent elements of taxation – object, subject, tax base, tax rate – against facts and circumstances of a specific case), they do not determine the route one has to follow between them: the way to proceed, i.e., the procedure leading from the identification of the problem to the establishing of the 'right answer' to it.

---

13 Article 217: "The imposition of taxes, as well as other public imposts, the specification of those subject to the tax and the rates of taxation, as well as the principles for granting tax reliefs and remissions, along with categories of taxpayers exempt from taxation, shall be by means of statute". Article 84: "Everyone shall comply with his responsibilities and public duties, including the payment of taxes, as specified by statute" (translation published at the official website of *Sejm* – lower chamber of the Polish parliament).

14 "There is no place for a consensual resolution of the case based on an agreement in the jurisdictional tax proceeding, where the law clearly states when a tax liability arises". Cf. also the observation that ADR, as they are conceived of in the Assumptions, "are associable unequivocally with private law and do not harmonize with public law, and in particular, with tax law" (comments made in the consultation process; tax academics).

15 This thesis in itself is debatable, and in fact debated and challenged by legal philosophers (Marmor, 2005; Endicott, 2000; Peczenik, 1989). 'One right answer' should be regarded as a regulative idea governing the practice of the interpretation and application of the law rather than as a concept which has substance – solid grounding in reality.

Articles 217 and 84 of the Constitution are provisions of the substantive, and not procedural, tax law. By contrast, an agreement (a settlement), and the procedure it is embedded in, provide a procedural solution: a mechanism of reaching valid answers concerning the relevant content of tax laws and facts of the case in cooperation with disputants rather than in conflict between them. It is not an institution of the substantive tax law that would interfere with the volume and allocation of tax burdens. It follows that these provisions constitute no obstacle to the introduction into tax procedures the opportunities for discussion and settlement with a party (a taxpayer).

This objection can also be construed as considering tax cases as self-evident by their nature – such that "there is nothing to talk about"[16]. It is true that the practice of complying with the law and applying it knows many situations which, in the theory of law, are called 'easy cases' – where a legal provision is directly understandable and facts of the case are established beyond doubt[17]. In reality, the majority of situations where taxpayers deal with tax law fall into this category. Nonetheless, if we assume (as we should) that participants of tax disputes act in good will and are competent[18] – as users of the Polish language in which tax law provisions are expressed and as the law addressees – we have to come to the conclusion that cases of tax disputes do not belong to this category. Tax disputes arise – often, if not as a rule – in cases which are far from obvious, are complex and discursively profound. In such cases, areas of discretion in solving contentious issues (not to be conflated with arbitrariness) open up (Barak, 1989). To deny that tax authorities have discretionary powers, and that 'difficult cases' do arise, is to misconceive the nature of the law. Such misconception leads to wrongly attributing self-obviousness to the law, and to its trivialisation. The resulting

---

16 Comment made in the consultation process (tax academic). Cf. also "A mediator in the tax assessment proceeding is needless, since wherever it is necessary to assess tax there is no area which can be subject to mediation. Substantive law provisions determine the amount of the tax base, and the tax rate – there is no place for mediation" (comment made in the consultation process; tax official).

17 In the routine practice of understanding and 'using' the law (be it complying with it by addressees or applying it by tax administration and courts), the majority of legal rules are immediately comprehensible and automatically followed. Their meanings are transparent to their users and devoid of discursive potential: agreed upon in an implicit consensus. Cf. the well-know Wittgenstein's comments: "There is a way of grasping the rule which is not an interpretation" and "When I obey a rule, I do not choose. I obey the rule *blindly*" (Wittgenstein, 1953, §§ 201 and 219). *See, for instance*, Marmor, 2005; Brożek & Zyzik, 2010.

18 A participant who acts in bad will or is ignorant may see doubts where there are none. However, the rules of legal discourse by which tax authorities are bound commit them to the assumption that this is not the case. This assumption not only satisfies the requirement of fairness but is also productive in assuring the accuracy of the resolution of the case: it enables the revelation of the discursive potential of the problem which otherwise might go unnoticed.

picture of the law, and of actions routinely undertaken by its users, seriously misrepresents the reality – it is *tout court* inaccurate. Because of that, one can contend that situations where a tax dispute has arisen are a natural environment for a settlement.

It is erroneous to believe that settling a case with a taxpayer detracts tax authorities from their regular duties which, in the normal course of events, would lead them to establishing the 'objective truth' – and as a consequence, that it distorts the outcome of the case and harms the accuracy of the resolution. These negative effects allegedly can occur due to restrictions on activities performed by tax authorities in order to collect evidence, or because of negotiation pressure from a participant in the dispute[19]. There are at least two remarks to make in this regard.

First, it is quite naïve to believe that tax proceedings typically lead to establishing the 'objective truth' about the content of tax law provisions: the facts of the case and the relationship between the two[20]. This is because there are many determinants of the process which leads to the resolution of the case. The process is even now, i.e. in a state without the possibility of using ADR, subject to factual limitations (e.g. linked to the language as a medium of communication used in law, cognitive biases of participants, pragmatic restrictions in the time that can be devoted to any tax proceedings, which is conducted up until in the perception of a tax authority that the point of 'saturation' is reached, etc.). The process is subject to normative limitations as well, e.g., related to restrictions in using evidence that has been acquired illegally ('fruit of the poisonous tree' is inadmissible). 'Objective truth' which is reached at the end of the proceedings is nothing but a construct whose alignment with reality – 'things-in-themselves' – is not guaranteed[21]. It is not clear whether in the realm of the statutory law any "thing-in-itself" exists, or whether the content of law is not a social construct, and therefore, something which by its very nature is negotiable (where negotiations are not necessar-

---

19 "Under the law in force everything that can contribute to elucidating the case can be admitted as a proof, it is therefore inappropriate to create instruments that restrict this principle in order to (…) make an agreement about the scope of evidence to be heard, it will in essence be a limitation of evidentiary proceeding" (comment made in the consultation process; tax official).

20 "Tax authorities do not issue final decisions in cases in which doubts [as regards facts] persist. (…) An agreement about the factual background of the case is a departure from the principle of objective truth" (comment made in the consultation process; tax official).

21 An important context to this thesis is provided by the observation that contemporary philosophy (also analytic philosophy) renders problematic the adequacy (or representation) relation allegedly held between a scientific theory and reality. This is so even though science is in our culture a paragon of rationality and truth.

ily carried out intentionally and consciously). The competence (authority) to settle the case – strike a deal with a taxpayer – does not imply the departure from the principle of objective truth. It is one of many legal determinants of this principle, dictating how this 'truth' is to be established.

Legal and factual state (background) agreed between disputants is where their common perception, and on the basis of all available arguments and proofs, 'represents' reality – which means that it is its closest approximation. In particular, tax authorities are not supposed or allowed to enter into deals consisting of accepting a formally agreed 'normative state' or 'factual state' that are known to be at variance with reality.

Second, it is unclear why discussions and settlements should render the final 'construct' more distant from the truth instead of bringing it closer to it. To be more specific: talks with a participant of the dispute undertaken in the intention of settling a case may shed new light on the legal issue that is in dispute, or allow the acquisition of new evidence which otherwise would have been unavailable because of the animosity between a taxpayer and a tax authority. As a result, truth may become more easily attainable than it would have been without cooperative interaction with a taxpayer.

The attitude of 'procedural solipsism', that is the reluctant communication with a party to tax proceedings, as potentially threatening the accuracy or legality of the outcome of the case, is wrong both from the legal perspective of the existing principles of tax procedure (the principle of enhancing trust in tax authorities; the principle of active participation of a party in the proceedings[22]), which dictate an open relationship with a taxpayer, and from the pragmatic viewpoint, which requires that proceedings be conducted in an effective and efficient manner.

Finally, it is interesting how the comments made in the consultation process related to this objection reveal the background belief in the specificity of the tax law: in that it differs significantly from other branches of law. It is commonly believed, and often asserted by tax academics, that in tax law less leeway or discretion of tax authorities is permissible than in administrative law (not to speak of all private law branches), and that it should be viewed as similar to the criminal law, with its narrow and rigid reading of legal provisions. The position of such 'tax exceptionalism' is as unfounded as it is widespread[23].

---

22 Articles 121 § 1 and 124 of the Tax Ordinance.
23 It has its disputants; e.g. , Menéndez rightly speaks against "conceptualization of taxes as equivalent to criminal laws with regard to their possible impact upon individual rights"

The principle of legality (rule of law)

An objection which is similar (yet not identical) to the one already discussed argues that concluding an agreement would be contrary to the rule of law principle – in Poland set out in Article 7 of the Constitution[24] and Article 120 of the Tax Ordinance[25].

This objection could be rebutted by asserting simply that settlements will be made only on the basis of[26] and within the limits (boundaries) of the law[27]. However it goes deeper than that, and therefore deserves to be discussed.

It seems that this objection is rooted in the supposition that settlements between taxpayers and tax officials involve bargaining the amount of tax. Admittedly, such bargaining is excluded by the provisions of the Constitution. Yet in the current proposal of ADR it is excluded as well. The new mechanisms that are being contemplated encourage disputants to engage in a legal discourse *ad meritum*: to exchange arguments on legal and factual aspects of the case with a view to reaching a consensus. An agreement reached as a result of this discourse will affect the amount of a tax liability only indirectly, i.e. in a manner mediated through what has been agreed on law and facts.

Importantly, consensus is not to be confused with compromise[28]. Settlement of a case does not necessarily rely on mutual concessions made by disputants with regard to, and in comparison with their initial positions. Where one of the parties is able to convince the other of the correctness of his/her viewpoint, an agreement may fully reflect his/her initial position. It is not so

---

and the maxim *in dubio contra fiscum*. "The principle was recycled by the formal paradigm of tax law as providing a further protection of individual rights against an institution that was clearly anomalous", whereas "[a] general theory of democratic tax law should assert that there is no basic difference between the application of tax norms or of any other norm. Tax laws are not exceptional norms" (Menéndez, 2001, pp.320-321). The general trend in tax jurisdictions seems to be against legal formalism (Thuronyi, 2003, p.149).

24 Article 7: "The organs of public authority shall function on the basis of, and within the limits of, the law".

25 "How can one reconcile the conciliatory forms with the constitutional principle of the legality of tax authority operations and with the fact that tax law provisions are legally binding?" (Comment made in the form of a rhetorical question in the consultation process; tax academic).

26 The legal ground will be provided by a general competence norm (authorising a tax authority to settle a case).

27 Let us note what the language suggests here: 'within the boundaries' means that the law delineates an area of its correct application, and not a point. Is it then true that in all cases one and only one answer is right (sufficiently justified or justifiable)?

28 This distinction is inspired by the ideas and framework of 'principled negotiations' – 'negotiation on merits' (Fisher & Ury, 1981).

that in such a case the other party gains nothing throughout the procedure, and thus leaves it empty-handed. Throughout his/her important interests may have been satisfied (also other than financial i.e. non-monetary ones). It is important to distinguish between positions and interests: a position in a negotiation is what a party in a conflict wants to achieve; an interest i.e. his/her desire or goal, which dictates why s/he wants to achieve it (Fisher & Ury, 1981). The sense of procedural justice (i.e. subjective procedural fairness) can be interpreted as one of the interests of a party. Consequently, a settlement can be made also in 'all-or-nothing' or 'binary' cases which do not allow for a compromise. Every contentious issue should be dealt with consensually on the basis of its own merit (without 'package deals').

Equality principle

Tax ADR are objected to also from the perspective of horizontal equity (the principle of equality – art. 32 of the Constitution[29]). An essential feature of legal rules – their attribute – is that they are universal: they apply indiscriminately to a category composed of similar cases[30].

The new institutions, as currently envisaged, will not modify or violate the principle that taxpayers similarly placed – who find themselves in legal and factual situations that are similar in all relevant aspects – should be treated equally by tax authorities. In particular, they should be qualified as eligible or not for a deal, in categories rather than individually. Entering into a deal with a taxpayer should be dependent on objective characteristics of their situation. The principle of equality requires similar (the same) situations to be treated similarly (in the same manner), but also to treat differently situations which are different. This principle is observed on condition that taxpayers are categorised properly.

Since settlements (whether made with the help of a mediator or without it) are to be entered into voluntarily by both parties, respecting the principle of equality will depend on the way tax authorities use in practice the authority (competence, capacity) vested in them to settle a case. The consistency of policies of the tax administration in this regard should be both based upon and reflected in the strategy, and announced publicly. The strategy should include in particular a declaration of will to enter into negotiations (and

---

29 Article 32: "1. All persons shall be equal before the law. All persons shall have the right to equal treatment by public authorities. 2. No one shall be discriminated against in political, social or economic life for any reason whatsoever".

30 It is an essential feature of all normative systems, as collections of rules. "The rule of law (…) implies the precept that similar cases be treated similarly. Men could not regulate their actions by means of rules if this precept were not followed" (Rawls, 1971, p.237).

possibly, deals or settlements) in cases belonging to the generally described categories, and of the lack of such will in other categories, enumeratively listed. It should also indicate rules of conducting negotiation and entering into agreements or settlements.

Equality concerns were raised (by the Ministry of Economy, among others) in particular with respect to the cooperation compliance program. The program will address the 'big business' sector only. The objection which argues that it should be extended to all taxpayers is based on the 'one size fits all' attitude. The choice to address the program to large, strategic taxpayers is not arbitrary but judicious – these entities possess characteristics which make their 'traditional' control difficult and/or ineffective and at the same time, they have a reliable internal tax control function. Moreover, they are particularly prone to tax avoidance, and an offer of 'certainty in exchange for transparency' could encourage their compliance with the spirit of the tax law. The same benefits as those gained by large taxpayers via the participation in the program, related to legal certainty, will also be available to other taxpayers, but they will be attainable through other legal means and mechanisms (in particular, through offering them assistance and support in complying with their tax duties; OECD, 2012).

Despite the above, it should be observed that the question asked by the Ministry of Finance: "Won't forms of mediation undermine the belief in equality and justice in the imposition of tax burdens?"[31] is legitimate. It is necessary to make sure that the public does not lose trust in the system: in that tax law is administered fairly, as a result of the way in which ADR are applied.

Model of tax procedure

Finally, it is argued that ADR do not concur with the model of tax procedure. Tax procedure is shaped as inquisitorial (non-adversarial), and the position of a tax authority is such that is has the capacity to unilaterally and imperatively determine the legal situation of a party to the proceedings (a taxpayer). It is contended that prohibits entering into deals (settlements) between tax authorities and taxpayers. This objection invites several comments.

First, it should be obvious that the authority (competence) to unilaterally decide on the legal situation of taxpayers does not rule out conducting dialog and negotiations. And conversely, negotiations and settlements do not contradict the nature of tax procedure. The proposal included in the

---

31 Comment made in the consultation process (the Ministry of Finance).

Assumptions does not eliminate the imperative character of an act issued at the end of the proceedings; as mentioned, this feature of the proposal has been decided in order to keep it as conservative as possible. Tax settlements are not to replace tax decisions; however, a tax decision is to be issued on the basis of a settlement and reflect its dispositions[32]. No dramatic or revolutionary departure from well-established procedural principles is postulated[33].

Second, a tax authority plays a double role in the tax proceedings. On the one hand, it is an authority conducting tax proceedings (and in this capacity, it is bound to be neutral and impartial). On the other hand, however, it is a creditor in the underlying legal relationship which is to be decided in the proceedings (and as such, it has its 'own' interests to safeguard). This 'duality' is a widely recognised phenomenon (Mastalski, 2004, p.267). It explains why a dispute can easily arise in the proceedings, and in what sense the proceedings are insufficiently characterised if asserted simply that it is 'non-adversarial' or 'inquisitorial'. 'Non-adversarial' does not mean in this case 'dispute-free'.

This duality of tax authority's roles may be subject to criticism, and is in fact criticised. One of the aspects rarely observed is that it can diminish the perceptions of subjective procedural justice[34]. An authority examining and resolving the case has a vested interest in its resolution to the advantage of the state budget, which unfavourably affects the perception of its impartiality (if not impartiality itself). One could even argue that ADR, where conflict between disputants and underlying tensions between their interests are brought to light, is more 'honest' in elucidating the contradictions of their positions and interests. It may be beneficial for fostering a sense of procedural justice.

Third, the domination of a tax authority and asymmetry in power between parties to the tax dispute are not such that they preclude making settlements.

---

32 This means that in a sense the alternative dispute resolution methods set out in the proposal are not that 'alternative', and that the proposal is quite balanced and moderate.

33 As mentioned above, ADR are currently being introduced also in the administrative procedure (the amendment to the respective act is in the legislative process). This demonstrates that the inquisitorial type of procedure does not preclude the implementation of consensual methods of dispute resolution. On the admissibility of alternative methods of dispute resolution in the area of administrative law see, ex multis, Kijowski, 2007; Recommendation Rec(2001)9 of the Committee of Ministers to member states on alternatives to litigation between administrative authorities and private parties of 5 September 2001.

34 Interestingly, there is research suggesting that adversarial procedure scores better that inquisitorial procedure in subjective procedural justice (Lind & Tyler, 1988, chs. 2 and 3).

Theories of negotiations and theories of legal discourse assume liberty and equality of entities who enter into negotiations, as well as their being interrelated (co-dependent). Admittedly, in tax proceedings a taxpayer is not placed on a par with a tax authority. However, despite appearances to the contrary, disputants are interrelated – a tax authority is not independent of a party to the proceedings. The procedural position of a tax authority is dominant, yet not absolute (Kmieciak, 2007). Tax authorities' actions are affected by the actions of a party (a taxpayer) who has tools to influence an authority, both through instruments to-the-merits (e.g. argumentation) and not-to-the merits (e.g. using persuasion instead of argumentation). One of the ways for a taxpayer to exert this influence is to file an appeal or a complaint.

Moreover, a tax authority has a number of interests which can motivate it to enter into negotiations and settlements. It is interested in ensuring tax compliance; it is the most fundamental public interest, and therefore, the interest of a tax authority. Furthermore, it has financial interests (as a tax creditor) related to efficient managing the workload of cases, proper allocation of tax audit resources, securing the position of tax administration in view of the uncertainties involved in the court proceedings, securing voluntary execution of a tax decision by a taxpayer (instead of its being enforced upon him/her, which is more costly and risk-laden), etc. This means that a tax authority can endeavour to reach a consensual closure of a case not (only) in the interest of a taxpayer but to safeguard its own interests – which does not contradict its dominant position.

As a result, while tax ADR may not exactly follow the model of negotiations or discourse (with disputants enjoying equal positions), in practice they come sufficiently close to this model to use the respective theories fruitfully, and to deserve their name of ADR.

Practical difficulties

Although there are no normative grounds on which applying ADR in tax procedure should be excluded, one can predict that the adoption and implementation of the proposal, and then the successful operation of ADR, will encounter practical difficulties. As much as the above normative objections are not valid, the mere fact that they have been raised (and by many respondents) is a significant factor to be taken into account in the assessment of the odds of success of the proposal.

First and foremost, these expected impediments relate to the perceptions and attitudes of tax dispute participants: tax officials, taxpayers, tax intermediaries. Certain beliefs which seem to be quite common[35] can diminish chances of success of the ADR proposal. An example is provided by the belief that conflict between taxpayers and tax authorities is 'structural' in nature and intractable: it is triggered by the irreconcilable interests of disputants[36]. This view ignores the fact that over and above conflicting interests, taxpayers and tax authorities (officials) have interests in common, principally to ensure tax compliance. Also, it seems (though this has not been supported as yet by empirical studies) that there are negative and antagonistic stereotypes of other participants of tax disputes – a stereotype of a tax official adopted by taxpayers, and of a taxpayer and a tax adviser adopted by tax officials[37]. Symptomatic of a cliché vision of a tax adviser may be one of recurring themes in the consultation: concerns that ADR will be 'abused' by tax advisers, e.g. to lengthen the procedure to bring about the ineffective closure of the case after the period of limitation[38]. Objectively, these concerns are exaggerated if not altogether unfounded: it is hardly imaginable how this can happen given that a tax authority will retain full control over the employment of ADR, including control over its duration[39].

---

35 There is mostly anecdotal evidence supporting this claim. The field of tax compliance is under-researched in Poland. To the best of my knowledge the only extensive analysis based on empirical studies (surveys) has been presented in Niesiobędzka, 2013. However, this study is useful for the present purposes only to a limited extent, since: i) it examines only the attitudes of taxpayers (and not other participants of tax life in Poland); ii) only those belonging to certain categories; and iii) it does not explore attitudes of participants of tax disputes but more generally, factors influencing tax compliance and evasion outside of any particular procedure and independently of whether a respondent has participated in any dispute. However, it is noteworthy that this study confirmed that procedural justice influences tax compliance (indirectly, through personal and social standards), and showed that the level of subjective procedural justice has been low among respondents (in fact, the more frequent contacts with tax administration, the stronger the sense of procedural injustice).

36 "Conciliation in public law, and in particular in tax law, will nonetheless always be an auxiliary form of a tax authority's operation, in view of the structural conflict of financial interests of the parties" (comment in the consultation process; tax academic). The same respondent underlined, quite philosophically, the 'egoistic' nature of a man in the modern society which discourages him from being compliant with the tax law. This Hobbesian vision of a man is an interesting view, yet unjustified in light of the body of economic psychology research showing that taxpayers are not (only) *homines oeconomici*.

37 This is what I infer from my own experience, having extensive contacts with tax advisers, tax academics, tax officials.

38 Cf. also: "One cannot doubt that taxpayers, in order to secure their interest, will be using this [i.e., consultation] procedure excessively (like it is the case with private tax rulings)" (comment made in the consultation process; tax official).

39 Another example is a comment regarding mediation: "It is a kind of a courtesy towards a certain group of professional attorneys who will get an opportunity for additional earnings (the costs of mediator's work are to be covered by the state budget), which in light of the difficult situation of the budget resulting in long-lasting "freezing" of salaries of tax authorities' employees is a disputable solution, to say the least" (comment made in the consultation process; tax official).

Participants of the Polish tax arena may have instrumental, reserved or pessimistic attitudes towards consensual methods of disputes resolution. The ADR proposal received many sceptical comments; if one and only strand were to be extracted from the heterogeneous body of critical comments received during the consultation process, it would be the expression of this sense of scepticism. It is feared that ADR regulation will become a 'dead-letter law', following mediation before the administrative courts. A variant of generalised scepticism is calling the proposal 'naïve', tainted with 'wishful thinking', or declaring disbelief in 'the world to be so beautiful'[40]. Also, the question was asked "[a]re our tax administration and our society prepared for new forms of cooperation?"[41]. Very relevant in itself, this question conveys scepticism. It goes without saying that these negative attitudes can work as a self-fulfilling prophecy.

Scepticism as to ADR's chances of success is inspired in particular by the failure of the mediation procedure before the administrative court (and this inspiration was visible in the comments). Also, it was often shrouded in the reserved attitude toward the possibility of adapting solutions employed in other jurisdictions to the Polish reality[42]. Furthermore, deficits of knowledge and experience in using consensual methods of conflict resolution[43] and (possibly) low interpersonal communication skills of all participants of tax disputes can work against ADR. This factor is not so much about attitudes but, more fundamentally, concerns basic knowledge and skills.

A theme that has been conspicuous in the consultation process (and highlighted by many respondents) relates to tax officials' worries about possible accusations they may face if they actively use ADR: accusations of arbitrariness, committing the *ultra vires* offense and/or corruption, or of the insufficient protection of public finances. It is a very important factor as these concerns may practically inhibit the operation of ADR. It is obvious that fears of personal responsibility for the *bona fide* employment of ADR can ruin the chances of the proposal. They can result in tax officials having recourse to formalism[44] – *modus operandi* which would be opportunistic or inertial, but

---

40   Comments made in the consultation process (tax academics; tax officials; tax advisers).

41   Comment made in the consultation process (the Ministry of Finance).

42   "One needs to consider whether it is a good idea to introduce to the Polish tax law system the solutions adopted in countries where the so-called common law – law of precedence – is used" (comment made in the consultation process; tax official).

43   Striking evidence of these deficits is that not all tax law professors understood the idea of mediation – some remarks received in the consultation process exposed this ignorance.

44   A defense mechanism of finding "escape in formalism", as a way to manage controversial decisions and workload of cases, has been observed with regard to judiciary in Galligan & Matczak, 2005, pp.38-39.

in view of the above preoccupations, quite understandable. These worries should be addressed in the first place, in order to encourage tax authorities (tax officials) to embrace the exercise of discretion in deciding cases[45].

More generally, one of the main interests of a tax official is their own personal security *sensu largo*: also in terms of being confident that the resolution of the case is the right one, i.e. aligned with tax law. Striving for this security motivates tax officials to refer cases to the administrative courts – through taking a position most advantageous for the state budget, and negative for a taxpayer, which the latter will surely challenge before a court – rather than take full responsibility for their resolution. Every tax adviser in Poland surely has heard a typical comment by a tax official: "I see the validity of the arguments you give; however, I prefer that the court decides on the merits of the case". This is in a way an escape from responsibility for deciding the case. This approach, which can be called 'opportunistic', 'self-effacing' or 'overcautious', obviously acts against ADR.

Finally, one should note that the background of low level of trust in Polish society in general creates an unfavourable environment for ADR. Trust, as a crucial constituent of social capital, affects many phenomena of social life. As remarked by Czapiński, Poles show very low values of trust in indexes of social capital. In the European Social Survey (hereinafter: the ESS) in 2006 and 2012 Poles ranked as one of the least trustful with respect to general trust (Czapiński, 2015, pp.351-352). In Czapiński's own survey (conducted periodically – every 2 years – within the "Social Diagnosis" project) 10.5% of respondents in 2003 and 2005, 11.5% in 2007, 13.4% in 2009 and 2011, 12.2% in 2013 and 15.2% in 2015 agreed with the opinion and "the majority of people are trustworthy"; the respective numbers in the ESS were 18% in 2012 and 16% in 2014. It is more than four times less than for Denmark, Norway and Finland.

The low level of trust is not easily manageable: one cannot ameliorate the situation overnight. On the one hand, it is clearly a hindrance to ADR. Tax authorities will be afraid that taxpayers or their supervisors will accuse them of an offence, misdemeanour or maladministration (as already mentioned); and conversely for taxpayers – that information they disclose in ADR procedure will then be used by tax authorities against them[46]. On the other hand, it

---

45 In this regard an interesting suggestion was made during the consultation process: that a representative of the appeal authority should be allowed to participate in the negotiations conducted in the first instance, in order to bolster and encourage the first instance authority to make use of the procedure (especially in the first years of its operation).

46 The observation that taxpayers may not be cooperative in their dealings with tax authorities out of fear that their openness will be abused, was made by colleagues from the Committee.

should by no means persuade legislators and policy makers to abandon the idea of ADR. Quite the contrary, it makes ADR even more desirable, as one of the ways to enhance trust in the long run.

Non-normative (factual) obstacles, and in particular, shared beliefs and perceptions concerning the nature of taxation, substantive tax law and tax procedure (the testimony of which are theoretical objections pointed out above) though not insurmountable, should not be discarded lightly. Additionally, as already mentioned, it has rightly been remarked during the consultation process that proper measures should be employed to prevent ADR from undermining taxpayers' belief in that tax burdens are imposed in an equitable and fair manner.

Is law sufficient? "To-do list"

General remarks

In view of the above it is imperative that the formal adoption of the proposal be complemented by a range of supporting activities able to aid the successful i.e. the effective, efficient and fair, implementation and operation of ADR. They should address in particular the non-normative obstacles to the ADR proposal that have been commented on above.

It is important to stress the need to be prepared 'from day one' for the legal accessibility of ADR[47]. ADR will naturally draw much public interest and incite curiosity in taxpayers. Presumably, they will also arouse hopes and expectations. The ADR proposal is a response to the real need of taxpayers, and to the common belief that the *status quo* in tax disputes resolution is lacking in many respects and cannot be maintained[48]. Also, it is a well-known fact that ADR are successfully used in many foreign jurisdictions, and that they are considered modern and advanced methods of dispute resolution. This could result in a 'fashion' for ADR – and hopefully, not a short-lived one.

It is worthwhile to capitalise on this interest and to familiarise taxpayers and tax authorities with the characteristics of ADR and the benefits they can offer[49]. The first experiences with ADR will be decisive for their overall chances of success. If these experiences are negative, the reception of the entire project will be negative as well, and in all likelihood ADR will quickly lose popularity.

---

47 This was highlighted also by other members of the Committee.
48 This observation was made also by other members of the Committee.
49 Several members of the Committee underlined this aspect.

It is therefore necessary to ensure a proper foundation for the operation of ADR in order to improve the odds of the project. "You cannot make a first impression twice", as the saying goes. This means that the actions pointed out below should be carried out even before the proposal (within a new tax ordinance) comes into force – they should precede its formal adoption. If possible, pilot projects of tax mediation and cooperative compliance will be realised before the adoption of a new ordinance (on the basis of a regulation which will be inserted in the 'old' Tax Ordinance for this purpose), and these projects should as well be preceded and accompanied by supporting activities. Otherwise, the potential of ADR will be negatively affected.

In this context the case of mediation before administrative courts – its practical failure – is instructive. First, reasons for this failure should be contemplated, so as not to commit the same mistakes twice[50]. There seem to be many such reasons, including flaws in legal regulation of this procedure (not a mediation strictly speaking, as the role of a mediator is assumed by a judge); too late in the proceedings for a mediation to be effective (when a conflict is already escalated and hardened); lack of competences in communication skills on the part of 'mediators' who were unfit for this role; lack of a negotiation mandate for tax authorities participating in mediation (sic!); relatively short waiting period for a trial before regional administrative courts (3-6 months), and therefore, limited incentive for a taxpayer to engage in mediation, etc. It is striking that some of these factors could have been avoided, had they been properly addressed prior the regulation on mediation before administrative courts has been adopted or concurrently with its adoption. It is a red-flag warning against implementing ADR in an unprepared and improvised manner.

Second, the example of mediation before administrative courts shows how impactful the failure of a legal institution can be. As mentioned before, the malfunction of mediation overshadows the current project and arouses intense scepticism toward it, which in turn is not without effect on its chances of success. Therefore, policy makers and legislators engaged in the current project bear a burden of responsibility[51]. Further failures of ADR, should they occur, would impair, if not altogether forfeit the chances of all similar mechanisms to succeed. How to 'set the stage' for tax ADR? The initiatives

---

50 This fiasco has been discussed in numerous articles; references to them would run for several pages.

51 This is the responsibility of the Committee members, but first and foremost of the Ministry of Finance. The work of the Committee consists solely in preparing a (draft) tax ordinance, and law is insufficient to attain desired social objectives.

suggested below concentrate on the tax administration. There are several reasons for this focus.

First, because tax authorities (tax officials) set the tone of tax proceedings, the entire climate of interaction with a taxpayer is dependent on the attitude they show. Taxpayers are in a way responsive to attitudes manifested by tax authorities. If not for other reasons, it is because in the inquisitorial procedure the authorities conduct the proceeding, and therefore, have a leading role in it. Second, tax authorities are more easily targeted, as constituting a centralised structure (taxpayers and tax advisers are more dispersed and more difficult to reach and therefore to influence as a group). Third, possible problems and obstacles linked to tax authorities are dominant among those in the consultation process. Interestingly, members of the Committee also pointed out issues related to the tax administration as the main potential obstacles to the success of ADR.

List of activities

A non-exhaustive list of activities supporting ADR should include the following.

'Tone at the top'

A clear message and commitment to ADR is necessary on the part of the Minister of Finance[52]. While such a declaration of will *per se* is insufficient, it is a starting point and an indispensable element of the entire project. Tax administration is a hierarchical, centralised and formal structure, and statements of the Minister of Finance are attentively listened to and respected. In practice, as attested by experiences of any tax adviser, this influence, and the resulting subordination of tax officials to the guidance coming from the Ministry of Finance, far exceeds the formal framework of law. Any technical position of the Ministry of Finance, irrespective of its form, is treated as an instruction equal to the law. The Minister of Finance should send a clear message to the tax administration that entering into deals with taxpayers is welcome. It should help in dissolving doubts as to whether it is admissible to settle cases with taxpayers, and in managing fears of being accused of corruption or maladministration.

More generally, the commitment of the Minister of Finance is particularly valuable in building the belief that for tax law to be effective, tax authorities should administer a range of both coercive and non-coercive mea-

---

52 The importance of this element was highlighted also by members of the Committee.

sures, according to the motto of the Dutch horizontal monitoring: "flexible when possible, strict when necessary". The Minister should be the leader of change. The example of Australia, and the successful transition from a culture of 'command and control' to the 'voluntary compliance' model, induced by the political decision at the top of the tax administration's management (Braithwaite, 2003; Braithwaite, 2005), is instructive and promising.

One should note that for the time being, such commitment of the Ministry of Finance is nowhere near. Currently tax policy issues are discussed exclusively in the context of tax evasion and tax avoidance, and actions are taken to strengthen the deterrence and control mechanisms with no balancing activities reinforcing the dimension of 'trust'. Consensual methods of dispute resolution are therefore not high on the agenda of tax policy.

The adoption by the Ministry of Finance of a litigation and settlement strategy

Such strategy would be a novelty in Poland, and a much needed one in general – quite irrespectively of the introduction of ADR. It would provide the governance framework for interactions with taxpayers, as well as formulate and explain general policy goals and attitudes of the tax administration[53]. Importantly, it would also give assurance to tax officials and provide internal guidance to tax administration staff on dealing with tax disputes, for them to know how to handle and resolve disputes in a consistent manner.

The British HMRC *Litigation and Settlement Strategy* (hereinafter: LSS) (2011) together with the accompanying documents (*Resolving tax disputes* (2012), *Commentary on the litigation and settlement strategy* (2013) and *Code of governance for resolving tax disputes* (2014)) are good examples to use, both in terms of their general principles (their focus on fostering a non-confrontational approach and collaborative working practices, and a striking proper balance between legality and pragmatism in tax authorities' operations[54]) and significant elements of their content related to tax ADR and tax settlements.

---

53 One of the possible explanations of the fact that no such strategy exists now is that not enough significance is accorded to non-binding documents in general, also as a way to communicate with stakeholders. Law, on the other hand, understood as a normative system, is overestimated as to its effectiveness. As a result, in time of trouble a new legal rule will be enacted rather than an 'old' one explained. Few are also official clarifications of new legal regulations coming into force. Belief that law can be self-explanatory is an illusion.

54 Reflected in, for instance, the concept of a cost-effective dispute, and in deciding which disputes to take up based on the analysis of potential of the case for litigation, with a number of factors to take into account: amount of tax at stake (in an individual case and similar ones); HMRC's chances of success; cost of litigation; if a deliberate attempt to undermine legislation is involved; if strategic points of policy or principle are involved.

In this latter respect, valuable elements of the British strategy (considered here as exemplary) are, among others, the commitment to resolve tax disputes in accordance with the law (to ensure that the right tax liability is assessed consistently with tax regulation), and fairly and even-handedly between taxpayers; measuring the potential for litigation – in 'strong' cases litigate and in 'weak or non worth-while' cases concede rather than pursue; excluding 'package deals' – requiring that each contentious point is resolved or settled on its merits[55]; excluding arithmetical splitting the difference in the case of the 'all-or-nothing' ('binary' or 'black-and-white') cases[56]; welcoming settlements in partial or procedural issues (e.g., to narrow down the points in dispute to be litigated, or jointly draft the statement of facts, etc.). All these elements can and should be reproduced in the Polish strategy.

Another British document valuable for tax authorities and taxpayers is *Resolving tax disputes. Practical guidance for HMRC staff on the use of alternative dispute resolution in large or complex cases*. Its special interest lies in the categorisation of large and complex cases, which gives guidance as to whether ADR are applicable and appropriate to be used to resolve them. Proper selection of cases is crucial to the success of ADR.

Adopting such policy documents in Poland would help to address concerns over equity in ADR application. In particular, they would provide guidance for the tax administration through setting reference points to facilitate the decision process in case of doubt whether, and if so, to what extent, a given case has characteristics making it appropriate for a settlement. This is very relevant, as during the consultation process many tax officials were expressing discontent with the generality of the provision of a new tax ordinance setting out the scope of possible settlements with taxpayers. In tax officials' view more guidance is needed[57], and such guidance should be provided by internal regulations produced by the Ministry of Finance and announced to the general public. It would also help in reassuring the public that the tax administration is equitable, fair and consistent in using ADR,

---

55 It excludes that a concession is made on one of the contentious issues in order to get a concession on other issues, as this would lead to compromising the legality of the resolution.

56 I appreciate also the fact that LSS allows for a possibility that any given case is only seemingly black-and-white, and invites to examine discursive potential of a case in collaboration with a taxpayer and/or to check whether it can be subdivided into smaller issues which can be dealt with separately. Cases which are genuinely 'all-or-nothing' can only be either fully settled or fully litigated.

57 It is necessary to "make the objective scope of possible settlements more specific. (…) The objective scope of a possible agreement should take the form of a closed list". "Non-exhaustive catalogue of areas of possible settlements gives rise to a risk of using this solution too widely" (comments made in the consultation process; tax officials).

which addresses the concern that ADR can undermine taxpayers' trust in the system.

Tax official's mandate and consultation

The Ministry of Finance should determine the 'decision path' in cases in which negotiations with taxpayers are conducted. It should state clearly who is entitled to settle a case, and in case of doubts, who (i.e. which body) can be consulted internally (possibly in the Ministry of Finance). Clear attribution of powers, along with open consultation channels, will give confidence to tax officials, ensure proper management of cases, and prevent deadlocks in negotiations or their becoming unproductive. This factor has been underlined in the PwC report:

> *[A]n official who is about to follow an amicable procedure must have an authorisation which is strong enough, on the one hand, to encourage the taxpayer's trust in the effectiveness of this procedure and, on the other hand, to offer the said official enough comfort with making decisions as to the contents of the settlement"* (PwC, 2013, p.8)[58].

This factor manifested itself in a visible manner also in the comments made in the consultation process[59].

It would be advisable to set up a separate organisational unit in the Ministry of Finance with a mission to review the cases referred to ADR and provide prompt consultations at the request of a tax authority directly involved in the procedure. It could also function as a supervisory authority in cases with a particularly material amount of tax at stake.

Training

The tax administration should be trained on the methods of alternative dispute resolution and interpersonal communication skills. Training courses

---

58 In the Report it has also been suggested that a negotiator "is not related organisationally to the persons involved in running the proceedings (irrespective of the stage) or the possible preparation of the decision" (*ibidem*). This requirement seems unnecessary. Besides, since the question of who will conduct negotiations in the name of a tax authority is not determined by the law, it is left to the decision of the Ministry of Finance.

59 "It is advisable that a representative of the appeal authority took part in the 'soft' procedures, in order to overcome fears about the admissibility of using these procedures, and of committing formal infringements. Excessive fears of corruption allegations and the resulting reluctance to entertain a close and un-formalised contact with a taxpayer in the case in dispute, fears related to the possible negative supervisory reaction, may result in the practical failure of these solutions. The presence of the supervisory authority in the course of these proceedings will significantly reduce these fears and reassure [tax officials] that they can use these procedures. It is important in particular in the first years of these procedures" (comment made in the consultation process; tax official).

should be organised in the first place for tax officials, and if possible, also for tax advisers and other tax intermediaries. The need for such training is apparent given that, as evidenced by comments in the consultation process, the dimension of procedural justice may be insufficiently appreciated by the tax administration. The crude comment particularly indicative in this respect is that "[i]t does not seem legitimate to transform a tax assessment proceeding into the field of exercises in interpersonal communication, as its objectives are meant to be different"[60].

It is important to put across the message that time spent communicating with a taxpayer is never lost, even whne there is failure to meet each other's expectations as regards the outcome of the process, and as a result, the failure to end the procedure with an agreement (settlement). Facilitating communication should be viewed as one of the objectives of the ADR proposal[61].

Financial and organisational preparations

Proper financial resources should be allocated to the implementation of ADR, and in particular to organising training courses and covering the costs of mediation. Also, practical preparations are needed, in order to ensure proper technical means and to put in place the infrastructure necessary to use ADR (e.g., dedicated rooms in tax authorities' premises adapted to discussing cases with taxpayers; accessible information on ADR in each tax office, on official websites of tax authorities and in social media, etc.). Last but not least, in each tax authority a team of 'ADR leaders' should be appointed, preferably consisting of volunteers only.

Competent mediators

The success of mediation is largely dependent on the competences, skills and personal qualifications of mediators. Therefore, again, proper funding is needed to attract the best in this profession[62]. Also, it seems a good idea to acquaint the mediators-to-be with the fundamentals of taxation (as according to the Assumptions they will not necessarily have a legal background,

---

60 Comment made in the consultation process; tax official.

61 Unfortunately this objective is not universally accepted. Cf. the comment concerning the passage from the Assumptions where the role of ADR in facilitating communication was highlighted: "This description is unequivocally associable with private law and does not correspond with the public law, and in particular, tax law. One can observe that this proposal lacks a systematic, holistic, view of the tax law, and in particular, of its legal essence" (tax academic). The myth of tax law specificity (tax exceptionalism) resonates in these words.

62 In the Assumptions neither the amount of mediator's fees nor the methodology of their calculation have been decided.

not to mention being specialists in tax law[63]). To this purpose technical trainings for mediators should be organised.

Support of tax academics and media for the proposal; information campaigns

Finally, it is advisable to gain support of tax academics and media for the proposal. It will help in the implementation of the proposal and in making it popular with taxpayers. In particular, social campaigns familiarising taxpayers with tax ADR and benefits attainable through them would increase the popularity of these methods.

The first experiences of using tax ADR, which are hoped to be positive, should be gathered and analysed. They should then be summarised in the information made publicly available, providing facts and figures demonstrating the effectiveness and efficiency of ADR as a way to resolve tax disputes.

Conclusion

Integrating alternative dispute resolution methods into Polish tax procedure is a difficult task. Contrary to what is commonly believed, the difficulty lies not in its alleged inconsistency with the nature of tax procedure or substantive tax law, but is linked to a host of factual determinants of how tax procedure is perceived and applied, and how tax cases are resolved. Therefore, the success of the 'ADR project' is not dependent solely, or even primarily, on the quality of regulation drafted by the Committee. However, its success is well within the realm of possibility; it can be brought about by good law in combination with supporting activities, which are well devised and executed with determination[64].

---

63 Despite the fact that in the consultation process some tax academics quite strongly stressed the need for a mediator to be "as qualified as a tax adviser" in terms of tax knowledge (comment made in the consultation process).

64 The reader may find interesting how the members of the Committee see the chances of the ADR project to succeed. I asked them (myself including) two questions: "How do you estimate the chances that the provisions we draft to regulate ADR forms of tax authorities' operation (in particular settlements and mediation), will come into force?" and "How do you estimate the chances that these provisions – provided that they enter into force – will be used in practice and will contribute to the efficient and fair resolution of tax disputes?". On the scale 1-10, where "1" means "almost impossible", and "10" – "almost sure", the average score for the first question was 7.18, and for the second question – 5.11.

References

Administrative Procedure Act of 14 June 1960 [ustawa z dnia 14 czerwca 1960 r. kodeks postępowania administracyjnego], consolidated text: Journal of Laws of 2016, item 23, as amended.

Administrative Court Procedure Act of 30 August 2002 [ustawa z dnia 30 sierpnia 2002 r. Prawo o postępowaniu przed sądami administracyjnymi], consolidated text: Journal of Laws of 2012, item 270, as amended

Ayres, I, & Braithwaite, J. (1992). *Responsive Regulation: Transcending the Deregulation Debate*. Oxford: Oxford University Press.

Barak, A. (1989). *Judicial Discretion*. New Haven, USA: Yale University Press.

Braithwaite, J. (2005). *Markets in Vice, Markets in Virtue*. Oxford: Oxford University Press.

Braithwaite, J. (2011). The Essence of Responsive Regulation. *UBC Law Review*, **44**(3), 475-520.

Braithwaite, V. (Ed.) (2003). *Taxing Democracy. Understanding Tax Avoidance and Evasion*. Aldershot: Ashgate Publishing Limited.

Brożek, B., & Zyzik, R. (2010). Reguły prawne z perspektywy dociekań filozoficznych. *Ruch Prawniczy, Ekonomiczny i Socjologiczny*, **2**, 113-132.

Brzeziński B. (2011). Relacje między administracją podatkową a podatnikami – od konfrontacji do współpracy. In P. Borszowski, A. Huchla & E. Rutkowska-Tomaszewska (Eds.), *Podatnik versus organ podatkowy* (pp.35-43). Wrocław, Poland: Uniwersytet Wrocławski.

Constitution of the Republic of Poland of 2 April 1997 [Konstytucja Rzeczypospolitej Polskiej z dnia 2 kwietnia 1997], consolidated text: Journal of Laws of 1997, item 78, as amended.

Czapiński J. (2015). Stan społeczeństwa obywatelskiego, Diagnoza Społeczna 2015, Warunki i Jakość Życia Polaków – Raport. *Contemporary Economics*, **9**(4), 332-372. DOI:10.5709/ce.1897-9254.191.

Dworkin, R. (1977). *Taking Rights Seriously*. Cambridge, USA: Harvard University Press.

Endicott, T.A.O. (2000). *Vagueness in Law*. Oxford: Oxford University Press.

Filipczyk, H. (2011). O elementach negocjacyjnych w sporach między podatnikami a organami podatkowymi. *Toruński Rocznik Podatkowy*, 142-162.

Fisher, R., & Ury, W.L. (1981). *Getting to Yes: Negotiating Agreement Without Giving In*. Boston, USA: Houghton Mifflin.

Galligan, D., & Matczak, M. (2005). *Strategies of Judicial Review. Exercising Judicial Discretion in Administrative Cases Involving Business Entities*. EY, Poland: Sprawne Państwo.

Hartner, M., Rechberger, S., Kirchler, E., & Schabmann, A. (2008). Procedural fairness and tax compliance. *Economic Analysis Policy*, **38**(1), 137-152.

HMRC (2011). *Litigation and Settlement Strategy*. Retrieved from Https://www.gov.uk/government/publications/litigation-and-settlement-strategy-lss.

HMRC (2012). *Resolving Tax Disputes. Practical Guidance for HMRC Staff on the Use of Alternative Dispute Resolution in Large or Complex Cases*. Retrieved from Http://webarchive.nationalarchives.gov.uk/20140109143644/http://www.hmrc.gov.uk/practitioners/adr-guidance-final.pdf.

HMRC (2013). *Resolving tax disputes. Commentary on the litigation and settlement strategy*. Retrieved from https://www.gov.uk/government/uploads/system/uploads/ attachment_data/file/387770/Commentary_on_litigation.pdf)

HMRC (2014). *Code of governance for resolving tax disputes*. Retrieved from https://www.gov.uk/government/uploads/system/uploads/attachment_data/file/387861/resolve-dispute.pdf

Kijowski, D. (2007). Problematyka regulacji prawnej stosowania form alternatywnych wobec aktu administracyjnego. In J. Zimmermann (Ed.), *Koncepcja systemu prawa administracyjnego* (pp.427-439). Warsaw, Poland: Wolters Kluwer.

Kirchler, E. (2007). *The Economic Psychology of Tax Behaviour*. Cambridge: Cambridge University Press.

Kmieciak, Z. (2007). *Mediacja i koncyliacja w prawie administracyjnym*. Warsaw, Poland: Wolters Kluwer.

Lind, E.A., & Tyler, T.R. (1988). *The Social Psychology of Procedural Justice*. Dordrecht, Netherlands: Springer.

Marmor A. (Ed.) (1995). *Law and Interpretation. Essays in Legal Philosophy*. New York, USA: Oxford University Press.

Marmor, A. (2005). *Interpretation and Legal Theory: Revised Second Edition*. Oxford: Hart Publishing.

Mastalski, R. (2004). *Prawo podatkowe*. Warsaw, Poland: C.H. Beck.

Matczak, M. (2007). *Summa iniuria. O błędzie formalizmu w stosowaniu prawa*. Warsaw, Poland: Wydawnictwo Naukowe Scholar.

Menéndez, A.J. (2001). *Justifying Taxes. Some Elements for a General Theory of Democratic Tax Law*. Dordrecht, Netherlands: Springer.

Montesquieu (1949). *Spirit Of The Laws*. New York, USA: MacMillan 1949.

Morawski, L. (2000). *Główne problemy współczesnej filozofii prawa. Prawo w toku przemian*. Warsaw, Poland: PWN.

Niesiobędzka, M. (2013). *Dlaczego nie płacimy podatków. Psychologiczna analiza uchylania się od opodatkowania*. Warsaw, Poland: Scholar.

Nita, A. (2014). *Porozumienia w prawie podatkowym. Horyzontalne metody determinacji powinności podatkowej*. Warsaw, Poland: Wolters Kluwer.

OECD (2008). *Study into the Role of Tax Intermediaries*. OECD Publishing.

OECD (2012). *Right from the Start: Influencing the Compliance Environment for Small and Medium Enterprises*. Forum on Tax Administration: SME Compliance Sub-Group. Retrieved from http://www.oecd.org/site/ctpfta/49428016.pdf.

OECD (2013). *Co-operative Compliance: A Framework. From Enhanced Relationship to Co-operative Compliance*, OECD Publishing.

Peczenik, A. (1989). *On Law and Reason*. Dordrecht, Netherlands: Springer.

Pietrasz, P., & Siemieniako, J. (2011). Przepisy ogólne prawa administracyjnego a realizacja zobowiązań podatkowych – wybrane zagadnienia. In H. Litwińczuk (Ed.), *Prawo europejskie – 5 lat doświadczeń w polskim prawie finansowym* (pp.489-504). Warsaw, Poland: Wolters Kluwer.

Pietrasz, P., Siemieniako, J., & Wróblewska, E. (2013). *Czynniki zmniejszające rolę władczych form działania administracji skarbowej w realizacji zobowiązań*. Warsaw, Poland: Oficyna Wydawnicza Aspra.

PwC (2013). *Tax ADR. Alternative methods for resolving tax disputes – an outlook for tax mediation in Poland*. Retrieved from https://www.pwc.pl/en/publikacje/assets/podatkowe-adr-raport-pwc-en.pdf.

Rawls, J. (1971). *A Theory of Justice*. Cambridge, USA: Harvard University Press.

Recommendation Rec(2001)9 of the Committee of Ministers to member states on alternatives to litigation between administrative authorities and private parties of 5 September 2001. Retrieved from https://wcd.coe.int/ViewDoc.jsp?p=&id=1103533& Site=COE&direct=true.

Supreme Administrative Court (2016). *Information on administrative courts' operation in 2015*. Retrieved from http://www.nsa.gov.pl/sprawozdania-roczne.php.

Tax Ordinance of 29 August 1997 [ustawa z dnia 29 sierpnia 1997 r. – Ordynacja podatkowa], consolidated text: Journal of Laws of 2015, item 613, as amended.

Tyler, T.R. (1990). *Why People Obey the Law: Procedural Justice, Legitimacy and Compliance*. New Haven, USA: Yale University Press.

Tyler, T.R. (2011). *Why People Cooperate. The Role of Social Motivations*. Princeton, USA: Princeton University Press.

Thuronyi, V. (2003). *Comparative Tax Law*. The Hague, Netherlands: Kluwer Law International.

Wittgenstein, L. (1953). *Philosophical Investigations*. Oxford: Blackwell.

5 How Effective is Islam on Tax Compliance Decisions of Muslims?

Recep Yucedogru

Abstract

The aim of this paper is to explore the effect of religion, specifically Islam, on tax compliance decisions. It starts with an overview of the literature that explores the relationship between religiosity and tax compliance. A qualitative approach was followed by utilising semi-structured interviews, which were conducted with 20 SME owner-managers in Turkey. The recorded interviews were thematically analysed using NVivo10. The paper stands out as one of the few works that provides an in-depth understanding of the effects of Islamic knowledge on tax compliance behaviour. In particular, findings shed a light on four critical issues for Muslim taxpayers, such as: Effects of their Islamic stance on tax compliance; rightful due concerns of tax evasion behaviour; comparison of Zakat with taxes; and the intervention of Islamic scholars on the tax compliance decisions of Muslims. Lastly, the paper contributes to the literature by further analysing the qualitative data through focusing on SME owner-managers, in which current literature offers very little about the effects of their religiosity on their tax compliance.

Introduction

The reasons for voluntary taxpaying behaviour have caught the attention of many scholars over recent decades. It has proved a fascinating debate because of the complicated nature of taxpayers' behaviour, which brings the relationship between the citizen and the state into focus. Additionally, it confronts citizens with a decision of whether to comply or not. Despite the significant impact of obligation on the decision to be tax compliant, ignoring the cultural and moral aspects would be remiss, and may lead to possible misunderstandings regarding the nature of the behaviour. Moreover, the literature that has emerged in recent decades has brought new approaches that might provide guidance for policy makers to generate more compliance-friendly policies on tax-related issues.

Many of the factors that influence voluntary tax compliance have been identified in the literature, such as: expected utility from tax evasion (Allingham and Sandmo, 1972); compliance costs (Hasseldine, 2001); fear of getting caught and facing tax penalties (McKerchar and Evans, 2009); auditing (Andreoni et al., 1998); equity and fairness of the tax system (Spicer and Becker, 1980); and tax ethics (Song and Yarbrough, 1978). Notwithstanding these factors, religion and religiosity have not been very widely discussed in the literature (Torgler, 2007). Yet the moral and cultural motivations of taxpaying behaviour, and especially the religiosity of people, are playing an effective role on taxpayers' compliance behaviour (McGee, 2006). Moreover, the effect of religion and its influence might be more deterministic than other factors because of its dominance over culture and society through the centuries. Furthermore, it could be claimed that such influences might be different in a Muslim-dominant society then a Christian-dominant society. In addition, some (Kurt, 2009) have claimed that Islam is more likely to be more influential and domineering on people's daily practices than Christianity and Judaism because of its daily prayer frequencies, such as a five times a day prayer requirement. Considering this point, Muslim societies should be investigated in a different way than Christian societies.

In a discussion of Muslim society, Turkey is a promising area for the literature and differs from many countries because of its historical roots, demographical characteristics and growing economic strength. In the last several decades, the importance of Turkey has become more prominent. In particular, Turkey's integration into the EU and successive high growth rates in recent years has drawn attention from many academic circles. Despite the attention gained, there has been little research about tax compliance in Turkey. Additionally, there are only limited studies on taxpayers' compliance behaviour in Muslim countries such as Malaysia (Phalil, 2010). Nevertheless, the considerable cultural heritage of Turkey and its effects on taxpayers have not been discussed widely in the literature. In our review, we could not find an example of a study on effects of religion and religiosity on tax compliance at a corporate level. Therefore, by focusing on Small and Medium Enterprises (SMEs), this research may shed a light on a previously untouched area.

Following the introduction, this paper provides an overview of the relationship between tax compliance and religiosity by summarising the main approaches that are discussed in the literature. Additionally it covers related literature with an Islamic focus that has not had many chances to appear internationally. Finally, it discusses the results of interview analysis under the subsections of: Islamic stance on tax compliance; rightful due concerns on tax evasion; contrasting tax law with Islamic values and a comparison of Zakat and taxes; and Islamic intervention on tax compliance decisions.

Literature Review

Tax compliance and religiosity

The relationship between religiosity and taxation can be traced back to Adam Smith, who counts religiosity as an internal moral enforcement mechanism (Anderson, 1988; Torgler 2006). Despite popular opinion in the 19th and 20th centuries, which sees religion as an irrational body of rules, supported by famous scholars such as Freud, Davis and Marx (Stark et al.,1996), the Rationality emphasis of Smith's approach has been followed by many others (Torgler, 2006).

Although religiosity started to be considered as a factor in taxation with Smith, the area has recently attracted attention in the literature after works of Torgler (2003), McGee (2006), Welch et al. (2005), Stack and Kposowa (2006) and Pope and Mohdali (2010). Studies related to religiosity generally rely on secondary data resources (Pope and Mohdali, 2010) and the literature mostly agreed that the level of religiosity is negatively correlated to the level of tax evasion (Torgler, 2007). Additionally, different societies and their religious practises should be analysed as differing religiosities while examining tax compliance. In other words, religious behaviours are different among Muslims, Christians and Jews.

Religiosity and Islam

There is substance to the claim that the literature on tax compliance and religiosity has been under-explored in Muslim countries. Although there are some works from the Islamic perspective about tax ethics, such studies are generally focused on Muslim countries' perspectives rather than the Islamic perspective (McGee, 1998). On this point, acknowledging the difference between the Islamic tax system and the tax systems of Muslim countries would be enlightening, because a considerable number of Muslim countries, such as Turkey, have very similar tax systems and revenue administration structures to Western countries.

In order to understand the Islam-tax relationship, it is helpful to look at the Islamic obligatory charity payment called Zakat. In Islam, rich Muslims, who have more than 80.18 grams of gold or equal wealth, exclusive of their living costs, have responsibility to pay Zakat annually to support the needy and the state at a proportion of 2.5% of their total wealth. Paying Zakat is considered as a prayer and has been mentioned in the Quran many times; indeed evading Zakat is counted as one of greatest sins in Islam (Choudhury, 1986). Moreover, an Islamic state has the right to force qualified people to pay their Zakat. In addition, obeying additional rules and orders of the Islamic government is also required in the Quran under some conditions, which attempts to improve obedience to the rulers in society. However, Muslims do not have a responsibility to follow every demand of the government or to pay any kind of additional taxes if the government engages any illegitimate functions or goes beyond the borders of the Islamic rules on the legislation (Yusuf, 1971). Furthermore, if Muslims realised that the government is engaged in non-Islamic acts then not complying with the tax system might even be considered a good deed. Although there are certain rules about Zakat in Islam, there are only a few countries that have embedded Zakat into their taxation systems such as Malaysia (Mohamed et al., 2008).

Religiosity and tax compliance in Turkey

The Turkish tax system has a changed configuration as part of its restructuring from an Islamic taxation to a Western taxation system over the last two centuries (Inalcik, 1994). Starting with the early Ottoman era, tax systems had formed with purely Islamic dynamics; however, it changed, occasionally according to the needs of the state, but mainly because of tax riots and financial needs (Maliye, 2000). After the imperial edict of Gülhane in 1839, the revenue administration started to be modernised and the tax system was improved, taking Western contemporary structures as an example. From the beginning of the new Republic in 1923, the revenue administration was introduced under a new Ministry of Finance, which became independent from the Ministry in 2006 to support the EU integration process. It can be claimed that the Turkish tax system has now a very similar structure to its counterparts in the West and its tax law is following a similar path.

Although the Turkish tax system has adapted itself to needs of the modern world, its roots are still heavily influenced by the dominant relationship between the taxpayer and the state. In addition, Turkey's majority Muslim population (officially 99% of the population) and considerably conservative structure enhance the influence of religiosity. According to research (Altug et al., 2010) conducted in Istanbul, 62% of taxpayers believe that tax evasion is related with the evader's level of ethics, while 67% think that paying taxes is a sacramental duty. The same research also revealed that 64% of taxpayers regard tax evasion as a sin, and 59% of taxpayers declared that Imams should be more effective in directing people to comply with the tax system. Overall, it is clear that religiosity and religion is influential on the majority of tax compliance decisions in Turkey.

Nevertheless, it would be difficult to claim that the Turkish revenue administration takes religiosity into account to increase tax compliance in Turkey. Controversially, some exceptions have occurred. One of these surfaced during the 2009 global crisis when the revenue administration and administration of religious affairs in Turkey cooperated on the preparation of a Khutba (sermon) which was given in all mosques in Turkey at the Cuma (Friday) prayers. The Khutba was given in February, a week before the annual income tax bill falls due, which aimed to remind taxpayers to comply with the regulations and help the revenue administration to meet their revenue collection targets. Moreover, the Khutba described complying with the tax system and paying taxes on time as an acquired merit in Allah's view. Other similar examples can be found on this subject.

Overall, religiosity and religion appears as an important factor in tax compliance policies that needs to be investigated. Therefore, this paper aims to explore the influence of Islam and its orders among the taxpayers (SME owner-managers) who are actively engaged with tax paying and the tax authority. Additionally, it contributes by summarising the views of participants regarding the main impact of Islam on tax compliance.

Methodology

This paper presents the results of the analysis of 20 interviews, which were conducted with SME owner-managers in Turkey. The qualitative, semi-structured interviews were conducted with companies from eleven different sectors; all had more than ten employees, and all interviews were recorded. Moreover, transcriptions of the interviews are thematically analysed by using the software NVivo 10.

Qualitative research attempts to understand the pattern of experience in lives (Dilley, 2000). This is because the perspective of others could be meaningful and can be made explicit (Patton, 1990). Thus, researchers conduct interviews to understand what is in and on someone else's mind (Patton, 1990). Furthermore, in this study, the use of interviews for data collection is considered appropriate since it reflects the emic approach (inside perspective) in understanding the effects of religion and on tax compliance behaviour in Turkey.

I chose semi-structured interviews to discover any other factors that may influence the SME's tax paying behaviour. Randomly selected SMEs who participated in the semi-structured interviews were contacted by telephone by the researcher, based on the details provided by SME support agency to explain about interviews. The details provided to 32 SMEs were their name, telephone number, sector, and employee number. Additionally, the demographics of participants are included as a list at the end of the paper.

The interviews were conducted in Turkish as English is not commonly used in commerce, especially among SMEs. Interviews were recorded using an audiotape recorder after gaining consent from the interview participants. To be consistent with the nature of the semi-structured interviews, I prepared an interview protocol, consisting of a list of questions based on several themes relevant to the study. Since the lack of standardisation in a semi-structured interview-based study may result in lack of reliability in its findings, the interview protocol could also be helpful in reducing the reliability issues (Saunders et al., 2003). Despite the themes being determined a priori in the interview protocol, the nature of a semi-structured interview is flexible (Bryman and Bell, 2011), allowing some freedom for other themes to emerge during the interview, which is relevant to understanding the tax compliance behaviour of SMEs.

In this study, the data was analysed using the steps suggested by Braun and Clarke (2006). Specifically, there were three main steps involved in the data analysis performed in this study. First, the researcher transcribed the recordings into written text. The second phase was the process of coding the data, finding related themes and analysing the themes to check for consistency.

Thematic analysis is the foundation method for qualitative analysis that involves finding repeated patterns of meaning from the data (Braun and Clarke, 2006). It is a method to identify, analyse and report the patterns in the data. Despite the argument that thematic analysis is perceived as 'anything goes', thematic analysis is still considered as essential due to its flexibility, ease of application, ability to capture similarities and differences across the data set, which could generate unanticipated insights (Braun and Clarke, 2006). Additionally, the data is analysed using NVivo 10 by using the codes that have been generated.

As the interviews were conducted in Turkish, all analysis was run in the same language and only the results of the analysis have been translated. At the same time when direct quotes are used, all paragraphs or text has been translated into English in order to avoid misrepresentation.

Since there is lack of standardisation in semi-structured interviews, the findings may be subject to the issue of reliability. Apart from using an interview protocol to reduce the issue of reliability, we also performed other procedures as suggested by Saunders et al. (2003), Braun and Clarke (2006) and Creswell (2009) to ensure that the findings in this study are reliable. Additionally, we repeatedly checked the transcripts to ensure that there were no obvious errors and compared the transcript against the recording.

Validity in qualitative research is defined as how accurate and reliable the data represents the realities of the interview participants in understanding the social phenomena (LeCompte, 2000; Creswell and Miller, 2000). One common method to determine validity in a qualitative study is to use the 'member checking procedure' (Creswell and Miller, 2000; Creswell, 2009). The member checking procedure is considered as establishing the validity of the qualitative study using the lens of the participant (Creswell and Miller, 2000). It is among the eight primary procedures frequently used to determine validity in qualitative studies (Creswell, 2009). Member checking involves requesting the interview participants to confirm the credibility of the information by asking the participants to check the data, whether the themes are correct and the overall information is accurate (Creswell and Miller, 2000). Following the suggestion by Creswell (2009), we requested that two participants check the refined transcript, the themes identified and provide feedback, as a procedure to determine the validity of the findings; all feedback received was positive.

Findings

The interviews started by investigating participants' personal views on their religion, Islam, and their tax compliance attitudes. They continued with an evaluation of sacred Islamic terms and values such as sin and rightful due. Further questions were focused on the relationship between current tax legislation and Islamic law, Zakat and tax comparisons, and lastly reaction to the intervention of imams on compliance issues. The analysis produced five interconnected clusters that are discussed in detail in this section.

Religion, religiosity and Islamic evaluation of tax compliance

Although religion and religiosity started to be considered as a factor in taxation with Adam Smith, they have recently attracted attention from tax academics with the works of Torgler (2003), McGee (2006), Welch et al. (2005), Stack and Kposowa (2006) and Pope and Mohdali (2010). The literature mostly agreed that the level of religiosity is negatively correlated with level of tax evasion (Torgler, 2007).

Participants were asked about whether their religious stance has an effect on their tax compliance decisions. The discussion started with understanding how participants evaluate tax evasion according to their religious beliefs. Considering the fact that twelve participants defined themselves as religious, it is expected that a majority of interviewees acknowledge tax evasion as a misdeed within the religion of Islam. Moreover, some of them declared that they considered tax evasion as a sin.

> *I am not an authority to decide but I understand tax evasion as sin (Haram).* Interviewee 2
>
> *I think all kind of tax evasions is sin. Nevertheless, I cannot define it as illicit completely, yet it is still a misdeed.* Interviewee 9
>
> *I clearly define tax evasion as a sin.* Interviewee 15
>
> *You have the money and you are not giving it to the state. Of course, it is a sin. It is a sin because; we are using common goods. If people are earning, they should pay. In this sense, we can say it is a sin.* Interviewee 12

Controversially, some participants raised the importance of public spending perceptions, which may affect tax compliance decisions dramatically. They claimed that obeying religious rules might make evading taxes necessary when a conflict occurred between them. Therefore, tax evasion might even be considered a good deed.

> *If taxes that I pay are returned to the people of this country then I must pay taxes. However, if they are wasted, then, for me, paying is committing sin.* Interviewee 20

Resistance on tax payments about non-religious tax subjects became more distinct especially among religious participants when an example rose about national lottery contribution. In Islam, gambling is defined as sin; naturally, this perception developed an antipathy for the national lottery itself. Although there is not an imposed contribution in the current Turkish tax system, participants seems to be confusing it with other compulsory contributions such as the broadcast contribution which assists Turkish broadcasting agency. Nevertheless, responses are providing different perspectives on religiosity and tax compliance relationship. Three participants indicated they would evade or refuse to pay taxes that are against Islamic orders if they were obligated.

> *I do not pay taxes that serve or are collected for non-Islamic purposes. Even gambling, I will not consider giving a kurus (penny). If they force me, I will*

definitely look for evading opportunities. Interviewee 15

Apart from the two former opinions above, some participants stressed tax-related issues should not be associated with religious concerns, as they believe running a business should be separated from religious concerns.

I think.... money is nothing to do with religion. If you are working in a small scale then you might think with religion. In a bigger scale, religion stays aside because we are all capitalists. Interviewee 10

I do not see paying taxes as a good deed for religion. I think it is a civic duty. It should not be seen as good deed or bad deed. Interviewee 8

Unexpectedly, some religious participants also supported tax evasion that is not related to religious perspective, but as a result of unfair tax system. This opinion is more common for religious participants than others.

Tax evasion might be an illicit if we are talking about fair tax system. Without fairness, there is no need to talk about good deed or bad deed or rights of taxpayers in Islam. (...) I believe we do not have fair tax legislation. Interviewee 17

Some underlined laicism, which is the constitutional political criteria in Turkey, as the reason of separating religious motives from state activities. Therefore, they found affiliating tax issues with religion as inappropriate.

Participants were also asked for their opinion about the effect of being religious on tax compliance. The majority, including some secular participants, admitted that religious people should comply more easily with the legislation. The reason for that as explained by two participants, aligns with Islam's commend to obey the head of state under Islamic rules; therefore obeying tax legislation could be understood as a religious obligation.

Religious people, normally, would wish to comply with the tax system and even pay more taxes if possible. As a religious individual, I am thinking in that way. Interviewee 15

Religious people, at least, would have a tendency to comply with the tax system. Interviewee 12

If you are religious, you should automatically not get involved with tax evasion or avoidance. Interviewee 4

Nevertheless, most of the interviewees added, in reality, religious people are not different from others. Furthermore, a few secular participants claimed that religious ones are more likely to evade. They explained this with the moral reasoning of tax evasion of religious taxpayers because of the state's restrictive policies for religious people such as the scarf ban in recent years.

> *They (religious people) used to have arguments for not paying taxes. I remember that someone said; "tax should not be paid to this infidel state".* Interviewee 12

Some religious interviewees also supported non-compliance as an idea. However, their motives are different from secular people. Some of them highlighted unfairness of the tax system as being a moral obstacle for them to comply with the tax system. Moreover, some interviewees claimed moral values and the tax burden should be in balance, otherwise the tax burden is more likely to prevent religious taxpayers to comply.

> *Our Islamic values and money should be in balance when we are deciding to pay our taxes. I am willing to pay but what happens if the cost is excessive for me. Balance is important but bearable cost with no values means nothing to me.* Interviewee 15

Seizing rightful due of other citizens

To evaluate the religious stance in the sample, participants asked whether they see tax evasion as seizing the rightful due of other citizens, to reveal their religious position on tax evasion. This question is similar to whether the interviewees see tax evasion as a sin; however terminologically it is referring to a different situation. In Quran, it is stated that sins can be forgiven by Allah but seizing a rightful due of an individual can only be forgiven by that individual; therefore it is considered as the worst deed that one can take to the afterlife. In other words, the fear of seizing someone's rightful due is more fearsome than committing a sin. To understand the difference, participants were asked their opinion on whether evading taxes can be understood as seizing the rightful due of others. Unusually, a large majority, including most secular participants, agreed that tax evasion is seizing a rightful due of others.

> *I think evading is definitely seizing other citizens' rightful due.* Interviewee 3
>
> *The state's money is poor orphans' money. We should see it like that. If I believe the state is totally rightful then I would say it is seizing other citizens' rightful due and there is no escape from that.* Interviewee 18
>
> *If you say I am earning money but evading. That is not right and certainly seizing my rightful due.* Interviewee 12
>
> *I am paying because I am considering tax issues through my religion. That is why I am paying more attention. If you seize someone's rightful due, you can find the man and ask his blessing about it. However how am I going to find 70 million (Turkey's population) and ask them.* Interviewee 18

Consequently, views on the rightful due revealed that religion is considerably effective on the compliance decisions of the participants in the sample. On the contrary, few participants highlighted that tax issues are not related to religion or seizing a rightful due; hence, they interpreted tax evasion as a business arrangement. Unexpectedly, few religious participants questioned the state's religious position and define the current state as secular; therefore, they concluded, it should not be involved in Islamic interpretations.

> *The issue of rightful due is a very sensitive one. If you jump on a bus without buying a ticket or gate-crash the tube this is seizing one's rightful due. For taxes, I cannot see any relevance. In which part of the tax law is mentioning rightful due or is there any Islamic concerns of this state?* Interviewee 11

> *All misdeeds in Islam is legal now in this country; prostitution, gambling etc. If you look through an Islamic frame, it is obvious that there is not a rightful due problem. The state is responsible here for all.* Interviewee 20

Additionally some participants declared that they see the borders of rightful due can only be drawn between the equal parts. Hence, the responsibility of rightful due is not valid because of mismanagement in the tax system.

Cooperation of Islamic orders with legislation

In further questions, participants were asked whether they would be more compliant if tax legislation took Islam's orders more into account. The majority agreed on the view that Islam-friendly tax legislation would encourage their compliance.

> *I believe if the tax law is designed in cooperation with Islam's orders, more tax revenue can be collected. I can pay my tax more freely in this way.* Interviewee 15

> *I would certainly be more compliant.* Interviewee 19

Some religious participants indicated that even though compliance levels would not increase, the possibility of evasion and avoidance would most likely decrease.

> *Tax collection is somehow a psychological dominant issue. Therefore, if the citizens see their taxes are spent in a good way they will comply more. At least their tendency for evasion will decrease.* Interviewee 12

Although supporters of the idea are mainly religious participants, some participants who define themselves as secular joined them with a slightly different point of view. They indicated that better tax legislation should consider the main concerns of the society; therefore tax legislation should be aligned with Islam.

Nevertheless, there were a considerable number of participants who seemed to disagree with this view. The main opposing views focus on two common points. The first view stresses that tax related issues should not to be considered with Islam because of different approaches in Islam on the issue. They feel different views can be confusing and even distracting. Additionally they feel that tax, a compulsory payment, should not be placed under sacred umbrella of Islam. Second, others find it difficult and rather absurd to talk about this issue in the constitutionally laic state of Turkey, a result of current secular society.

Additionally participants generally tend to believe that the current tax legislation does not cooperate with Islamic values.

Comparison of Zakat and taxes

Zakat is one of the five fundamental obligations of Islam; it is a compulsory charity payment that is collected from the wealthy. In Islamic law, Shari'ah, the word Zakat refers to a determined share of wealth prescribed by Allah to be distributed among deserving categories. It is also used to describe an action of payment of this share (Qaraḍāwī, 1999). A wealthy individual is defined as one who is in possession of a minimum amount of wealth called Nisab[1] for an entire lunar year, and these individuals are obligated to give 1/40 (2.5%) from their personal and business wealth (CIOGC, 2005).

Historically, Zakat was collected by the government and distributed to the needy in Muslim countries. Ottomans followed the same principal as some of their contemporary counterparts who are ruled by Shari'ah (Inalcik et.al., 1997). However, Turkey is not currently following Shari'ah law and the government is not involved in the Zakat collection. Although Zakat is not the part of Turkish tax system, some religious taxpayers understand Zakat and taxes in the same way as a result of the compulsory nature of both payments. Furthermore, the tax system has been criticised in some religious circles by not considering the Zakat payments. To support this, some of the participants expressed Zakat as 'double taxation' during the interviews.

> *I wonder whether I can count my tax payments in my Zakat. I am paying Zakat and as well as that I am paying my taxes. It feels like I am being*

---

1   Nisab is roughly accepted as the expandable wealth outside of daily needs. Islam does not impose Zakat on all amounts of growing wealth. There is a minimum required for Zakat, which is called among jurists 'nisab'. Sayings of the Prophet exempt anything that is less than five camels, forty sheep, two hundred dirhams of silver, or five wasq of grain, fruits, or agricultural crops. For more information please look at *"Fiqh az-zakat:* a comparative study", Qaraḍawi, Y. (1999)

double taxed. Interviewee 19

In light of the explanations above, participants are asked about their views on taxes and Zakat. Participants seemed to be grouped in two different views. The first one is appeared to give more importance in Zakat and they support the idea that the tax system should embrace it. The second view considers taxes and Zakat as two different concepts and insists that they need to be interpreted differently. Although possible bias might direct the reader to predict participants in the first group as religious people and the second as secular, it appears that there are mixed views on the participants of each group.

The participants in the first group, who are the majority in the sample, declare that they treat Zakat more sensitively than taxes. In other words, they are more compliant with Zakat.

If you ask me about Zakat and taxes, I say that you can pay taxes in one way or the other but, for me, I would be more careful about my Zakat. Interviewee 8

In addition, some participants mentioned that their Zakat payments are legitimising their income in terms of their religious beliefs. More specifically, they expressed that they see the Zakat as purification of their income from 'Haram' (sinful) resources. Therefore, compliance of the Zakat differs from tax compliance, even though they are mainly understood as closely related. Additionally, a few participants stressed that their perception of being treated in an unjust tax system is preventing them from complying with the tax system because they think that there is no religious legitimacy to taxes. This point can be considered as a unique insight that might shed a light on improved compliance policies in cooperation with religion.

Muslim capitalists have some duties to fulfil. They need to give Zakat. If they do not, they cannot legitimise their income, no matter how much taxes they have paid. Interviewee 11

Additionally, some participants explained that Zakat is bringing happiness to its payers not only because of religious perspective but also from a sense of a direct contribution to society. More importantly the majority of participants indicated that Zakat is more helpful to society in comparison to taxes. In other words, participants doubt the return of taxes to society and therefore feel that Zakat is more constructive on meeting society's needs.

I am paying my taxes but I do not know how they are going to return (to) me. Or, are they returning (to) me? I am waiting for them to build road in a year or so. However, in Zakat you find the needy and solve the problem directly. I think Zakat is more efficient. Interviewee 13

Alternatively, a few participants are agreed that taxes are more effective for society because of their scale and commonness. Nevertheless, the overall conclusion can be reached that for better tax compliance rates, policies should be more careful about informing taxpayers about the spending of taxes and increasing public spending efficiency by considering Islamic concerns in Turkey.

For the second group of participants, Zakat and taxes should be treated differently and should not be considered the same because of their nature. They feel that Zakat and taxes should not be compared. These participants stressed that these payments stand for the divine (Zakat) and material (taxes) sides of the world; therefore they are not rivals.

> *Zakat is a charity payment and it is a prayer. I do not think they (Zakat and tax) can replace each other. Their rates and their system are completely different.* Interviewee 6

Further discussions in the interviews undercover the relationship between Zakat and taxes in the minds of the interviewees. Some of them pointed out that paying Zakat and taxes together without the integration of the Zakat into Turkish tax system is unjust, as mentioned above: "double taxation". Although Zakat is not compulsory under the Turkish tax system, some mentioned that trying to pay Zakat alongside taxes is increasing tax avoidance or even tax evasion.

Another point raised by both of the groups is to integrate Zakat into the tax system. Although religious and secular participants agree on the same point, their incentives are different. The interviewees who defined themselves as religious insist the Zakat should be recognised by the state and somehow integrated into tax system. Apart from double taxation concerns, religious participants have focused on two main benefits of integrating Zakat. The first one stresses an increase in the willingness to pay. They explained that being recognised by the state with all aspects of being a Muslim citizen and taxpayer would increase confidence and trust in the government; therefore they would pay their taxes more voluntarily. Moreover, some of them stressed that integrating Zakat into the tax system would bring together state and religion without having a religious state.

> *I think integration of my Zakat with taxes is a brilliant solution for tax avoidance. For me, I see two holy and sacred things coming together; Zakat and taxes. Tax evader Muslims and even Zakat evaders might start paying both.* Interviewee 20

> *If the state absorbs Zakat in the tax system, not all of the Zakat even half or less would be enough, I would trust my government more and pay more*

Zakat and I would try to pay my taxes more appropriately. Interviewee 19

The second point is stressed by religious interviewees, as integration might be beneficial for achieving social welfare equality. Moreover, by incentivising Zakat payments, which induce an increase in social transfer payments, public spending on social transfers could be reallocated. Therefore, the economy might grow faster. Although the calculation seems raw, it may be achievable in theory.

Secular interviewees approach integration of Zakat from a different perspective. First, they mention their concerns about the accountability of Zakat payments. In other words, these participants are apprehensive about the decentralised structure of Zakat organisations, which concerns them about distribution of Zakat money. Second, some participants mentioned that the tax legislation should consider these concerns and the beliefs of all taxpayers which might increase tax compliance; therefore Zakat should be included in the tax system. Nevertheless, most of the secular participants agree that integration of Zakat should be limited and it should not be taken from tax paid but it might be extracted from the taxable base. Lastly, one secular participant opposed the idea of integration because he found it against the constitutional criteria of laicism, therefore taxes and Zakat should be kept completely separately.

Overall, the common agreement among the participants seemed to be on the integration of the Zakat into the tax system. Although there might be some concerns about it, such as the possible injustice between taxpayers who choose to pay and not to pay Zakat, and proposed methods of integration, in general, interviewees agreed that integration might increase tax compliance. Nevertheless, the effects of integration on revenue levels and the methods integration are still vague.

Imams' interventions and Tax compliance decisions

Lastly, participants were asked whether they would be influenced by inculcations of religious bodies, especially imams, about tax compliance. This question is asked to understand whether the findings of Altug et al.'s research (2010) are valid within SMEs in the sample. The research, which was carried out on individual taxpayers, revealed that 59% of taxpayers agreed that Imams should be more effective in directing people to comply (Altug et al., 2010). Surprisingly, the large majority of interviewees did not support the idea that imams' intervention would be positive on compliance issues. A number of reasons appear to cause this stance. First, it is observed that the influence of imams is not significant as a result of unsatisfactory public appearances and their background. Moreover, some participants declared that they do not find their advice thoughtful. Controversially, some of them indicated that advice from more reliable people such as Islamic scholars, presidents of religious affairs, or community leaders might be more influential than imams in encouraging tax compliance. Second, some participants explained their concerns about using Islamic values and Islamic figures to fulfil government business. They found it inappropriate and discouraging of compliance policies.

> *To my mind, there is no difference between announcing state propaganda from loudspeaker and hearing it from an imam. People are not buying misuse of religious values for the state's own interest.* Interviewee 14

The last concern that was expressed was generally about the negligence of the constitutional criteria of laicism. Although some participants admitted that advice from Imams might be effective on some taxpayers, they refused this action because of their acceptance of the secular state. Overall, interviewees seemed to disagree with the research findings of Altug et al. (2010).

Conclusion

Despite the fact that religion is slowly gaining importance in tax compliance studies, it is obvious that it has a significant influence on taxpayers' tax compliance decisions. Moreover, considering there are only a few studies on Islam about tax compliance in contrast with its growing number of followers in many countries, it would not be wrong to claim that this research is shedding a light on a gap in the literature. Furthermore, it presents a new perspective on the Islam and tax compliance relationship, apart from analysing religion as a wider term. Although the qualitative research applied has its own drawbacks, such as low sample size, this research has provided some insights on tax compliance from the taxpayers' perspectives on the effects of Islam on their behaviours, which are new to the literature.

Despite the common agreement in the literature that religion and religiosity encourages compliance, the research has observed that if there is conflict between the state's acts and Islamic beliefs, religion and religiosity might prevent taxpayers from complying, even though the majority had predicted that religious people would be more compliant. However, the paper found evidence, despite a common agreement, that religious people are not different from others; religious participants showed a tendency for high levels of non-compliance when there is a controversy between state rules and Islam.

Additionally, participants seemed to agree on viewing tax evasion a sin. Furthermore, they understood it as seizing another citizen's rightful due which is more fearful for Muslim taxpayers. Considering the fact that the majority is concerned about rightful due, regardless of their religious or secular stance, generating tax policies by taking account of this issue might lead to better tax compliance policies.

The Zakat and tax relationship appeared to be another significant issue between taxpayers. They considered that ignorance of the Zakat in the tax system is causing 'double taxation'; therefore they feel it is unfair. The solution suggested is integrating Zakat into current tax system which would encourage religious taxpayers to comply by increasing sensibility into Zakat and tax calculations by developing a sacred or divine identity to taxes. Surprisingly, secular participants supported the idea as it would bring accountability to Zakat collections. Obviously, there are opposing views as it raised concerns of laicism as the constitutional criteria and concerns of fairness to others who do not follow Islam.

Overall, evaluating Islam and its values seems to be an important parameter for the countries which have a majority Muslim population. Moreover, creating tax compliance policies that consider Muslim values seems to be promising for encouraging taxpayers to comply. However, taking Islamic values into account seemed to be ignored by policy makers in Turkey and may be many other countries. Nevertheless, larger scale studies might be more enlightening for policy makers and researchers in terms of generalisability concerns of the findings of this study. Additionally, this research sheds a light on the inner directions of the religiosity phenomena that needs further evaluation and promises a valuable discussion despite its drawbacks.

References

Allingham, M. G., & Sandmo, A. (1972). Income tax evasion: a theoretical analysis. *Journal of Public Economics*, **1**(3-4): 323-338.

Altug, F., Cak, M., Seker, M. & Bingol, O. (2010). Turkiyede Vergi Bilinci Istanbul Arastirmasi, *ISMMO publications*, no.134

Anderson, G.M., (1988). Mr. Smith and the preachers: the economics of religion in the wealth of nations. *Journal of Political Economy*, **96**, 1066–1088.

Andredoni J. Erard E. & Feinstain B. (1998). Tax Compliance. *Journal Of Economic Literature*, **26**, 818-860

Braun, V., & Clarke, V. (2006). Using thematic analysis in psychology. *Qualitative Research in Psychology*, **3**, 77-101.

Bryman, A., & Bell, E. (2011). *Business Research Method* (3rd Ed.). New York: Oxford University Press.

Choudhury, M. A, (1986). *Contributions to Islamic Economic Theory: Study in Social Economics*, New York, St. Martin's Press.

CIOGC, The Council of Islamic Organizations of Greater Chicago (2005) Central Zakat Committee. "The institution of zakat." The Council of Islamic Organizations of Greater Chicago(CIOGC), Accessed at: http://www.zakatchicago. org/ZakatBook. pdf

Creswell, J. W. (2009). *Research Design: Qualitative, Quantitative and Mixed Methods Approaches* (3rd Ed.). California: Thousand Oaks.

Creswell, J. W., and Miller, D. L. (2000). Determining Validity in Qualitative Inquiry. *Theory into Practice*, **39**(3), 124-130.

Dilley, P. (2000). Conducting successful interview: Tips for intrepid research. *Theory into Practice*, **39**(3), 131-137.

Hasseldine, J. (2001). Linkages Between Compliance Costs and Taxpayer Compliance Research. In *Taxation Compliance Costs: A Festschrift for Cedric Sandford*. Prospect Media.

Inalcik, H, (1994) *Osmanlı Imparatorluğu'nun Ekonomik ve Sosyal Tarihi*, Cilt 2, Eren, Cambridge University Press

İnalcık, Halil, Suraiya Faroqhi, and Donald Quataert. (1997) "An Economic and Social History of the Ottoman Empire, Vol. 1." : 162-167.

Kurt, A. (2009). *Işadamlarinda dindarlık ve dünyevileşme*. Istanbul: Emin Publishing.

LeCompte, M. D. (2000). Analyzing Qualitative Data. *Theory into Practice*, **39**(3), 146-154.

Maliye, (2000) *Osmanlı Maliyesi Hakkinda Ingiliz Raporları (1861-1892)*, Ankara APK publications, p.355

McGee, R. W., (1998). The Ethics of Tax Evasion in Islam: A Comment. *Journal of Accounting, Ethics and Public Policy*, **1**(2), 162-168

McGee, R. W., (2006). Three Views On The Tax Ethics Of Tax Evasion?, *Journal of Business Ethics*, **67**, 15-35

McKerchar, M., & Evans, C. (2009). Sustaining growth in developing economies through improved taxpayer compliance: Challenges for policy makers and revenue authorities. *eJournal of Tax Research*, **7**(2), 171-201

Mohamed, S. A. R., Arifin, M. S., & Abdul, G. B. (2008). Incorporating zakat into the national taxation system: Its effect to the Malaysian government revenue. *Ikaz International Journal Of Zakat*, **1**(1), 143-152

Patton, M. Q. (1990). *Qualitative Evaluation and Research Methods*. California: SAGE Publications Inc.

Phalil, M. R. (2010) *Tax Knowledge and Tax Compliance Determinants in Self-Assessment System in Malaysia* unpublished PhD thesis in Birmingham University, http://etheses.bham.ac.uk/1040/1/Palil10PhD.pdf (accessed: 01.01.2012)

Pope, J., & Mohdali, R. (2010). *The Role of Religiosity in Tax Morale and Tax Compliance*. Australian Tax Forum, 25(4), 565-596

Qaraḍāwī, Y. (1999). *Contemporary fatawa: current issues in Islamic fiqh : Fatāwá muʿāʿirah = Fatawa of recent times [sic]*. Newark, NJ: Islamic Book Service.

Saunders, M., Lewis, P., & Thornhill, A. (2003). *Research Methods for Business Students*. England: Pearson Education Limited.

Song, Y. & T. Yarbrough, (1978), Tax Ethics and Taxpayer Attitudes: A Survey, *Public Administration Review*, September/October, 442-452

Spicer, M. & L. Becker, (1980), Fiscal Inequity and Tax Evasion: An Experimental Approach, *National Tax Journal*, June, 171-175.

Stack, S., & Kposowa, A. (2006). The Effect of Religiosity on Tax Fraud Acceptability: A Cross-National Analysis. *Journal for Scientific Study of Religion*, **45**(3), 325-351.

Stark, R., Iannaccone, L.R., & Finke, R., (1996). Linkages between Economics and Religion. *American Economic Review*, **86**, 433–437

Torgler, B. (2003). Tax Morale, Rule Governed Behaviour and Trust, *Constitutional Political Economy*, 14, 119-40.

Torgler, B. (2006). The Importance Of Faith: Tax morale and religiosity. *Journal of Economic Behaviour and Organization*, **61**(1), 81-123

Torgler, B. (2007). *Tax Compliance and Tax Morale: A Theoretical and Empirical Analysis*. Cheltenham, UK: Edward Elgar Publishing, Massachusetts

Welch, M. R., Xu, Y., Bjarnason, T., Petee, T., O'Donnell, P., & Magro, P. (2005). But Everybody Does It: The Effects of Perceptions, Moral Pressures, and Informal Sanctions on Tax Cheating. *Sociological Spectrum*, **25**(1), 21-52.

Yusuf, S.M., (1971). *Economic Justice in Islam*. Sh. Muhammad Ashraf, Lahore.

6 The Role of Software Systems in Tax: An Empirical Evaluation

Menno van Werkhoven, Reinout Kok and Felienne Hermans

Abstract

In the recent years, the role of information technology has increased in the lives of non-technical professionals. Finance is a highly number-driven part of businesses, in which automation plays a major role. One particular part of finance, tax, is currently under increasing scrutiny by both governments (OECD, 2015a) and the public eye. This paper explores how IT is used in practice by non-technical professionals, focusing on a particular group of people: tax professionals employed by multinationals. By performing 14 semi-structured interviews and analysing the results, first the educational background of the interviewees and their previous educational experience with IT is explored. Second, the programs that the interviewees use for their daily work is examined. Third, we explore what the perceived issues of interviewees with IT use are, and finally the educational requirements from an IT perspective are assessed. The outcomes of this explorative research will be used to identify areas of focus for future research.

Keywords: information technology, tax, finance

Introduction

In a world where businesses of all sizes are increasingly making use of information technology (IT) (Taruté and Gatautis, 2014), and the use of IT has even been referred to as the 'third industrial evolution' (Ollo-López and Aramendía-Muneta, 2012), the impact of IT has been much discussed. The goal of this research in general is to explore the impact of IT, and the challenges it can bring to non-technical professionals, focusing on a specific group of employees. Finance is highly number-driven and, as such, has been part of many automation efforts over the last two decades. One particular area of finance is tax. Since the start of the most recent economic downturn, the tax departments of multinational enterprises (MNEs) have been the focus of both public investigations, as well as receiving worldwide attention of the media, due to alleged tax avoidance (Barford and Holt, 2012). This paper studies the IT tools that are used by employees of MNEs working at tax departments in the Netherlands – the tax professionals – and the issues they encounter (or expect to encounter in the future) while using IT. In addition, the paper explores the interviewees' educational experience with IT, as well as current educational requirements around the subject of IT. This was done by conducting a set of 14 semi-structured interviews with professionals working in tax, and encoding and aggregating the interview results.

The results indicate that the most significant tool that professionals use is the Microsoft Office suite (and in particular Excel), followed by the consolidation and ERP systems in place at the company. In addition professionals use a wide array of different (and sometimes custom made) IT solutions for parts of their work. The most cited IT challenge that professionals have is compliance with upcoming legislation and how to provide the correct dataset to tax authorities, which is an issue for 80% of the interviewees. The second most cited issue is getting access to the right dataset to allow professionals to do their jobs, which was indicated by 70% of interviewees. Another challenge indicated by a little under half of the interviewees was the need for them to be included early in IT processes in various other departments of the MNE. Excel risks, transfer pricing (TP) requirements, the need to manage tax-related risks, and friction with the IT department on the priority of the tax department's requirements were each mentioned as being challenges by one-third of interviewees. On average, interviewees spend between five and six hours of their daily working time using a PC or laptop, including the use of email.

According to the study, the current educational offerings by universities in the Netherlands are perceived to be somewhat insufficient in regards to the professional requirements of the respondents. In particular, the perception by interviewees was that current graduates have little or no knowledge of corporate IT systems in place at MNEs, which is not reflective of the central position that these systems have in everyday work.

This paper is organised as follows. We start by describing the background of the respondents, then outline the methodology of the research. The results of the research are presented, and then discussed, while threats to validity of the research are considered next. We then provide an overview of related work, and finish with concluding remarks, including a summary of the contributions and directions for future research.

Background of the research field

Tax professionals are responsible for managing the daily tax affairs that effect a typical MNE including (but not limited to) corporate income taxes, value added taxes (VAT), customs and import duties, and withholding taxes. Although formally being part of the finance team, the role of this professional is a distinctly separate one, due to the specific knowledge and background education required for the specialist nature of the job. Other than answering direct questions and challenges in regard to national or international tax positions, tax professionals also have an obligation in internal and external reporting processes on the amount of taxes due. In addition, tax professionals are tasked with monitoring tax risks and providing information and insights to the Dutch tax authorities (DTA) and auditors, as part of their law-embedded task of reviewing and signing of on the annually presented figures of the MNE.

Although the finance departments of MNEs have rapidly become automated since the late 1990s – for example, the financial consolidation at all interviewed companies is done using a dedicated system instead of MS Excel – the tax teams have kept using their own systems and methodology. Because of the very specific knowledge of the professionals staffing the tax departments, there has not been a defined focus on automating the functions of the tax department in the past. In addition, tax automation is considered a niche for most of the larger software developing companies.

The focus changed as a result of the worldwide economic downturn that started in 2008. Subsequently tax authorities worldwide began work to replenish the treasuries of countries hit hard by increased spending on welfare on the one hand, and a decrease in taxable revenue on the other (Unger, 2013). One of current projects of the Organization of Economic Cooperation and Development (OECD, 2015b) is base erosion and profit shifting (BEPS), i.e. the practice of corporate taxpayers reducing the taxable base by shifting profits to another – lower taxed – jurisdiction, thus reducing their amount of payable tax (OECD, 2013). Part of the project are the country-by-country-reporting (CbCR) requirements, consisting of sharing financial and company data with the local tax authorities of the countries where a MNE has a presence, and providing local tax authorities with an enhanced insight of the tax structure of MNEs (OECD, 2015). These developments on an international level reflect the increased focus on MNEs who are seen as not paying their 'fair share' in the eyes of governments. Public opinion spurred a renewed interest in the tax departments of MNEs and their way of operation, with the general public demanding increased transparency on when, where and how much taxes are paid (Dyreng et al., 2015). It is not to be expected that the amount of company, financial and tax data shared between taxpayers and tax authorities will decrease in the future. As such, lawmakers will need to take into account the manageability and safe keeping of the large amounts of data received.

Previously conducted research has indicated that the amount spent on general IT by companies has an effect on taxes paid (Hamilton and Stekelberg, 2016), and is as such a factor of influence.

Methodology

Now that the background of the topic has been examined, the scope of the research is defined, including data sources, research questions, and corresponding methodology.

Context

To acquire data on the current usage of IT by tax professionals, a qualitative approach was followed, collecting and analysing data from different sources to investigate different aspects relevant to the study: (1) a review on literature on how the (tax) professional uses IT, (2) 14 interviews with tax professionals working at MNEs with a sizeable presence and profile in the Dutch market, (3) the encoding of interviews using cards and accumulating results.

The selection criteria for the interviewees were:

- The interviewee is working as tax professional for a MNE active in the Netherlands. This MNE has a sizeable presence (i.e. having a minimum of a 1000 staff employed in the Netherlands) in the country, and has a dedicated tax department to cater to the requirements of the Netherlands. The rationale for these criteria is to exclude potential interviewees with dual roles (the other role being mainly finance focused) and interviewees working for smaller, local enterprises. The employee in a more finance-focused role usually has a different educational background compared to the dedicated tax professional, and is as such not a representative of the respondents. Smaller, local enterprises have different tax requirements and usually do not employ dedicated tax professionals.
- The interviewed party has at least three years of experience working as a tax professional at an MNE. The rationale for this criterion is that interviewees should have a good understanding of the requirements

of the tax department they are working in. More junior professionals, often with a background as a tax advisor at an advisory firm before joining an MNE, are usually less experienced in coping with the different tax challenges an MNE has and would thus be less able to answer the interview questions in the detail required.

- Between interviewees there is enough diversity of industry verticals between the various MNEs where the interviewees worked. The participating industry verticals were: banking, insurance, software, travel, food, (high-tech) manufacturing, pharmaceutical, oil & gas, real estate, chemicals, and retail. The rationale for this criterion was to have an interview base that had experience with different industry verticals, thus not being unintentionally focused on only two or three industry verticals.

Research method

Interviews with professionals employed by MNEs

The tax professionals were selected according to the criteria mentioned above, and were interviewed for about 45 to 60 minutes each (on average 55 minutes). Each interview was semi-structured in its approach. This form of interviewing uses an interview guide that contains general groupings of topics and questions, rather than a predetermined exact set and order of questions. The 'to be discussed' topics were shared with interviewees up to several weeks before the interview in an effort to enable interviewees to gather their thoughts on the topic. With consent, and assuring the interviewees of anonymity, the dialogues were recorded in all but one case. After creating an interview report based on the recording, the report was sent to the interviewee for validation, to ensure that the interview report reflected the input of the interviewee during the interview correctly. The interviews were held between March and July 2015.

Encoding the interviews

To analyse the interview data, the validated interview reports were encoded by reading through them, identifying relevant pieces of content and subsequently writing these down on a small piece of paper, creating a card. This resulted in 362 cards containing a short summary, linked to the context (e.g. the question asked) and the interviewee's name. These cards were analysed and comparable content was grouped together (Schade and Janis, 2000). Cards containing similar messages were aggregated in a spreadsheet, creating a total of 99 different topics. A diagram was created linking the topics and interviewees, thus making it possible to connect the related concepts and derive the main themes.

Research questions

The interviews were performed face to face or (in one case) over the telephone with professionals selected following the above mentioned criteria.

Table 6.1: Interview set-up

Interview conducted how?	Number of interviewees
Face to face	13
Telephone	1

The interviews were structured around four research questions (RQ) or themes. Below are the research questions, including the high-level corresponding interview questions and the rationale for these questions. The detailed interview questions are publicly available[1].

[RQ1] What is the educational background of tax professionals?

The high level interview questions were:
- What is your educational background?
- How did you gain your relevant IT knowledge?

The reason for this question is to investigate whether the typical tax professional can be considered as an educated IT user or not. It is also interesting to validate whether an education in IT (or some training courses) can be related to a more in-depth use of IT systems as part of one's work.

[RQ2] What is the current IT use of tax professionals?

The high level interview questions were:
- Can you describe what software programs you use for your work, excluding email?
- Can you describe your use of these individual programs in more detail?
- Can you estimate how much of your time is spend using IT (including email) on average?

The reason for this question is to get a clearer insight into the different programs and tax systems that professionals use for their work, and to what end a particular program or system is used to tackle the highly specific challenges of the tax department of a MNE. This to determine and evaluate the

---
1   www.lerp.nl/images/softwaresystems.pdf

current state of IT usage by the respondents. The use of email was excluded from the research because of its acceptance as a standard communication tool. The use of email was included, however, in the question on estimated time spent by interviewees because it was very difficult to segregate email use and use of other software, which are often intertwined.

[RQ3] What are the issues and/or wishes concerning the use of IT by tax professionals?

The high level interview questions were:

- Do you feel there is an IT need that is currently not adequately addressed?
- How would your ideal IT world look like?

The reason for this question is to get a better insight on the potential issues and challenges that professionals have with IT and where further research could be beneficial. It also gives an idea on the level of ability around using IT by the respondents.

[RQ4] What are the (future) educational requirements of tax professionals concerning IT?

The high level interview questions were:

- Do you feel that your education adequately prepared you by providing relevant knowledge required for the daily tasks of professionals working at a MNE?
- In your opinion, would there be a need for more specialised education on IT within tax education?

The reason for this question is to get a better insight into the perceived requirements of a university education in relation to IT, and to be able to provide universities with some awareness of what the state of their education is versus the perceived requirements in practice. This could help universities which teach tax specific courses to adjust their curriculum to improve the matching of requirements and to potentially improve the market value of their students.

Results

In this section the results from the interviews that were set-up using the methodology above, are presented.

[RQ1] What is the educational background of tax professionals?

All interviewees had a university education around tax, either fiscal economics or tax law. One interviewee had both a degree in fiscal economics and in tax law. In addition one interviewee did not formally complete a master degree and just had a bachelor degree. Seven interviewees also held a separate bachelor degree. Only two interviewees had any contact with IT in their formal education and an additional five, including one of the IT educated interviewees, had completed courses on IT in their professional careers. These courses ranged from an expert Excel course to a dedicated course on how to interact with an ERP system in place at one's place of work.

Table 6.2: Educational background

Type of education	Number of interviewees
Tax law	9
Fiscal economics	5
Separate bachelor degree	7
IT in education	2
IT in courses	5

All interviewees indicated that most of their relevant IT knowledge was gained by 'learning on the job'. Thus while the average time spent on IT by the interviewees (including email) was between 60% and 75% (or approximately five to six hours daily, and even more during peak times for half of the interviewees), only a minority had any education or a relevant course on IT. Another observation was that of the seven interviewees who had completed an education or a relevant course, six had a separate bachelor degree.

[RQ2] What is the current IT use of tax professionals?

The answers to the question: 'which types of software programs do you use for your work' are in the Table 3:

Table 6.3: Which types of software do you use for your work?

Type of software	Number of interviewees
Excel	14
Word	14
PowerPoint	12
Enterprise systems	10
Dedicated tax software	8
Tax information databases	8
Auditor platform	4

Excel

Looking at the results of the current IT programs in use, all interviewees indicated using Excel. *Eight interviewees indicated using Excel as their primary, most used, IT tool.* All interviewees indicated using Excel with data sourced from another system. The results of what Excel was specifically used for are in the Table 6.4:

Table 6.4: For what purpose is Excel used

What function is performed in Excel?	Number of interviewees
Tax accounting	11
Bridge between enterprise systems and tax team	11
Financial analyses	4
Tax planning	2
Internal reporting	2
Transfer pricing	2
Work-cost arrangement	2
Correspondence tax audit	1
Calculate stock options	1
Legal entity manager	1
Calculate US state taxes	1
Monitor compliance	1

Microsoft Office and PowerPoint

From the Microsoft Office suite (other than Excel), all interviewees indicated using Microsoft Word and twelve indicated using Microsoft PowerPoint. The specified use of both MS Word and PowerPoint was standard usage, e.g. on stand-alone basis as a word processor and presentation tool respectively. One interviewee described the use of PowerPoint as such: *'PowerPoint is a 'waving-around' type of document where one can wave it round and show that one has been busy – more focused on presentation than on actual content'*. The percentages of use around the combined Microsoft Office suite make it the most used software suite for tax professionals.

Enterprise Systems

Other frequently used software systems by interviewees was in the category of enterprise systems that were available at the respective MNEs, such as ERP systems containing transactional data and the consolidation system containing aggregated data for financial reporting purposes. As stated in Table 6.3, ten interviewees accessed these systems indirectly via Excel. For example: they had a colleague from the finance team exporting data from the

ERP system into an Excel file and delivering that to them for further processing. *In addition six of the interviewees indicated that they would access these enterprise systems themselves* to gather and export data or use internal modules in these systems to perform calculations.

Dedicated tax software

Eight interviewees indicated using some form of a dedicated tax-related software solution either bought off-the-shelf or having been custom built for purposes shown in Table 6.5:

Table 6.5: Dedicated tax software

What type of tax solution?	Number of interviewees
VAT solution	4
Tax accounting solution	3
Local customs systems	2
Tax filing solution	2
Information management solution	2
Tool for the work-cost arrangement	2
Calendaring tool	1
Transfer pricing documentation tool	1

Tax information databases and audit platforms

Tax information databases like Kluwer Navigator[2] or the IBFD portal[3] were indicated as being actively used by eight interviewees. Dedicated platforms or websites provided by the auditor for communication and the status of tax filings and other on-going assignments were used by four of the interviewees.

[RQ3] What are the issues and/or wishes concerning the IT use of tax professionals?

When prompted with the question about where potential issues with IT usage and work are manifesting themselves, a variety of answers were provided – but with two central themes: the changing role of the tax department in MNEs including higher pressure (both internally and from the DTA) to be compliant; and to 'not rock the boat' too much from a tax structuring perspective. The other theme identified was the difficulty in accessing the relevant data quickly and accurately. In Table 6.6 are the ten most frequently indicated topics:

---

2   www.navigator.nl
3   www.ibfd.org

Table 6.6: Observations

Issues and/or wishes	Number of interviewees
BEPS including CbCR	11
Difficult to access underlying data	10
Changing role of the tax department	6
Excel is a risk	5
Need VAT software	5
Need transfer pricing software	5
Need a risk management system	5
IT department doesn't prioritise tax	5
Big data	3
Difficulties in creating software	3

Base erosion and profit shifting including upcoming country-by-country reporting requirements

External compliance initiatives like BEPS and CbCR require MNEs to hand over specific company and financial data, which is usually captured in a variety of different IT systems, to local tax authorities. Interviewees indicated that extracting the required data would create challenges, as some of the requested data is not accessible by the tax department at the time of the interview. Not only was gathering the required data itself perceived to be an issue, but also the way that tax authorities handle and communicate IT requirements to MNEs was questioned by 11 interviewees. One quote of interest around this topic was: 'In the new – more technical web-enabled – world of the tax professional and the discussion that is unfolding around BEPS, it is clear that the classic fiscal concepts are not captured any more by traditional means and the professional group should have an answer to that eventually'.

It is difficult to access underlying data

Difficulty in accessing the required data and the desire for one dataset was indicated by ten of the interviewees. The wish for one dashboard for related IT systems, where professionals could drill into the lowest level of transactional data and access various components, is closely linked to this issue and was indicated by five interviewees. One interviewee described it as such: 'The more fragmented the IT landscape is, the higher the chance of errors – super dangerous'. Another interviewee put it like this: 'It shouldn't matter how I get the relevant information; as long as it is correct. At the same time I shouldn't have to depend a lot on others for gathering that information'.

The changing role of the tax department

The changing role of the Tax Department in general and the Tax Manager in particular was indicated by six interviewees. The wish of the interviewees to be able to influence and advise on company processes (which are captured by IT systems) from a tax perspective, including new enterprise systems so relevant data can be more easily extracted, was of particular note.

Excel is a risk

Five interviewees indicated that using Excel is a risk in itself. Some of reasons given which contributed to that perception of risk were:

- Excel is susceptible to formula errors that are difficult to identify due to user error. There are methods to counter these errors but these still require some detailed knowledge.
- Excel is usually locally stored and not very accessible by multiple users at the same time. A more cloud-based approach would be preferred.

An interesting quote by one of the interviewees was 'Excel cannot be the basis for the future'. Another quote was 'Effective automation reduces risks, and the current way of working with Excel is risky'.

In need of dedicated VAT software

Software that could deal with data on a transactional level for VAT purposes, combining international requirements for VAT retrieval and giving insight in potential unnecessary VAT-related losses was indicated by five interviewees.

In need of dedicated transfer pricing software

Transfer pricing software that could handle both operational TP requirements (gaining insight in current profit allocation and making corrections according to the economic function of an entity) and create TP documentation – both of which are currently time and labour intensive. This wish was indicated by five interviewees.

In need of a risk management system

The wish to create a dedicated IT system that could cope with risk management and give insights in potential tax-related risks via a 'red flag' system was indicated by five interviewees. A red flag can consist of a message and/or a visual indication that, at that moment in time, a certain tax-related outcome is outside of pre-established parameters and thus warrants further investigation.

The IT department does not prioritise the IT needs of the tax department

It was perceived by five interviewees that IT departments of MNEs were not giving the IT needs of the tax departments the desired priority. According to interviewees, this was part of a trend that reduced IT departments in general were having difficulty coping with fulfilling requirements that are perceived as more pressing (like operational IT needs). One interviewee put it as such: 'Tax shouldn't be last in line from an IT perspective'.

Big data

Big data, and the question on how exactly to define it, and how to approach it, was indicated by three interviewees. One interviewee described it as follows: 'I find big data to be somewhat of a buzzword, but there are very interesting sides to it that could affect business companywide'.

Difficulties in getting effective software

The difficulty in formulating IT requirements to an IT department or software supplier that does not have any relevant tax knowledge; and the difficulty communicating as a professional without any understanding of IT or its potential pitfalls, and yet get a system that actually works, was indicated by three interviewees.

As a final query around this research question, interviewees were asked to provide input to the theory that *'tax compliance is data management'*. This thesis was provided by one of the interviewees when discussing participation in the interview, and was appealing because it focused on an IT perspective in the strictest sense of the word.

Table 6.7: 'Tax Compliance is Data management'

Agreed with theory: tax compliance is data management	Number of interviewees
Yes	7
Yes, but...	6

When asked, half of the interviewees fully agreed with the theory. Six interviewees partially agreed with it: all of them indicated that although having the correct data is an important element, the hypothesis was too strict; there is also a strong component of relevant knowledge involved with tax compliance. One interviewee wasn't asked the question due to timing constraints during the interview.

[RQ4] What are the (future) educational requirements of professionals regarding IT?

When asked about the educational requirements of future tax professionals, the answers were less diverse than the answers provided by the previously discussed research question. All interviewees indicated that a university education on tax should focus on theory because of the scientific foundation of a Dutch university education. Although several years had passed since some had graduated from university, all interviewees could relate to the question and had a view on the topic. This was also driven by experiences with junior colleagues who had just graduated and started working in the tax departments of MNEs. The results are in Table 8:

Table 6.8: Educational requirements

Issues with current education	Number of interviewees
Little focus on IT	8
Students need soft skills	8
Teach about the corporate tax filing	3

There is little focus on IT in tax education majors of Dutch universities

Eight interviewees indicated that information technology and the role that it has in the working life of current professionals is insufficiently addressed in existing university teachings. Although the extent to which this was perceived to be the case differed from person to person, there was an agreement that there should be more focus on IT than is the case today. Basic knowledge like the concept of an IT infrastructure within an MNE is virtually unknown to current graduates. While interviewees agreed that skills like these can be picked up on the job as well, a more solid foundation could go a long way in the pace of acquiring such skills. Three of the interviewees even indicated that graduates should have a basic understanding of where they can get the data relevant to the requirements of the future job when they leave university with their master degree.

Students need communication (and other soft) skills

Another frequently mentioned topic was the changing role of the tax department and the need for tax professionals to cooperate with (or influence) other parts of an MNE, including the IT department. This requires communication skills and an understanding of the business in general. A university education should also focus on the relevant 'soft skills' of the tax graduates, according to eight interviewees.

Universities need to teach more regarding the processes of a corporate tax filing

Three interviewees also indicated that the current tax graduate has little knowledge around the – mostly IT-driven – process of actually doing a corporate tax filing. The Dutch corporate tax filing process usually consists of gathering relevant tax data from various enterprise systems and generating a pre-formatted file that is shared electronically with the DTA[4].

Since doing a tax filing, and managing the process around it, is a paramount element of the tax department's mission and subject to much supervision (and subsequent penalties) by the DTA (Booij et al., 2015), there could be more attention on this topic by universities.

Discussion

In this section, the research findings and potential areas for future research are identified.

Tax professionals rarely have an IT education in addition to their formal tax education

While professionals spend a lot of time behind their PCs and use Excel and other dedicated software tools extensively, relatively few have received any education on how to actually use the IT means at their disposal. An interesting observation by the interviewer while conducting the interviews was that the tax professionals who had a more economics-focused background (like a master degree in fiscal economics) generally appeared to be more adept at using software and were less reliant on other departments providing data than the professionals with a legal background. This observation was far from absolute and was not fully captured (or explored) in the interviews.

While not a trend unique to the respondents and seen in many different groups of (higher educated) employees, it was interesting to see that in a changing environment, professionals had to rely on their ability to learn on the job (and personal interest in the topic of IT) to keep up with demands. The difficulties in accessing the right data and the wish for one dashboard and one dataset are a result of the highly diverse and complicated IT infrastructure in place in most MNEs. Also, a lack of IT knowledge is reflected by the frequently indicated issues around the relationship with the

---

4   http://www.belastingdienst.nl/wps/wcm/connect/bldcontenten/belastingdienst/business/tax_return/filing_digital_tax_returns/how_do_you_file_digital_tax_returns/how_do_you_file_digital_tax_returns

IT department – and the difficulty met by some interviewees to effectively work together with that department to create effective solutions.

One of the ways to counter these issues is for post-doctoral professional education, like those provided by the Dutch Order of Tax Advisors (NOB), to try to increase the IT knowledge of tax professionals in the field. Another potential approach could be for tax professionals to have increased interactions with IT technical professionals in a more educational setting while on the job, thus providing mutual benefits.

Tax professionals use Excel as their dominant software tool

Every interviewee pointed to the use of Excel for a variety of work-related tasks. A majority indicated using Excel as the most predominant tool. Eleven interviewees were reliant on Excel to provide them with the required data to use as a base for their work-related calculations. Six indicated only using Excel and not using any other dedicated tax solutions. This information is even more interesting when combined with the fact that the visibility of tax, both internally and externally, is increasing, and the finding that only a very limited number of interviewed professionals ever completed an education or a course on how to use IT in general or Excel in particular. There has been research on Excel and its widespread use by analysts (Winston, 2001) and its prevalence in the financial industry (Panko, 2006). The quote of one of the more IT-savvy interviewees comes to mind: 'we've looked for Excel replacements many times but nothing has been found yet'. The same interviewee continued with: 'but we're doing our best to keep up with IT developments and are looking at least twice a year for potential replacements'.

Dedicated research into how spreadsheets are used by tax professionals could provide answers on where improvements can be made, either by improving spreadsheets or replacing them with other software solutions. Although there has been research on how professionals use spreadsheets, the requirements of the tax professional are different on some points due to the specialised nature of their jobs. Nevertheless it is expected that generic tools to improve spreadsheets could also benefit the respondents.

Tax professionals are in the centre of discussions around IT and external tax compliance

The most frequently indicated worry or issue (indicated by eleven interviewees) were external compliance initiatives like BEPS and CbCR and what the tax authorities would do with that additional data in an audit situation. The way that tax authorities could use received data outside the scope of its purpose could be a disruptive element in the relationship between tax authorities and the corporate taxpayer, something that needs to be considered from a tax policy perspective. Nonetheless, research by a tax software vendor indicates that an increasing number of corporate taxpayers are gearing up for compliance with CbCR (Thomson Reuters, 2016).

From a tax policy perspective, clear guidelines on how data is handled, including an open dialogue between the DTA and other tax authorities and corporate taxpayers on this particular point, could help to gain mutual understanding and appreciation. In addition, an effective cooperation between tax lawmakers and tax professionals and an understanding of IT limitations could be beneficial in achieving the goal of more effective transparency.

Dutch tax education does not fully match the working environment

Current tax-related education in Dutch universities does not fully reflect the present day requirements of the tax professional employed by an MNE. The perceived lack of focus on the changing role of tax departments and its increasing drive towards tax compliance is not reflected in structured education. The lack of relevant 'soft skills' by graduates, and the lack of understanding around the workings of an MNE and what the relevant functions are, are other potential points of attention for universities. On the other hand, interviewees also indicated that a scientific education should stay mainly scientific; however, with some effort towards more practical skills, graduates would be better prepared for working life. Finally, the lack of any IT component in university education in an ever-changing but increasingly IT-focused working environment was also perceived as a missed opportunity.

A potential approach for Dutch universities could be to include more IT components in their non-technical courses, creating a stronger foundation of basic IT knowledge that could be expanded on after graduation. In addition, an approach similar to that suggested for the tax professionals already working in the field, could be to provide graduates with more interaction with IT technical professionals working in the field via e.g. dedicated IT-focused internships during university.

Threats to reliability

A threat to the external reliability of this evaluation concerns the representativeness of the selected set of interviewees. While being representative of a specific group of financial professionals and in the most general sense non-technical professionals, some of the findings are very specifically tax-related issues. In addition the group of interviewees was small, consisting of only 14 interviewees. One step that was taken to maximise representability was the selecting of interviewees working in different types of industry verticals. In addition, interviewees had varying educational tax backgrounds, being educated in different universities and having completed different tax-related studies.

Regarding the qualitative aspects, gauging the validity of findings is a difficult undertaking (Golafshani, 2003). The coding process leads to increased processing and organisational capacity at the loss of accuracy of the original response.

Social desirability bias (Furnham, 1986), meaning the respondents' possible tendency to appear in a positive light, may have influenced the interviewees. To mitigate this risk, the interviewees were informed that, while their names would be known to the interviewer, it was guaranteed that they could not be identified in resulting papers and articles.

Related work

In 2002, Schäfer and Spengel examined the consequences of the increased use of IT on international corporate taxation, namely on the tax attributes in the resident and source country, as well as on the scope of taxation (Schäfer and Spengel, 2002). While they researched the impact generated by IT on the effective taxation of tax income streams and the potential challenges that lay ahead, it took the OECD some time to respond with the (earlier mentioned) action plan around BEPS, in particular action number one, named *Addressing the Tax Challenges of the Digital Economy* (OECD, 2014). These research efforts focus on the impact of IT on taxation, including the challenges around using IT for possible tax avoidance. The research discussed in this paper takes the non-technical user as a starting point, and provides insights into how they use IT in their tax-related day to day work.

Ming Ling and Hidayah Ahamad Nawawi (2010) explored integrating IT skills and tax software in the Malaysian tax education (Ming Ling, L. and Hidayah Ahamad Nawawi, N. 2010). Schwartz and Stout (2001) did the same for the United States, as did Miller and Woods for the UK (2000). They concluded that most new graduates were not well prepared in the area of taxation when they started to work. Although related, the previous research is focused on different countries, while this paper is focused on the Dutch experience, but the findings are similar.

Concluding remarks

The use of IT by a specific group of professionals – tax professionals employed by a MNE – was investigated in an effort to gain a better insight in how IT is used, and to better define what the potential issues are for this group around IT usage. The key contributions of this paper are:

- A series of interviews with non-technical professionals working in tax departments on how they use IT, what the perceived issues with IT usage are, and providing insight into potential improvements from an educational point of view.
- Encoding the input provided at these interviews and performing a qualitative analysis to generate results.
- Discussing these results and distilling the major points of focus, thus indicating where future research could be concentrated.

The interviewees provided valuable input, and several potential possibilities for follow-up and more in-depth research were identified. From a technical IT perspective more research on what this particular group of non-technical professionals does with spreadsheets could be considered. From a more tax-centred perspective, additional research in the number one issue – the developments around IT and external tax compliance – could be considered as well.

Acknowledgment

I owe my gratitude to the participants in the interviews and appreciate the fact that they reserved some of their scarce time for me. Thank you so much for your time and input!

References

Barford, V. & Holt, G. (2012, December, 4). *Google, Amazon, Starbucks: The rise of 'tax shaming'*, BBC News Magazine.

Booij, A., Hemels, S. & Bikkers, C. (2015). Surcharges and Penalties in Tax Law: The Netherlands. In R. Seer (Ed.), *Surcharges and Penalties in Tax Law*, IBFD.

Dyreng, S., Hoopes, J.L. & Wilde, J.H. (2015). *Public Pressure and Corporate Tax Behavior*. Fisher College of Business Working Paper No. 2014-02-003.

Furnham, A. (1986). Response bias, social desirability and dissimulation, *Personality and Individual Preferences,* **7**(3), 385-400.

Golafshani, N. (2003). Understanding reliability and validity in qualitative research, *The Qualitative Report,* **8**(4), 597-607.

Hamilton, R. & Stekelberg, J. (2016). The Effect of High Quality Information Technology on Corporate Tax Avoidance and Tax Risk, *Journal of Information Systems*, **3**(2), 83-106

Ming Ling, L. & Hidayah Ahamad Nawawi, N. (2010). Integrating ICT skills and tax software in tax education. *Campus-Wide Information Systems*, **27**(5), 303-317.

Miller, A.M. & Woods, C.M. (2000). Undergraduate tax education: a comparison of educators' and employers' perceptions in the UK, *Accounting Education*, **9**(3), 223-41.

OECD (2015a). *Action 13: Country-by-Country Reporting Implementation Package*, OECD Publishing, Paris.

OECD (2015b). *Explanatory Statement*, OECD / G20 Base Erosion and Profit Shifting Project. OECD. Retrieved from www.oecd.org/tax/beps-explanatory-statement-2015.pdf

OECD (2014), *Addressing the Tax Challenges of the Digital Economy*, OECD/G20 Base Erosion and Profit Shifting Project, OECD Publishing, Paris.

OECD (2013). *Action Plan on Base Erosion and Profit Shifting*. OECD Publishing, Paris.

Ollo-López, A. & Elena Aramendía-Muneta, M. (2012). ICT Impact on competitiveness, innovation and environment. *Telematics and Informatics*, **29**(2), 204-210.

Panko, R. (2006). Facing the problem of spreadsheet errors. *Decision Line*, **37**(5).

Schade, J.O.E. & Janis, S.J. (2000) *Improving Performance Through Statistical Thinking*, Mcgraw-Hill.

Schwartz, B.N. & Stout, D.E. (2001). A comparison of practitioner and educator opinions on tax education requirements for undergraduate accounting majors, *Issues in Accounting Education*, **2**, 112-26.

Schäfer, A. & Spengel, C. (2002) *ICT and International Corporate Taxation: Tax Attributes and Scope of Taxation*. ZEW Discussion Paper No. 02-81.

Taruté, A. & Gatautis, R. (2014). ICT impact on SMEs performance. *Procedia – Social and Behavioral Sciences*, **110**, 1218-1225.

Thomson Reuters, (2016). Global BEPS Survey Report. Retrieved from: http://tax.thomsonreuters.com/BEPS/survey-report-2016/

Unger, B. (2013). *How to Finance A Social Europe?* Roadmap to a Social Europe, Pages 95 – 97.

Winston, W.L. (2001) Executive education opportunities. *OR/MS Today*, **28**(4)

7 The Role of Social Norms in Tax Compliance Decisions

Riad Cheikh, Emer Mulligan and Breda Sweeney

Abstract

Tax non-compliance behaviour is a significant problem in many societies. In order to tackle this behaviour, tax authorities are arguably required to go beyond the traditional approach of ensuring tax compliance through enforcement and deterrence systems. The literature suggests the need to also consider a socio-psychological approach, thereby adding 'tax morale' to the tax compliance equation. Tax morale is commonly referred to as the intrinsic motivation to pay taxes and this can be shaped by several factors such as personal norms, social norms, and religion. This chapter focuses on the role of social norms in a tax compliance context. There is not a consensus regarding the precise definition of social norms, and no consensus has been reached on how to operationalise these norms in tax compliance studies. This chapter examines the definition and underlying dimensions of social norms, a necessary prerequisite to carrying out any in-depth study on this topic. It presents a review of the relevant literature on the theory of social norms and on ethical behaviour (specifically moral intensity). By drawing together these different strands of literature, the chapter unpacks the dimensions of social norms and their role in tax compliance decision making, while also identifying the need for further research in this area.

Introduction

Tax non-compliance behaviour is a significant problem in many societies. In order to tackle this behaviour, tax authorities are arguably required to go beyond the traditional approach of ensuring tax compliance. This traditional approach claims that a better compliance level can only be achieved through enforcement and deterrence systems (penalties and/or auditing). However, based on daily observations and common sense, it could be argued that an individual would abstain from non-compliance behaviour, exactly as from speeding, breaking the law and polluting the environment, not only as a result of potential penalties or prison but as a result of social and ethical considerations (Sandmo, 2005). In addition, convincing arguments are emerging in the literature that criticise the narrow traditional approach of understanding tax compliance behaviour and proposing a wider approach, which is the socio-psychological approach. This approach proposes considering the same traditional tools (such as penalty, audit, and enforcement) plus non-traditional tools (such as social and personal norms etc.). It complements the traditional view (economic view) by adding another dimension to the compliance equation, namely 'tax morale'. Tax morale is widely accepted as playing a vital role in shaping tax compliance behaviour and there is a consensus in the literature around the need to address tax morale in any study that examines tax compliance, evasion or avoidance (Bobek et al., 2013; Cummings et al., 2009; Feld & Frey, 2007; Frey & Feld, 2002; Frey & Torgler, 2006; McKerchar et al., 2013; Torgler, 2004; Torgler, 2007; Wenzel, 2007). Tax morale is commonly referred to as the intrinsic motivation to pay taxes (Torgler, 2002; Torgler, 2006; Torgler & Schneider, 2009). This intrinsic motivation can be shaped by several factors such as personal norms, social norms, and religion. In particular, social context is considered to be one of the main drivers of the intrinsic motivation to comply with a tax system (Bobek et al., 2013; Torgler & Schneider, 2007; Wenzel, 2004b). For instance, Torgler (2003) found that interactions between taxpayers themselves are significant in the context of the tax compliance decision, and Davis et al. (2003) emphasised that suspicion that a person's relatives and acquaintances are evading will enhance the probability of that person also engaging in tax evasion (non-compliance behaviour).

Despite these empirical studies, a consensus regarding the precise definition of social norms and how to operationalise these norms in tax compliance studies has not yet been reached. As noted by Torgler (2002, p.663) "When working with social norms, we have the difficulty of specifying their exact meaning". Therefore, prior to any in-depth study on this topic, there is a need to examine the definition and underlying dimensions of social norms. The chapter aims to address this by reviewing relevant literature on the theory of social norms and on ethical behaviour (specifically moral intensity). By drawing together these different strands of literature, the chapter unpacks the dimensions of social norms and their role in tax compliance decision making; it also identifies the need for further research in this area.

The remainder of the chapter is organised as follows. The next section discusses prior research on the role of social norms in the tax compliance field as well as the wider ethical behaviour field. This is followed by an outline of social norms theory and the four components of social norms. The differences between general and specific social norms are then discussed, and the final section provides a brief summary and identifies future research opportunities in this area.

Prior studies on social norms

Accepting social norms as a motivation mechanism implies that an individual would evaluate his personal behaviour alongside what is approved or disapproved within a community or group – in other words, the social norms of the group. The threat of social sanctions means that following such social norms would be considered rational behaviour. However, following social norms is not temporarily or partially dependent on self-interest; as Max Weber emphasised "a social norm is not like a taxi from which one can disembark at will, followers of a social norm abide by it even when it is not in their interest to do so" (noted by Elster, 1989). The next two sub-sections provide a review of prior studies in tax compliance and ethical behaviour literature which addresses the role of social norms in decision making contexts.

Tax compliance literature

In tax compliance literature, many studies provide strong evidence that the compliance behaviour of a taxpayer's peers is significantly correlated with individual compliance level (Bobek & Hatfield, 2003; Sandmo, 2005; Scholz et al., 1992; Spicer & Becker, 1980; Torgler, 2004; Torgler, 2008; Wenzel, 2004a). Earlier studies indicated that a taxpayer's perception of significant others is related to compliance intentions (Bobek & Hatfield, 2003). Indeed, a study conducted by Scholz et al. (1992) found that the opinions of others are extremely important with respect to a taxpayer's decision to comply. Sandmo (2005) confirmed that the tax compliance decision is related to the individual's perceptions of the behaviour of others. Furthermore, Torgler (2003) asserted that a taxpayer's decision to comply is not isolated from the other taxpayers' decision, stating that "individuals with tax evaders as friends are more likely to be evaders themselves" (Torgler, 2008 : p.1251).

Social psychologists attempted to explain the reasons why through knowing tax evaders, honest taxpayers would consider evading tax themselves. For instance, Montada and Lerner (1998) explained it by the feeling of justice, whereby individuals need to believe that the world is just and that justice is enforced by punishing the harm-doer; compensating; blaming or at least denying injustice, and supporting it with justice in the afterlife. If this does not happen, taxpayers will engage in tax evasion to seek justice by themselves (Spicer & Becker, 1980; Tyler, 1990).

7: The Role of Social Norms in Tax Compliance Decisions

An alternative view, presented by Cooter (1988) suggests that in general, individuals choose conformity as a behavioural standard, and violating this standard will incur a psychological cost of guilt even if the violation was not observed by others. In cases where the violation was made by a taxpayer of high moral character, it may cause the taxpayer to change his/her behavioural standard. Indeed, Kaplan and Reckers (1985)'s findings supported this view and provided evidence that the probability to evade will increase when a taxpayer observes a high moral character[1] in the evader (descriptive norms). Taxpayers' perceptions of the probability of being caught when evading tax are much higher than the actual probabilities of detection (Feld & Frey, 2007). However, it seems that this misperception is not sustainable over a long time horizon, as the interaction of individuals and the sharing of knowledge about the ability of others to evade taxes will impact personal compliance behaviour (Feld & Frey, 2007). This argument was supported by Orviska and Hudson (2003) who provided evidence that tax evasion is actually condemned by the majority of taxpayers, who are at the same time ready to reconsider it when they observe others evading.

In contrast, another argument was presented by Wenzel (2005) that taxpayers generally overestimate other taxpayers' acceptance of tax evasion. So, taxpayers become evaders under this misperception. This view was supported by a number of studies that suggested that individuals with more non-compliance behaviours perceived tax evasion to be more prevalent among their acquaintances (De Juan, Lasheras, & Mayo, 1994; Wallschutzky, 1984; Webley, Cole, & Eidjar, 2001)[2]. McAdams (1997) claimed that social norms can affect one's compliance level through the reputation of a taxpayer image within a specific group. In particular, McAdams pointed out that an individual is inclined to seek the respect of others which enhances his personal compliance level in response. Alm (1991) found strong evidence that social norms have a significant impact on the tax compliance of taxpayers. He added "those who believe that others cheat are more likely to cheat themselves, and that an individual's perception of how he or she is treated relative to others affects compliance" (Alm, 1991, p.591). Furthermore, a study by Wenzel (2004a) confirms the previous studies and suggests that tax compliance is affected by the taxpayer's commitment to the social norm of compliance.

---

1   In their study Kaplan and Reckers (1985: p 100), manipulated the moral character in which a high moral character refers to "the taxpayer who generally is regarded as an 'upright' businessman". Whereas, a low moral character refers to "the taxpayer who generally is regarded as a 'shrewd' businessman".

2   Those studies were cited by Wenzel (2004a and 2004b).

Blanthorne and Kaplan (2008) suggested that social norms have an indirect impact on the evasion behaviour through ethical beliefs. To further clarify, Elster (1989) pointed out that the effect of social norms on tax compliance would be observed even without exposition to external sanctions. In addition, once the norms are internalised, norms will be followed despite the possibility that the violation is undetectable or unobservable. Also, once the social norms are internalised, shame or anticipation of it (internal sanctions) would be the driver and take over from the external sanctions. In this regard, Polinsky and Shavell (2000) conducted a large-scale study which promoted social norms as an alternative to the deterrence system in shaping the person's behaviour. This could be achieved by enforcing internal sanctions (guilt, remorse and shame) or social sanctions (gossip and ostracism) which are the consequences of violation of social norms.

In response to this argument, Gordon (1989) developed the 'psychic cost' concept which refers to the cost that an individual will incur if he engages in tax evasion as a result of potential social sanctions by the community or specific group. So, increasing the level of tax evasion will increase psychic cost. Moreover, the variation of taxpayers' assessment of psychic cost is a source of division in the population between evaders and non-evaders. Jon et al. (2003) argued that an enforcement system and social norms will both place a great pressure on evaders to become more compliant.

There is no consensus among scholars about how society motivates taxpayers to either comply or not. Torgler (2004) argued that the contribution of society is the main driver behind taxpayers' compliance with taxes, while Davis et al. (2003) concluded that the pressure that honest taxpayers impose on evaders would force them to comply. They found that the greater the proportion of honest taxpayers within a population, the greater the pressure on tax evaders to switch back to honest compliance behaviour. At the same time, honest taxpayers should be protected as Frey and Feld (2002) emphasised that if honest taxpayers comply with tax rules and they realise that other society members are evading taxes, they may sense that they have been cheated by those evaders who disrespect the basic rules of citizenship duty (Frey and Feld, 2002).

However, evidence from Blanthorne and Kaplan (2008) showed that the opportunity to evade tax is unrelated to social norms, contrary to what the authors expected. However, this finding could be explained by the extent to which an individual identifies himself/herself within a group. Wenzel (2004a) pointed out that social norms would have absolutely no impact on tax compliance levels for individuals who did not categorise or identify with a group or community. In contrast, "the effect of social norms for those who are identified strongly with the group was mediated by the internalisation of the social norms as personal norms" (Wenzel, 2004a, p.224). Hence, in order to understand the role of social norms in enhancing tax compliance level, there is a need to examine the extent to which individuals identify themselves within a group, community or society.

To sum up, strong evidence was provided by these empirical studies on the role of social norms in impacting an individual's compliance level. However, the mechanisms by which these norms impact on tax compliance is still not fully understood which could be due, in part, to different definitions of social norms in various research studies. Therefore, the next section looks to the ethical behaviour literature to provide additional insights into how society impacts an individual's ethical behaviour and also examines how social norms are defined in that field.

Ethical behaviour literature

Most of the theoretical frameworks in the ethical behaviour literature included social norms as one of the key driving factors impacting on the ethical decision-making process. For instance, Trevino (1986) in her person-situation interactionist model, argued that the evaluation stage of the ethical decision making process is moderated by individual and situational factors. She listed social norms under the organisational culture sub-group and claimed that social norms will moderate the relationship between ethical evaluation (cognitions) and actual behaviour. Likewise, Ferrell and Gresham (1985) proposed a contingency framework for ethical decision making in marketing and claimed that an ethical issue or dilemma emerges from the social and cultural environment. They also included social norms (significant others) as one of the main factors that shapes the ethical evaluation stage. Built on the popular theory of reasoned action (Ajzen & Fishbein, 1975), Dubinsky and Loken (1989) developed an alternative ethical decision making model where they devoted great attention to the role of subjective norms (significant others). They hypothesised that significant others will directly impact the intention to engage in ethical/unethical behaviour. They presumed that the perception of the individuals about whether significant others think they should or should not perform the behaviour is important in the process of forming the behavioural intention towards the situation.

Jones (1991) in his significant contribution to the literature on 'moral intensity' clearly included the social context in his model. According to Jones

(1991), the moral imperative to act in an event is related to the degree to which there is social agreement that an action is ethically evil or good, that is 'social consensus'. He also included five other dimensions, namely, magnitude of consequences, probability of effect, temporal immediacy, proximity, and concentration of effect. He emphasised that the combination of these dimensions describe the moral intensity of a particular issue and each of these dimensions would directly impact the ethical decision-making process. Most empirical studies that examined Jones's model claimed that the two dimensions of moral intensity (social consensus and magnitude of consequences) matter more than others when it comes to shaping the ethical decision making process. Jones (1991, p.375) defined social consensus as "The degree of social agreement that a proposed act is evil (or good)". He claimed that the social group or culture shares norms and values which affect the perceptions of the goodness of different behaviours/actions which in turn create an agreement that an action/behaviour is either morally acceptable or unacceptable (Chia and Lim, 2000). A high degree of social agreement would lead to reducing the ambiguity around the concerning issue where the moral agent may otherwise struggle to decide on the ethicality of behaviour. Therefore, a strong social consensus makes the situation more concrete (Harrington, 1997). Furthermore, a strong social consensus against unethical action clarifies the situation for the moral agent to classify the consequence into approved/unapproved categories by the others.

Although Jones (1991, p.375) described the social consensus as social agreement, he never precisely specified what is meant by 'social agreement'. Social agreement can refer to significant others (subjective norms) as other authors mentioned above. Or it could be widened to refer to most people (injunctive norms) or be widened even further to the behaviour of society as a whole (descriptive norms). To accurately measure and understand the social consensus, a precise definition of this concept needs to be provided.

All in all, there are convincing arguments pointing to the importance of social context in shaping an individual's compliance level. However, the explanations of how this context impacts the compliance level were inconsistent through the empirical studies, which could be due to different definitions or operationalisation of social norms in these studies. For instance, some of the studies were examining and demonstrating the effects of 'significant others' on the individual compliance level, while others took a wider definition of social norms as meaning general members of the society. Hence, a precise definition and operationalisation of social norms need to be provided in order to enable researchers to draw conclusions from different studies on how and whether social norms have an impact on an individual's compliance level. Most importantly, the different components of social norms need to be untangled and the effects of each of these components need to be examined.

Social Norms Theory

Cialdini and Trost (1998, p.152) defined social norms as "rules and standards that are understood by members of a group, and that guide and/or constrain social behaviour without the force of law". Elster (1989) argued that social norms need to be distinguished from a number of other norms such as moral norms, legal norms, private norms, habits and compulsive neuroses. Elster built his differentiation on who is enforcing the norms. For instance, unlike social norms, which are enforced by members of the general community, legal norms are enforced by specialists (and it is their duty to do so), and private norms are self-imposed. In contrast to other norms, social norms are externally grounded. Following the same theoretical premises, social norms can also be unpacked into four constructs depending on different general community reference groups. For instance, if we are referring to significant others (people close to the person), this norm can be labelled as subjective norms. If we are referring to most people in the society, the norm can be labelled as injunctive, and descriptive norms refer to the observations of what other people do (behave) in any given situation. On the other hand, personal norms refer to the internalisation of the social norms which makes them an individual's own standards or norms. This segmentation is well discussed in the social norms theory developed by Cialdini and Trost (1998). The definition and the importance of each of these components of social norms are discussed in the following sub-sections.

Descriptive norms

Descriptive norms refer to the perceptions of what others do in a given situation. It stems from the desire to be accurate in personal choices and behaviours by observing how others in society behave in novel or ambiguous situations. In a tax context, taxpayers are likely to base their compliance decisions on the observations of others' behaviour and decide on the most effective course of action when they face a novel, ambiguous, or uncertain tax situation. Under this theoretical premise, the descriptive norms are theoretically deemed to have effects on the individual compliance level. Specifically, if the tax situation is viewed as an ambiguous or novel one, then the descriptive norms (what others do in this situation) will matter more. In addition, if the evasion or compliance is performed by someone of a high moral character, the individuals will be more tempted to behave similarly (as discussed earlier). Some empirical studies such as Cialdini (2007); Bobek et al. (2013); and Scholz and Pinney (1995) provided evidence on the role of descriptive norms in shaping the individual compliance level.

Injunctive norms

Injunctive norms refer to the perception of what most people in society think others should or should not do in a given situation. It can be considered as the moral rules of the majority of society members which dictate what should be done (what is approved or disapproved) in a given situation. It stems from the desire of building and maintaining social relationships as well as conforming to the societal norms. In the tax context, taxpayers are likely to conform to societal norms around the tax situation to avoid social stigma or to gain social rewards. These norms might be more powerful when they are made salient. There is empirical evidence to support the positive relationship between injunctive norms and individual tax compliance level (Bobek et al., 2007; Cialdini, 2007; Wenzel, 2004b; Wenzel, 2004a).

Subjective norms

Subjective norms refer to the perception of what those significant others (e.g., friends, family, co-workers ... etc.) think that a person should or should not do in a given situation. It is similar to the injunctive norms; however, it refers more to the norms around the significant others or referent others. The significant others are likely to impact the feeling of guilt and shame. In particular, conformity is more likely among these significant others. In the tax context, taxpayers are likely to share their tax compliance choices with the important others to seek conformity and support. Most empirical studies in tax compliance literature devote greater attention to the subjective norms compared to the other two norms (descriptive and injunctive norms). These studies found a significant relationship between the subjective norms and tax compliance intention stage, with some empirical studies basing their approach on the theory of reasoned action (Bobek & Hatfield, 2003; Langham et al., 2012; Wenzel, 2005).

Personal norms

Personal norms are self-based values and standards that stem from internalisation of social norms. Wenzel (2004a) referred to personal norms as the individual's own injunctive norms. He argued that personal norms need to be understood as a dynamic concept and this concept is highly correlated with social norms and the exterior world. He added that studies which investigate the effect of personal norms on tax compliance may fail to distinguish between the personal and social norms which would underestimate the role of social norms in tax compliance generally and in tax morale in particular. So, due to the overlap of personal and social norms and based on theory of social norms, personal norms can be categorised as one of the four components of social norms. Cialdini and Trost (1998) showed in his social norms theory that social norms can be unpacked into four components: personal, subjective, injunctive, and descriptive norms. Furthermore, Wenzel (2004a, p.214) stressed that: "Personal tax norms are certainly to a large part based on processes of social learning and absorption from the environment and thus have a social basis". Hence, all studies that are concerned with or aim to examine tax compliance and the role of social and personal norms need to take into account that these concepts can be part of one construct or at least that they are very highly correlated.

Specific and general social norms

Generally, when it comes to measuring social norms, most of the studies in tax compliance fail to distinguish between general social norms (towards a general aspect of tax system) and specific social norms (toward a specific tax situation). The two types of social norms are theoretically different. For instance, Jones (1991) claimed that specific social norms toward the specific situation (he labelled it as 'social consensus') described one of the dimensions of moral intensity which theoretically and empirically has a significant impact on the decision-making process toward this issue or situation. In contrast, Ferrell and Gresham (1985) acknowledged that ethical issues emerge from a social and cultural context (general social norms) and they did include another type of social norms (specific social norms) in their model (a model that demonstrates the ethical decision making process) and claimed that these specific social norms (subjective norms) are likely to impact the decision making of the moral agent. Therefore, social norms can be separated into two types: general and specific. General social norms refer to those that are concerned with a general aspect of the situation (for example, in a tax context, underreporting income tax). Whereas, specific social norms refer to those that are concerning with a specific issue or situation (for example, in a tax context, underreporting a certain amount of income such as tips.)

There has been a call in the tax compliance literature for studies to examine the attitudes and norms around the specific issue rather than (or in addition to) general attitudes and norms. For example, Hageman et al. (2011, p.4) state "our findings also emphasize the need to tailor scale items to measure the specific behaviour being examined (as opposed to only measuring general attitudes and beliefs)". Therefore, any conclusions and implications in prior research about the role of social norms in tax compliance which ignored the separation of the social norms into general and specific may be limited or somewhat misdirected.

Summary

Building on social norms theory and empirical evidence from tax compliance and ethical behaviour literature, social norms are explored and a more comprehensive definition and segmentation of social norms are proposed. More effective approaches to study the role of social norms in enhancing the individual tax compliance level were also recommended. Social norms need to be differentiated into general social norms and specific social norms (social consensus). Each of these two types has its unique impact on the decisions around tax compliance. For instance, social consensus could have a direct impact on the intention to comply with the tax system, whereas general social norms would have an overall effect on the perception of the tax compliance situation and classification of this situation into an ethical or unethical situation (approved or disapproved by society).

Also, social norms need to be unpacked into four components which are highly inter-correlated. These four components are: personal norms, subjective norms, injunctive norms, and descriptive norms. Each component would have its own effects on how taxpayers perceive and act when they face a tax situation. For instance, the descriptive norms in a given society could be against tax compliance, whilst the subjective norms (the significant people around the person) could favour tax compliance, which would put more pressure on the taxpayer to be compliant. Hence, unpacking social norms into these four components will help to better understand the relative effect of each component on tax compliance and will enable an understanding of the complex relationship between social norms and tax compliance decisions at an individual level.

This chapter provides a direction for future tax compliance research which should examine the role of social norms in tax compliance decisions. There is a need to better understand why and how these social norms impact on tax compliance levels. Social norms have a potentially powerful role to play as a complementary system to the enforcement tools and formal/

informal sanction system traditionally employed by tax authorities. Future research should consider the complexity of the effect of social norms on tax compliance decisions as this effect could be mediated by personal norms as mentioned earlier.

In summary, this chapter provided an understanding of the definition and the potential role of social norms (unpacked into its different components) on the tax compliance level of individuals. Also, the important distinction between general social norms and specific social norms (social consensus) was made explicit. Finally, the chapter called for further research on tax compliance which draws on the theory of social norms.

References

Ajzen, I. & Fishbein, M. (1975). *Belief, Attitude, Intention and Behavior: An introduction to theory and research.* Reading, MA: Addison-Wesley.

Alm, J. (1991). A perspective on the experimental analysis of taxpayer reporting. *The Accounting Review,* **66,** 577-593.

Blanthorne, C. & Kaplan, S. (2008). An egocentric model of the relations among the opportunity to underreport, social norms, ethical beliefs, and underreporting behavior. *Accounting, Organizations and Society,* **33,** 684-703.

Bobek, D., Hageman, A. & Kelliher, C. (2013). Analyzing the role of social norms in tax compliance behavior. *Journal of Business Ethics,* 115, 451-468.

Bobek, D., Roberts, R. & Sweeney, J. (2007). The social norms of tax compliance: Evidence from Australia, Singapore, and the United States. *Journal of Business Ethics,* **74,** 49-64.

Bobek, D. D. & Hatfield, R. C. (2003). An Investigation of the theory of planned behavior and the role of moral obligation in tax compliance. *Behavioral Research in Accounting,* **15,** 13-38.

Chia, A. & Lim, M. (2000). The effects of issue characteristics on the recognition of moral Issues. *Journal of Business Ethics,* **27,** 255-269.

Cialdini, R. (2007). Descriptive social norms as underappreciated sources of social control. *Psychometrika,* **72,** 263-268.

Cialdini, R. B. & Trost, M. R. (1998). Social influence: Social norms, conformity and compliance. In D. T. Gilbert, S. T. Fiske & G. Lindzey (Eds.), *The Handbook of Social Psychology* (pp.151-192). New York, NY, US: McGraw-Hill.

Cooter, R. D. (1988). Expressive law and economics. *Journal of Legal Studies,* **27,** 585-607.

Cummings, R. G., Martinez-Vazquez, J., McKee, M. & Torgler, B. (2009). Tax morale affects tax compliance: Evidence from surveys and an artefactual field experiment. *Journal of Economic Behavior and Organization,* **70,** 447-457.

Davis, J. S., Hecht, G. & Perkins, J. D. (2003). Social behaviors, enforcement, and tax compliance dynamics. *The Accounting Review*, **78**, 39-69.

Dubinsky, A. J. & Loken, B. (1989). Analyzing ethical decision making in marketing. *Journal of Business Research*, **19**, 83-107.

Elster, J. (1989). Social norms and economic theory. *The Journal of Economic Perspectives*, **3**, 99-117.

Feld, L. P. & Frey, B. S. (2007). Tax compliance as the result of a psychological tax contract: the role of incentives and responsive regulation. *Law & Policy*, **29**, 102-120.

Ferrell, O. C. & Gresham, L. G. (1985). A contingency framework for understanding ethical decision making in marketing. *Journal of Marketing*, **49**, 87-96.

Frey, B. & Feld, L. (2002). Deterrence and morale in taxation: An empirical analysis. *CESifo Working Paper Series No. 760*.

Frey, B. S. & Torgler, B. (2007). Tax morale and conditional cooperation. *Journal of Comparative Economics*, **35**(1), 136–159.

Gordon, J. P. P. (1989). Individual morality and reputation costs as deterrents to tax evasion. *European Economic Review*, **33**, 797-805.

Hageman, A. M., Kelliher, C. F. & Bobek, D. D. (2011). The social norms of tax compliance: scale development, social desirability, and presentation effects, in *Advances in Accounting Behavioral Research, Vol 14*, Emerald Group Publishing Limited, pp.37-66.

Harrington, S. J. (1997). A test of a person – issue contingent model of ethical decision making in organizations. *Journal of Business Ethics*, **16**, 363-375.

Jon, S. D., Hecht, G. & Jon, D. P. (2003). Social behaviors, enforcement, and tax compliance dynamics. *The Accounting Review*, 78, 39-69.

Jones, T. M. (1991). Ethical decision making by individuals in organizations: An issue-contingent model. *Academy of Management Review*, 366-395.

Kaplan, S. E. & Reckers, P. M. J. (1985). A study of tax evasion judgments. *National Tax Journal*, **38**, 97-102.

Langham, J. A., Paulsen, N. & Hartel, C. E. J. (2012). Improving tax compliance strategies: Can the theory of planned behaviour predict business compliance? 10, 364-402.

McKerchar, M; Bloomquist K. & Pope, J. (2013). Indicators of tax morale: an exploratory study. *eJournal of Tax Research*, **11**, 5-22.

McAdams, R. H. (1997). The origin, development, and regulation of norms, *Michigan Law Review*, **96**, 338.

Montada, L. & Lerner, M. J. (1998). *Responses to Victimization and Belief in a Just World*, New York, Springer.

Orviska, M. & Hudson, J. (2003). Tax evasion, civic duty and the law abiding citizen. *European Journal of Political Economy,* **19,** 83-102.

Polinsky, A. M. & Shavell, S. (2000). The economic theory of public enforcement of law. *Journal of Economic Literature,* **38,** 45-76.

Sandmo, A. (2005). The theory of tax evasion: a retrospective view. *National Tax Journal,* **58,** 643-663.

Scholz, J. T., McGraw, K. M. & Steenbergen, M. R. (1992). Will taxpayers ever like taxes?: Responses to the U.S. Tax Reform Act of 1986. *Journal of Economic Psychology,* **13,** 625-656.

Scholz, J. T. & Pinney, N. (1995). Duty, fear, and tax compliance: the heuristic basis of citizenship behavior. *American Journal of Political Science,* **39,** 490-512.

Spicer, M. W. & Becker, L. A. (1980). Fiscal inequity and tax evasion: an experimental approach. *National Tax Journal,* **33,** 171-175.

Torgler, B. (2002). Speaking to theorists and searching for facts: tax morale and tax compliance in experiments. *Journal of Economic Surveys,* **16,** 657-683.

Torgler, B. (2003). To evade taxes or not to evade: that is the question. *The Journal of Socio-Economics,* **32,** 283-302.

Torgler, B. (2004). Tax morale in Asian countries. *Journal of Asian Economics,* **15,** 237-266.

Torgler, B. (2006). The importance of faith: Tax morale and religiosity. *Journal of Economic Behavior and Organization,* **61,** 81-109.

Torgler, B. (2007). *Tax Compliance and Tax Morale: A Theoretical and Empirical Analysis,* Edward Elgar.

Torgler, B. (2008). What do we know about tax fraud? an overview of recent developments. *Social Research,* **75,** 1239-1270.

Torgler, B. & Schneider, F. (2007). What shapes attitudes toward paying taxes? evidence from multicultural European countries. *Social Science Quarterly,* **88,** 443-470.

Torgler, B. & Schneider, F. (2009). The impact of tax morale and institutional quality on the shadow economy. *Journal of Economic Psychology,* **30,** 228-245.

Trevino, L. K. (1986). Ethical decision making in organizations: a person-situation interactionist model. *The Academy of Management Review,* **11,** 601-617.

Tyler, T. R. (1990). *Why People Obey the Law: Procedural justice, legitimacy, and compliance.* New Haven, CT: Yale University Press.

Wenzel, M. (2004a). An analysis of norm processes in tax compliance. *Journal of Economic Psychology,* **25,** 213-228.

Wenzel, M. (2004b). The social side of sanctions: personal and social norms as moderators of deterrence. *Law & Human Behavior (Springer Science & Business Media B.V.),* **28,** 547-567.

Wenzel, M. (2005). Misperceptions of social norms about tax compliance: From theory to intervention. *Journal of Economic Psychology*, **26**, 862-883.

Wenzel, M. (2007). The multiplicity of taxpayer identities and their implications for tax ethics. *Law & Policy*, **29**, 31-50.

8 Tax and Social Policy: The Case of the Irish Pension System

Dinali Wijeratne, Emer Mulligan and Michelle Maher

Abstract

This chapter employs the Irish pension system as a case study through which to examine the relationship between taxation and social policy. It describes the Irish pension system, discusses different pillars of the system with reference to coverage, benefits and financing of each, and reviews the gendered impact of the current pensions system. The trajectory of reform in Irish pensions is outlined and reflects a move towards encouraging individual responsibility for income security in old age via private saving. Current drivers of reform, such as sustainability, coverage, the European Union, as well as concerns over security of income are discussed. The recent consideration of the rate of income tax reliefs for incentivising retirement saving is also addressed. Overall this chapter examines the interface between tax and pensions, setting a foundation for further study in this area, and specifically highlights the need to evaluate the appropriateness, role and effectiveness of tax incentives as used in the pension's context.

Keywords: Pension reform in Ireland; reform drivers; sustainability; coverage; gender; European Union; pension policy; pensions and taxation

Introduction

Taxation and social policy are inextricably linked, and recognition of this enhances the study of both. As Boden observes, taxation represents one of the major tools directly or indirectly deployed by governments in the implementation of social policies (2004, p.107). A major area of social policy in most countries is its pension system. This is because it affects all residents of a country whether as current or future contributors to, and beneficiaries of, the system. In most countries with a developed pension system, it consumes a significant portion of a country's welfare spending resources[1]. As taxation is the primary means of raising resources for social spending,

---
1   The average social spending across the OECD is 21 per cent of GDP, of which pensions is 7.9 per cent (OECD, 2016).

the relationship between taxation and pensions raises interesting questions for policy makers. On one hand, the cost of public pensions, as well as the cost of subsidising private pensions by way of tax reliefs, brings economic concerns to the fore. On the other hand, tax reliefs are arguably central to promoting wider coverage of private pensions – a regular policy prescription for addressing pension adequacy concerns as well as averting a future over-reliance on public pensions. The first section of this chapter reviews the Irish pension system and its trajectory of reform in terms of pension pillars and gender related matters. This is followed by a section which provides a brief history of pension reform in Ireland, and deals with specific drivers of reform, namely, sustainability, coverage, the European Union's role, and security of income in old age. The direct interface of taxation and pensions, by way of tax relief for pension contributions, is then addressed before making some concluding remarks. The aim of this chapter is to employ the Irish pension system as a case study of how taxation and social policy are interlinked, and set the stage for future research in this area, to include evaluating the appropriateness, role, and effectiveness of tax reliefs as used in the pension's context.

The Irish Pension System

The Irish pension system is classified in pension system typologies as a first generation multi-pillar system (Natali, 2008, p.73). This designation categorises Ireland's system as one with a long-standing role for private pensions within the overall design. The pension system in Ireland began with the United Kingdom's Old Age Pensions Act of 1908 which introduced a state flat-rate means-tested pension payable from age seventy. In 1960, in line with the post-war trend across Europe for welfare state expansion, Ireland's state pension was structurally augmented with the introduction of a mandatory contributory pension. This too was, and remains, a flat-rate pension, which is paid to all insured workers who satisfy the social insurance contribution criteria. The original flat rate means-tested pension is retained as a safety net for those without adequate social insurance contributions.

Individuals who wish to supplement their state pension, and who are in a position to save, can do so through a pillar two occupational pension or a pillar three personal pension. These pillars are voluntary, although some employers make membership a condition of employment, e.g. in the public service. The main design features of the Irish pension system are summarised in Table 8.1.

Table 8.1: The Irish Pension System

	Pillar One	Pillar Two	Pillar Three
Coverage	Mandatory social protection public pensions for the entire workforce	Voluntary occupational pensions sponsored by employer	Voluntary individual private pensions. The two main types are retirement annuity contracts (RACs) and personal retirement savings accounts (PRSAs).
Benefits	Flat rate pension based on social insurance contribution record. Means-tested alternative for those with insufficient contributions.	Were defined benefit but increasingly switching to defined contribution (except in the public sector which remains defined benefit [1]	Defined contribution.
Financing	PAYG principle [2]. Social insurance contributions paid into the social insurance fund	Predominantly funded, the exception being public sector pensions, which operate on the PAYG principle.	Funded

Pillar one, the state old age pension

A full social insurance contribution record qualifies a worker for the top rate of the state contributory pension and there are bands of reduced pension for those with incomplete records. To qualify for a state contributory pension, an individual must have paid social insurance contributions, referred to in Ireland as pay related social insurance (PRSI). At retirement, the number of accumulated contributions is averaged over an individual's working lifetime, and different flat rate pension amounts are paid depending into which band the average falls. The bands and current pension amounts are set out in Table 8.2 below, as well as the impact of a policy decision in 2012 to increase the average contributions required for the higher bands of payment.

Table 8.2: The current bands and pension amounts. *Source* Bassett (2017, p.14)

Band and annual averaged contribution	Weekly level of payment pre-2012	Post-2012 changes
Average 48+	€230.30 (maximum)	€230.30 (maximum)
Average 40-47		€225.80
Average 30-39	€225.80	€207.00
Average 20-29		€196.00
Average 15-19	€172.70	€150.00
Average 10-14	€115.20	€92.00

The Minister for Social Protection explained the rationale behind the band changes in parliament:

> *The State pension is a very valuable benefit. Therefore, it is important to ensure that those qualifying have made a sustained contribution to the Social Insurance Fund over their working lives. Recent changes to State pension supports the direct link between contributions made and the rate of pension received which underpins State pension policy. By aligning the rate of pension paid with the contribution made ensures that those who contribute more during a working life benefit more in retirement than those with lesser contributions.* (Burton, 2011)

This discourse serves as an example of the overall thrust of pension policy in Ireland towards increasing the work-relatedness of outcomes from the pension system. It also highlights how gender-blind policy making can be in Ireland. Women are over-represented in the lower bands (Bassett, 2017, p.15), and the National Women's Council of Ireland (NWCI) argue that this policy change effectively amounts to a protection of state pensions for men while women suffer severe reductions (NWCI, 2015). Despite the adverse impact of this change on women, researchers have noted how "surprisingly challenging" it has been to ascertain the savings made for the Exchequer, with estimates ranging from €10 million to €45 million (Bassett, 2017, p.15).

Most European pension systems make some allowance for years spent outside the workforce caring for children (as distinct from credits based on maternity leave linked to giving birth or adoption). In Ireland, this happens within pillar one and takes the form of the homemaker's scheme, introduced in 1994. Individuals with prior social insurance contributions, who spend up to 20 years out of the work force caring full time for children up to the age of 12, or an incapacitated adult, can have these periods disregarded when working out the yearly average social insurance contribution for the state contributory pension. The lack of retrospection on introduction means that it benefits current retirees, while ignoring an older cohort of women, some of whom were compelled to leave employment under the pre-1973 marriage bar[2].

The state contributory old age pension is financed by employer, self-employed, and employee PRSI contributions to the Social Insurance Fund. The fund also serves contingencies such as unemployment, maternity, incapacity, illness, and bereavement. There is a subvention from the Exchequer to the fund when there is a gap between income and expenditure. We examine the ongoing sustainability of the social insurance fund in the face of changing demographics as a driver of pension reform later in this chapter.

---

[2] Up until 1972, legislation was in force that required female civil servants to leave state employment upon marriage.

In Ireland, state transfers offer significant social protection for older people, with the exception of the top income quintile. In the 'Celtic Tiger'[3] years the state pension was substantially increased in the annual budget and older people moved from being a category most at risk of poverty to one of the categories least at risk.

The current (January 2016) rate of the contributory state pension is €233.30 per week for a person with a full PRSI record. This equates to 33 per cent of the average weekly wage, and is just shy of the government's target of 35 per cent set in the *National Pensions Framework*[4] (DSFA, 2010). The decision to maintain the rate of state pensions when other welfare benefits were cut during austerity measures post the 2008 financial crisis provided on-going social protection for pensioners.

Pillars two and three, occupational and personal pensions

There is no compulsion for employers to provide a pension for their employees. Neither is it mandatory for the self-employed or individuals to have a private personal pension to supplement their state pension. In a 2015 survey, the Central Statistics Office (CSO) found that 47 per cent of persons in employment had pension coverage. 18 per cent of workers had a personal pension; 98 per cent of these identified as self-employed and assisting relatives (CSO, 2016).

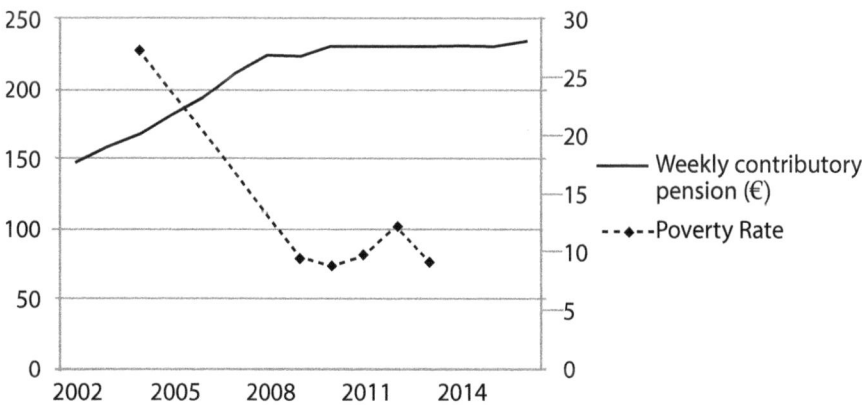

Figure 8.1: Correlation between weekly pension rate and risk of poverty

Source: Department of Social Protection (various years); CSO 2013, 2015

---

3   The Celtic Tiger is a phrase used to capture the period of Ireland's rapid investment growth and high employment growth in the 1990s and into the 2000s.

4   The National Pensions Framework is the most recent policy document on the Irish Pension System. It drew on public debate following the publication of a Green Paper on Pensions in 2007. Published in 2010, circumstances had changed dramatically in Ireland in the interim.

In the private sector, occupational pensions are financed by employer and employee contributions to a pension fund established under trust. Public sector pensions are primarily paid from the Exchequer on a PAYG basis. It is uncommon for employers to contribute to personal pensions, but by law they must facilitate the deduction and submission of pension contributions being made by an employee to a Personal Retirement Savings Account (PRSA). The state makes a substantial contribution to private pensions through tax reliefs in a traditional Exempt Exempt Taxed (EET) approach. Employees get tax relief on contributions at their marginal rate of tax, subject to overall limits. Employer contributions are deductible as a business expense. The investment income and capital gains of pension funds are exempt from tax. Certain lump sums payable on retirement and death are tax-free. Tax is paid on pensions in payment (with state and private pensions being amalgamated for tax calculation purposes). However, the prevalence of tax-free lumps sums, tax relief on contributions at an individual's marginal rate of tax, tax relief on assets, and the lower amount of pension income relative to salary, makes the government tax subsidy unlikely to be recovered in full from tax on pensions in payment. This makes the current system of subsidies via the tax system a valuable incentive to individuals.

Data from the latest *Thematic Report on the Elderly* from the CSO (2013) confirms that the vast majority of pensioners derive most of their income from state transfers. A gender gap is evident in this data as demonstrated in Figure 8.2.

Figure 8.2: Sources of pensioner income by gender
Source: CSO 2013

Elderly males have higher average earnings and occupational pensions than elderly females. In 2011, more than 70 per cent of the gross income for elderly females came from social transfers compared with just over half for elderly males (CSO, 2013, p.4).

Gender and Pensions

Older women having lower income from occupational pensions reflects how a pension system can reproduce gender inequality in the labour market and mitigate against women achieving a decent pension. Unsurprisingly, unpaid caring work and childrearing in particular emerges as the main factor determining the amount of retirement income for women (Ginn, 2004, p.124; Marin, 2010, p.16). In an EU survey which compared the gender gap in pensions of women with children relative to the average for all men, it was confirmed that having children leads to pension disadvantages across Europe. In most cases, the 'children penalty' increases linearly with the number of children (Bettio et al., 2013, pp.60-62). For lone mothers (divorced, never married or widowed) the problem of obtaining affordable childcare is more acute than for married mothers, magnifying the difficulties in reconciling motherhood and employment (Ginn, 2004, p.124). In Ireland, women almost exclusively carry the responsibility for unpaid care work within families. Consequently, it is harder for them to build up adequate contributions in both the public and private pillars of the pension system. Individuals with prior social insurance contributions who subsequently spend up to 20 years out of the work force caring full time for children up to the age of 12, or an incapacitated adult, can have these periods disregarded when working out the yearly average social insurance contribution for a state contributory pension. There is still a requirement to have paid 520 (i.e. ten years) social insurance contributions to qualify for the contributory state pension, which can be difficult for women who are part-time and for those in precarious employment.

Occupational pension coverage for women and men in employment is almost equal with men at 47 per cent and women at 46 per cent (CSO, 2016). Yet this statistic masks an underlying disparity in pension system outcomes. The CSO's 2014 report *Men and Women in Ireland 2013* showed a marked difference in labour force participation between men and women. Overall, fewer women than men participate in the labour force and for those that do, women work fewer hours per week than men. In a pension system with an increasing emphasis on occupational pensions, these statistics identify serious gender implications in the outcomes from the system. Plans to introduce an automatic enrolment system will improve coverage for women who qualify for inclusion, but the positive effect of coverage is likely to be tempered by hours worked and salary scales. Married men work longer in paid employment than married women with 44.1 per cent of married men working 40 hours or more per week compared with 16.8 per cent of married women and 15.2 per cent of widowed or divorced women (CSO, 2014). One example of the potential impact of such disparities is evident in data from the UK where automatic enrolment is in place in the private pillar of their pension system. There, the entry level salary for inclusion in the automatic enrolment system is £10,000 p.a. This threshold excludes 4.6 million workers who earn less than this amount. Of these, 3.4 million (or 74 per cent) are women (TUC, 2016, p.7).

In Ireland, a similar disparity is evident in the statistics for recipients of the state pension. Currently almost twice as many men than women satisfy the requisite number of social insurance contributions to qualify. The statistics for the means-tested alternative is almost exactly reversed, see Figure 8.3 below. This demonstrates that women's unequal participation in the labour market has direct implications for them in retirement.

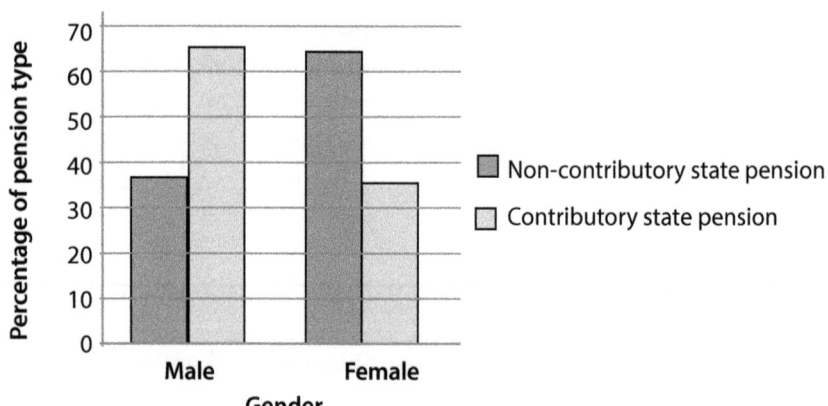

Figure 8.3: State pension recipients by type of pension and gender
Source: Department of Social Protection 2015, p.61

The current state pension recipient statistics strongly suggest that if eligibility for a state pension is a policy consideration, then it should be the opposite of what is currently being considered to include rather than exclude more women.

Pension Reform in Ireland

A brief history

There has been little structural change to the Irish pension system since its inception. For decades, various plans to alter the system have been formulated by the government. These are summarised in Table 8.3.

Table 8.3: The reform trajectory of the Irish pension system 1960-2016

1960s	1970s	1980s	1990s	2000s	2010s
Introduction of Social Insurance	Plans to strengthen Pillar 1	Regulatory concerns	Plans to strengthen Pillar 2, voluntary	National Pensions Framework	Plans to strengthen Pillar 2, mandatory

Source: Maher, 2016

The only real structural change to the Irish pension system happened in 1960 with the introduction of a contributory social insurance pension. During the 1970s in Ireland, pension policy was on a strong trajectory towards further strengthening of the first pillar of the system, with plans to introduce a mandatory earnings related component to the state pension. The economic climate of the early 1980s saw a number of company closures leaving insolvent pension funds in their wake. This drew attention to the lack of any regulation on minimum funding standards for occupational pensions, trustee reporting, or disclosure of information in Ireland. Thus the main focus on pensions in Ireland became directed towards creating an appropriate and effective regulatory environment for private pensions. This culminated in the passing of the 1990 Pensions Act and the creation of the Pensions Board. The Pensions Board largely contained all statutory pension regulation, compliance, and policy advisory functions in a single agency. Up until March 2014 it remained the only institution with statutory responsibility for providing advice to the Minister for Social Protection on all pension matters, either on its own initiative or at the Minister's request.

As part of its 2012 Public Service Reform plan, the government undertook a critical review of the case for integrating the regulatory functions of the Pensions Board with the Central Bank. In recognition of a view in submissions that interests from the pensions industry had become over-represented, the Pensions Board was restructured in 2014 (Government of Ireland, 2013, p.15). Interest group representation was removed from the Board, and it was renamed the Pensions Authority. It retained its regulatory oversight and advisory function. A separate Pensions Council was established to advise on the formulation of pensions policy, and its membership has been constituted to give the pension system a far greater consumer focus (Turner et al., 2015, p.28)

The 1980s also represented a critical juncture in policy terms. With the main focus on the regulatory environment for private pensions, Ireland switched paths to one of shifting responsibility for adequate social protection in old age away from the state. Instead, individuals were encouraged to look to individual market based solutions, with continuing tax relief incentives as outlined earlier. The main policy recommendations in this period emanated from a National Pensions Policy Initiative, which commenced in 1997 (Edmundson et al., 1997). The Initiative's 1998 report Securing Retirement Income endorsed the idea that income adequacy in old age would best be achieved through encouraging private savings. It recommended that a new personal pension instrument be introduced into the Irish system to improve the numbers of those with private pensions, and in response the Personal Retirement Savings Account (PRSA) was launched in May 2003. However PRSAs have proved ineffective at improving coverage, with the Department of Social Protection noting that:

> *Despite the considerable efforts to incentivise participation in supplementary pensions, the marginal changes in coverage over the last 20 years indicates the voluntary approach to participation is not achieving the desired goal in terms of increasing coverage to an appropriate level* (Department of Social Protection, 2015, p.3).

A further review of the system was undertaken in 2007 with the publication of the *Green Paper on Pensions*. This resulted in the 2010 publication of the *National Pensions Framework*. It recommended that an element of compulsion was required to widen coverage of occupational pensions and reduce a future over-reliance on the state. To this end, a Universal Retirement Savings Group was established in February 2015. The group was tasked with bringing forward recommendations in the form of a roadmap and an estimated timeline for the introduction of a universal retirement savings scheme, based on the principles of individualisation of risk in market-based solutions.

Drivers of reform in Ireland

Having provided an overview of the trajectory of reform in Ireland, this section moves to the present day issues. In this section, we identify the four main drivers of reform, viz. sustainability, coverage, the EU's contribution to pension policy-making in Ireland, and income security from old age pensions. Academic literature, social commentators, government bodies and the pensions industry are in agreement that a reform of the pensions system is needed (Murphy and McCashin, 2008; Moloney and Whelan, 2009; Department of Social and Family Affairs, 2010; Milliman, 2015; Irish Association of Pension Funds, 2015; Hughes and Maher, 2016). The dominant narrative constructed within public discourse identifies sustainability of the state pension as the main driver of reform to be addressed through private pension coverage, which in turn will improve overall adequacy of income. Less visible in the debate are inequities in government support for private pensions and the gendered nature of system-generated outcomes as highlighted in this chapter.

Sustainability

Population ageing is the primary concern facing all pension policy-makers in the developed world. While Ireland's population is ageing, it still enjoys very favourable demographics when compared to others in the EU. Eurostat (2016) confirms that Ireland has the highest share of young people (22.1 per cent against an EU28 average of 15.6), and the lowest share of older people (13.0 per cent, compared to 18.9). The fertility rate is 1.94 live births per women, second only to France at 2.01, and well above the average of 1.58 (Eurostat, 2016).

Despite relatively favourable demographics, the Irish population is ageing. This places attention on the ability of the social insurance fund to continue to ance fund from which state contributory pensions are paid produces annual statements and an actuarial review every five years. The latest available actuarial report sets out the position at 31 December 2010 (DSP, 2012, p.1). The fund had an estimated shortfall of expenditure over income at 31st December 2010 of €1.5 billion. Projections estimate the shortfall increasing over the medium to long term, requiring significant exchequer subvention (ibid, p.1). The predominant expenditure from the fund is pension related, and the report expects future demographic developments (an ageing population and increasing pensioner dependency ratio) to exacerbate the funding position (ibid, p.2). Previous reports showed surpluses of €0.5 billion at 31st December 2005 (DSFA, 2007a) and €0.6 billion at 31st December 2000 (DSFA, 2002), but all three reports estimate deficits by mid-century requiring in excess of six per cent of GNP as a subvention to meet commitments. The actuarial valuation at 31st December 2015 has not been published at date of writing (January 2017).

There was a brief attempt to deal with this sustainability challenge and counter the demographic impact on state financing of pensions by creating a quasi-funded approach to future pension liabilities arising from both public sector and state pensions. Following from a recommendation in the National Pensions Policy Initiative (1997-1998), a National Pension Reserve Fund (NPRF) was created in April 2001. Funded from the proceeds of the privatisation of the state's telecommunications company Telecom Éireann, and an ongoing annual contribution of 1 per cent of GDP, the NPRF's aim was to meet state pension liabilities from 2025 onwards (Slattery, 2010). By the end of 2010, the fund held assets to the value of €15.06 billion but the 2008 financial crisis saw the government direct €10 billion of this to the recapitalisation of Allied Irish Bank and Bank of Ireland, and to fund part of Ireland's agreement with the Troika (OECD, 2014, p.70). The remainder is in the process of being transferred to the Ireland Strategic Investment Fund which was established in 2014 to support economic activity and employment.

Alternative ways of addressing sustainability and correcting deficits in the Social Insurance Fund such as increasing pay related social insurance, directly reducing the amount of pensions paid, or redirecting some of the tax subsidies that support the private element of the system, have so far proved politically unpalatable.

Coverage

The key idea informing pension reform in developed countries is to promote retirement saving in private pensions. The government's plan for the future of pensions in Ireland is set out in the *National Pensions Framework* (DSFA, 2010). The report opens on the question of coverage. Policy is framed around a target of having 70 per cent of the working population aged between 30 and 65 making private provision for their retirement (ibid, p.1). This target was established by the National Pensions Policy Initiative in 1998, at which time 46 per cent of persons in employment had pension coverage (defined as an occupational pension, a personal pension, or both – Pensions Board, 1998, p.45). As noted earlier, coverage is currently assessed at 47 per cent, demonstrating that additional private pension vehicles such as the introduction of PRSAs in 2003, and the incentive provided by tax subsidies have not proved effective at increasing coverage on a voluntary basis.

Given that the desired coverage target has not been achieved through private pensions, it is surprising that the government has neglected to thoroughly investigate what value the State is getting for subsidising private pensions through the taxation system. Retaining tax relief on employee contributions at the marginal rate benefits the higher rate tax payer. This was highlighted as problematic by the 2009 Taxation Commission because "it gives the greatest level of support to pension provision to those with the highest level of income while those most in need get the least support" (Department of Finance, 2009, p.387).

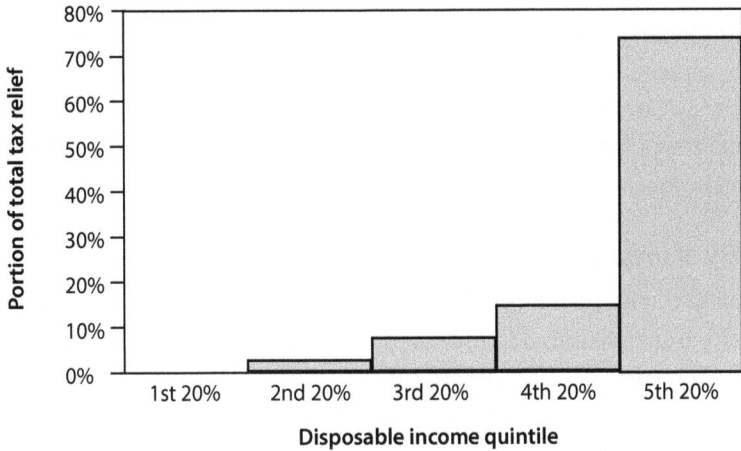

Figure 8.4: Distribution of tax relief on employee and individual contributions by income quintiles (2014). *Source:* Collins and Hughes 2016

The concentration of pension tax reliefs on the highest earners is detailed in Figure 8.4 above. Those outside the tax net do not receive any subsidy towards their pension. A gender breakdown of tax reliefs is not available. However the existence of a well-documented gender pay gap (see for example Dept. of Justice and Equality, 2017) strongly suggests that a gendered analysis of tax relief data would identify an inequitable distribution between men and women.

The European Union and pension policy in Ireland

Largely absent from the narrative on pension policy in Ireland is the role of the European Union as a driver of reform. This absence can possibly be explained by Ireland's well-established multi-pillar system and record of promoting private pensions; a system corresponding to recommendations in the *White Paper on Adequate, Safe and Sustainable Pensions* published by the European Commission in 2012. Having said that, following the 2008 financial crisis, EU attention did focus on Ireland's pension system, as well as that of the other most indebted members of the Eurozone (Matthias and Anderson, 2014, p.320). As part of the austerity measures agreed with the Troika[5] in November 2010, and in line with recommendations in the National Pen-

---

5   A tripartite committee led by the European Commission with the European Central Bank and the International Monetary Fund that oversaw the measures attached to the financial support provided to Ireland in November 2010.

sions Framework (Department of Social and Family Affairs, 2010), the state pension age was increased in 2011. The age at which people will receive their state pension increases to age 67 in 2021 and to age 68 in 2028. This change to the pension system was introduced with relative ease. Justified as one solution for longer-term pension system sustainability, the opportunity for any robust opposition was eclipsed by the unrelenting and multi-dimensional nature of Ireland's financial crisis (Considine, 2012). Later in this chapter we examine the policy position taken on the Troika-required reform of a reduction in tax reliefs for private pensions.

Security of income

Increasing the numbers of individuals with private pensions does not automatically translate into adequate and secure pensions. Since the turn of the century, there has been a marked difference in the financing mechanisms for funded private pensions, with a shift from defined benefit to defined contribution. Defined benefit schemes were once the norm. The switch is associated with the equity holding of Irish pension funds. Up to 2000, most defined pension schemes were in surplus having enjoyed approximately ten years of 14 per cent returns per annum. This allowed employers to take a 'contribution holiday', meaning they were paying little or no contributions. While the dotcom crash of the early 2000s reduced asset values, the Irish economy was mid-Celtic Tiger so employers were in a position to recommence paying, or increase the rate of contributions, and accordingly filed recovery plans with the Pensions Regulator at the Pensions Board. This was the first time that the Pensions Regulator had empirical data relating to the asset allocation of Ireland's pension funds, and it would appear to have sounded alarm bells, prompting the Pension Regulator (Pensions Board CEO, Brendan Kennedy) to comment in his 2006 annual report (published in July 2007).

> *Most defined benefit schemes remain heavily invested in equities...there is risk that poor performance in equity markets would have a significant impact on the funding level of those schemes. It is not clear to the Board that trustees are aware of the investment risks they are taking* (Pensions Board, 2007, p.11).

However, under pension legislation, the Pensions Regulator lacks any power to impose restrictions on trustee decisions, and his warning was largely ignored by those advising trustees.

By 2008, employer contributions were high in order to erase the dotcom deficit, leaving little room in a failing economy to provide any further remedy. In 2007, nearly 73 per cent of DB schemes were adequately funded. In 2008, the second fall in equity markets in a decade had a dramatic impact on Irish pension funds. By 2011 as many as 80 per cent were in deficit, with an estimated aggregate €10 billion shortfall (OECD, 2014). The OECD pointed to Ireland's real losses of 37.5 per cent in 2008 as "the worst investment performance for private pensions in the 30 OECD countries" (OECD, 2009). They cited the reason as being "because of the share of equities in pension fund portfolios: around two-thirds of assets before the crisis hit compared to an average of 36 per cent in the 20 OECD countries where data are available" (ibid.).

Employers unable or unwilling to continue supporting their DB schemes, closed them. Unusually in a European context, Ireland does not have any debt on the employer legislation, meaning that employers were not legally obliged to make good any deficit. In extreme cases, such as Waterford Glass, the double insolvency of both the employer and the pension scheme saw employees entitlements severely curtailed to between 18 and 28 per cent of what they were expecting. This led to a European Court of Justice ruling in 2011, which found that the Irish State was in serious breach of its obligations under article 8 of European Directive 2008/94 which protects employees in the event of insolvency of their employer (ECJ, 2011), and under which the former employees of Waterford Glass received a settlement from the state.

Where employers have continued a pension scheme for employees, it has largely been on a DC basis. The change from DB to DC threatens future replacement ratios, individualises investment risk, and leaves future pension income dependent on the capriciousness of the market (Whelan, 2005, p.9). There is no longer any degree of certainty about the level of retirement income that can be delivered from an occupational pension. Adequacy would not be an issue if employers continued to contribute to defined contribution schemes at the average level required for defined benefit schemes. Data from the pensions industry strongly suggests that this is not the case. The average employer contribution to DC schemes in 2014 was 5.7 per cent of pensionable salaries (IAPF, 2014), compared to the average employer contribution rate to DB schemes prior to the 2008 financial crisis and its impact on funding levels of 16.8 per cent (Mercer, 2006).

Pensions and Taxation

This concluding section returns to the question of taxation. At the interface of pensions and taxation, civil servants are tasked with competing priorities. On one hand, in Ireland the strong policy trajectory since the 1990s has been to encourage private pensions as a way to improve coverage and avert increased reliance on the public pillar. Most income tax systems in OECD countries give preferential treatment to pensions, and tax incentives are intended at least in part to modify pension savings behaviour (Marriott, 2010, p.598). On the other hand, discourse around the cost of employees obtaining tax relief at their marginal rate of income tax has emerged, culminating in the Troika recommending standardisation of tax relief at the lower income tax rate as an austerity measure.

Relief on employee contributions in Ireland has always been at the employee's marginal rate of income tax. The taxation system and pension policy was first formally examined in the 1988 National Pensions Board report on the tax treatment of occupational pension schemes. It concluded that it saw no justification for changing the current tax status for pensions unless it was decided to fundamentally alter the present system by discouraging occupational pension schemes, and providing income related pensions through an extended state scheme (1988, p.60). Neither a further report in 1993 on the future of the Irish pension system, nor the 1997-1998 National Pension Policy Initiative examined the tax spend on the pension system to establish whether it represented the most efficient way of meeting the income requirements of all older people.

In the 1990s the idea of tax reliefs as an incentive to encourage private pension savings was reinforced with the introduction of an increase in the maximum contribution to a pension that could be made with full tax relief. The 1997 Taxes Consolidation Act introduced age related limits to replace a blanket 15 per cent rate.

An innovation, approved retirement funds (ARFs) were introduced to the pension system in 2000 with implications for the taxation of pensions. Those with pillar three personal pensions (subsequently expanded to include PRSAs and AVCs) could transfer money at retirement into an ARF subject to them having an alternative source of income of at least €12,700. Capital gains and investment income in the ARF were not subject to tax. Withdrawals were taxed at the holder's marginal rate of tax. Unlike a conventional pension product, an ARF formed part of the estate on the death of the holder. This meant, for example, that an ARF could transfer to a spouse tax-free. This fundamentally changed personal pensions from being a vehicle for retirement savings into a scheme "for the accumulation of wealth which they could spend or leave as a bequeath to their heirs" (Hughes and Stewart, 2009, p.182).

Table 8.4: Limits on employee contributions

Age	Limit on employee contributions as a per cent of remuneration
Under 30	15
30-39	20
40-49	25
50-54	30
55-59	35
60+	40

Concerns within the Department of Finance prompted the Minister for Finance to instigate a major review of various tax incentive schemes in 2005. In relation to pension tax reliefs the Department of Finance found that two ARFs were valued at over €100 million and a further 6,000 averaged in value at €235,000 each (Department of Finance, 2007). Most ARF owners did not draw down any income. Hughes (2011, p.13) argues this demonstrated that they did not need to rely on the ARF to provide for their post retirement income, meaning they served purely as devices for avoiding tax. In response to such findings, the Department of Finance made a number of changes to taxation policy in the mid-2000s. An annual earnings cap was introduced in the calculation of the maximum employee contribution enjoying tax relief of €254,000 in 2003. In 2005 another cap was introduced on the capital value of a tax relieved pension benefit of €5 million. This second cap is referred to as a standard fund threshold, and was introduced to stem abuse of topping up pension benefits via unlimited employer contributions. The tax avoidance capability of ARFs was curtailed in 2005 by introducing a notional annual distribution of 3 per cent of the ARF's value, taxed at the holders' marginal rate of tax.

The 2007 Green Paper on pensions asked whether the existing structure of tax reliefs provided value for money and drew attention to the vertical inequities of the current system (Department Social and Family Affairs, 2007b, p.107-108). It specifically asked whether tax reliefs should be given at a marginal, standard or hybrid rate (p.118). Three separate reports issued between 2009 and 2010 all took a strong policy position and recommended a single 33 per cent rate of tax relief for employee and self-employed pension contributions. The first was a Taxation Commission report in 2009, followed later that year by the Renewed Programme for Government, and finally the following year the National Pensions Framework.

Coinciding with this policy position on tax relief was the 2008 financial crisis, and the subsequent arrival of the Troika into the pension and taxation policy space. This resulted in three different policy positions being taken in the space of six months in relation to taxation and pensions. The period is summarised as follows.

Table 8.5: Policy positions being taken in the space of six months in relation to taxation and pensions. *Source*: Maher 2016

Date	Event	Tax and pensions policy
24 November 2010	Fianna Fail/Green Party government publish the *National Recovery Plan 2011-2014*	Tax relief on employee contributions will be gradually standardised between 2012 and 2014 (Policy position 1)
28 November 2010	Programme of financial support for Ireland agreed with the EU, the ECB and the IMF	The *Memorandum of Understanding* governing the Troika agreement reiterated that tax relief would be gradually standardised between 2012 and 2014 (reiteration of policy position 1)
7 December 2010	Minister for Finance Brian Lenihan makes Budget speech in the Dail	No adjustment made to tax relief rates. Instead work would be undertaken with stakeholders to develop workable solutions
25 February 2011	General Election	Fine Gael and Labour form a government
6 March 2011	Fine Gael/Labour government publish *Programme for Government 2011-2016*	Declared "we will cap taxpayers' subsidies for all future pension funds for politicians (and indeed everybody) that deliver income in retirement of over €60,000 (Policy position 2)
11 May 2011	Jobs Inititiave launched	To be funded by a third pension fund levy of 0.6 percent of assets for the four years 2011-2014 inclusive (Policy position 3)

Given the government was dealing with a deep and multifaceted crisis, yet was still prepared to listen to alternatives from stakeholders to policy position 1 (in Table 8.5 above) speaks to how well supported the policy position on retaining marginal tax relief on pension contributions is in government. They remained intact, meaning savings had to be made instead by bringing in a complicated addition to the standard fund threshold (policy position two, above) and the imposition of an unpopular levy.

Conclusion

The narrative of pensions and taxation in Ireland is one of a tax system providing the revenue for social assistance pensions, subventions to the social insurance fund, and incentives to private pensions. The Irish pension system has social insurance and assistance pensions at its core, which constitutes the primary source of income for the majority of older people. State pensions are supplemented by private occupational and personal pensions. Recommendations from the Pensions Board over the last quarter of a century have driven policy decisions to focus on expanding the private pillars of the system to meet sustainability concerns. Academic literature, social commentators, government bodies and the pensions industry are in agreement that a reform of the pensions system is needed (Murphy and McCashin, 2008; Moloney and Whelan, 2009; Department of Social and Family Affairs, 2010; Milliman, 2015; Irish Association of Pension Funds, 2015; Hughes and Maher, 2016). The dominant narrative constructed within public discourse identifies sustainability of the state pension as the main driver of reform to be addressed through private pension coverage, which in turn will improve overall adequacy of income. Less visible in the Irish debate also are inequities in government support for private pensions and the gendered nature of system-generated outcomes as highlighted in this chapter. The long-standing system of tax reliefs has been shown to be inequitably distributed, and provide no assistance towards retirement savings for those outside the tax net. In providing an account of the primary interface of pensions and taxation in the area of incentives to promote private savings, this chapter provides a foundation for future research to evaluate the appropriateness, role, and effectiveness of tax reliefs as used in the pension's context.

Acknowledgements

This work is carried out through the H2020 FairTax project funded by the European Commission. We are grateful for comments and suggestions from the audience following our presentation at Tax Research Network 25th Annual Conference in Roehampton, London, UK.

References

Bassett, M. (2017). *Towards a Fair State Pension for Women Pensioners*. Dublin: Age Action.

Bettio, F., Tinios, P. & Betti, G. (2013). *The Gender Gap in Pensions in the EU*. Luxembourg: European Commission, Directorate-General for Justice.

Boden, R. (2004). Taxation Research as Social Policy Research. In M. Lamb, A. Lymer, and J. Freedman (Eds.) *Taxation: An Interdisciplinary Approach to Research.* Oxford: Oxford University Press.

Burton, J. (2011). Statement by Minister for Social Protection Joan Burton TD, Social Protection Budget' Dáil Éireann, 5 December. Retrieved from http://www.welfare.ie/en/pressoffice/Pages/Statement-by-Minister-for-Social-Protection-Joan-Burton-T.D.aspx

Central Statistics Office. (2013). *Survey on Income and Living Conditions. Thematic Report on the Elderly 2004, 2009, 2010 (Revised),* and 2012. Dublin: CSO.

Central Statistics Office. (2014). *Women and Men in Ireland 2013.* Dublin: CSO

Central Statistics Office. (2015). *Survey on Income and Living Conditions. 2013 Results.* Dublin: CSO.

Central Statistics Office. (2016). *Quarterly National Household Survey: Pension Provision Quarter 4 2015.* Dublin: CSO.

Collins, M. & Hughes, G. (2016). *Tax Expenditure on Occupational Pensions in Ireland, Cost and Distribution.* Nevin Economic Research Institute Seminar. Dublin, 28th September.

Considine, M. (2012). Increasing the State Pension Qualification Age, Pension System Reform and the Impact of Austerity: Ireland in Context. *Paper presented at the ESPAnet Conference, 6th-8th September 2012, University of Edinburgh.*

Department of Finance. (2007). *Budget 2006 - Review of Tax Schemes,* Dublin: Department of Finance

Department of Finance. (2009). *Commission on Taxation Report.* Dublin: Department of Finance.

Department of Justice and Equality. (2017). *National Strategy for Women and Girls 2017-2020: Creating a better Society for All.* Dublin: Department of Justice and Equality.

Department of Social and Family Affairs. (2002). *Actuarial Review of the Financial Condition of the Social Insurance Fund.* Dublin: Stationary Office.

Department of Social and Family Affairs. (2007a). *Actuarial Review of the Social Insurance Fund as at 31 December 2005.* Undertaken by Mercer Human Resource Consulting. Dublin: Stationary Office.

Department of Social and Family Affairs. (2007b). *Green Paper on Pensions.* Dublin: Stationary Office.

Department of Social and Family Affairs. (2010). *National Pensions Framework.* Dublin: Stationary Office.

Department of Social Protection. (2012). *Actuarial Review of the Social Insurance Fund 31 December 2010,* Undertaken by KPMG. Dublin: Stationary Office.

Department of Social Protection. (2015). *Statistical Information on Social Welfare Services 2014*. Retrieved from http://www.welfare.ie/en/Pages/Annual-SWS-Statistical-Information-Report-2014.aspx.

European Commission. (2012). *White Paper. An Agenda for Adequate safe and Sustainable Pensions*. Luxembourg: Office for Official Publications of the European Communities.

European Court of Justice. (2011). *Judgement in Case C-398/11Congress*. Retrieved from http://curia.europa.eu/juris/document/document.jsf?docid=136782&doclang=EN.

Eurostat. (2016). *Key Figures in Europe 2016 Edition*. Luxembourg: Publications Office of the European Union.

Government of Ireland. (2013). *The Public Service Reform Plan Critical Review. Integration of the Regulatory Function of the Pensions Board with the Central Bank and Amalgamation of the Pensions Ombudsman with the Financial Services Ombudsman*. Retrieved from https://www.welfare.ie/en/pressoffice/ Cheltenham: Edward Elgar Publishing. pdf/Report-of-the-Critical-Review.pdf.

Ginn, J. (2004). European Pension Privatisation: Taking Account of Gender. *Social Policy and Society*, **3**(2), 123-134.

Hughes G. & Stewart, J. (2009). Conflicting Objectives in Personal Pension Provision and Personal Savings in Ireland. In J. Stewart & G Hughes (Eds.) *Personal Provision of Retirement Income. Meeting the Needs of Older People?* Cheltenham: Edward Elgar Publishing

Hughes, G. (2011). *Executive Directors' and Employees Pensions: A Level Playing Field? Pension Policy Research Group Working Papers*. Dublin, Trinity College.

Hughes, G. & Maher, M. (2016). Redistribution in the Irish Pension System: Upside down? In M. Murphy & F. Dukelow (Eds) *The Irish Welfare State in the Twenty-First Century. Challenges and Change*. Basingstoke: Palgrave Macmillan.

Irish Association of Pension Funds. (2015). *IAPF Submission on a Universal Retirement Savings Scheme*. Dublin: IAPF.

Irsih Association of Pension Funds (2014) *DC Contribution Survey*, Dublin:IAPF

Maher, M. (2016). *The Politics of Pensions in Ireland*. Unpublished PhD Thesis, Maynooth University. Retrieved from http://eprints.maynoothuniversity.ie/8781/

Marin, B. (2010). General Trends in Pension Reform around the Millennium and Their Impact on Women. In B. Marin and E. Zolyomi (Eds.) *Women's Work and Pensions: What Is Good, What Is Best?* London: Ashgate.

Marriott, L. (2010). Power and Ideas: The Development of Retirement Savings Taxation in Australasia. *Critical Perspectives on Accounting*, **21**, 597-610.

Matthias, S. & Anderson, K. (2014). Pension Reform in the European Periphery: The Role of EU Reform and Advocacy. *Public Administration and Development*, **34**,320-31.

Mercer. (2006). *Defined Benefit Survey 2006*. Dublin: Mercer.

Milliman (2015). *Research Report on the Financial Sustainability of the State Pension in Ireland*: Prepared for the Society of Actuaries in Ireland and Publicpolicy.ie. Retrieved from https://web.actuaries.ie.

Moloney, M. & Whelan, S. (2009). Pension Insecurity in Ireland. *Journal of the Statistical and Social Inquiry Society of Ireland*, **38**, 75-104.

Murphy, M. & McCashin, A. (2008). *Pensions: What Women Want. A Model of Pensions That Guarantees Independence*. Dublin: NWCI.

Natali, D. (2008). Pensions in Europe, European Pensions. The Evolution of Pension Policy at National and Supranational Level. Brussels: P.I.E. Peter Lang.

National Pensions Board. (1988). Report on the Tax Treatment of Occupational Pension Schemes. Dublin: Stationary Office

National Women's Council of Ireland. (2015). *Submission to Public Consultation on a Universal Supplementary Retirement Savings Scheme*. Dublin: NWCI.

OECD. (2009). *Ireland. Highlights from OECD Pensions at a Glance*. Paris: OECD.

OECD. (2014). *OECD Reviews of Pension Systems: Ireland*. Paris: OECD

OECD. (2016). *Social Spending Update*. Paris: OECD

Edmondson, J., Ireland. Department of Social Welfare, Pensions Board, & Davy Kelleher McCarthy Ltd. (1997). *National pensions policy initiative : Consultation document*. Dublin: Pensions Board.

Pensions Board. (1998). *Securing Retirement Income. National Pensions Policy Initiative*. Dublin: Pensions Board.

Pensions Board. (2007) Annual Report, 2006, National Pensions Authority, Dublin: Stationary Office.

Slattery, L. (2010). The National Pensions Reserve Fund: An Obituary. *Irish Times*, November, 30.

Trade Union Congress. (2016). *Unfinished Business: Building a Fresh Consensus on Workplace Pensions*. London: TUC

Turner, J, Hughes G. & Maher, M (2015). The Economics of Complexity in the Allocation of Governmental Authority for Pensions. *Journal of Economics and Management*, **21**(3), 21-34.

Whelan, S. (2005). *Pension Provision in Ireland for 21st Century. Report prepared for the IAPF*. Retrieved from http://citeseerx.ist.psu.edu/viewdoc/download?-doi=10.1.1.495.1532&rep=rep1&type=pdf.

9

The EU Notion of Abuse of Law and the Italian Tax Legal System: Towards an Enhanced Horizontal Interaction among National GAARs?

Daniele de Carolis

Abstract

In the preface to the seminal book "Prohibition of Abuse of Law – A New General Principle of EU Law?"[1] Prof de la Feria relies on the metaphor of 'reverberation' in order to account for the creation and development of an EU principle of abuse of law and its impact on the different Member States' national legal systems. Building on this idea, this paper shows how the reverberation metaphor can effectively be used to explain the impact of the EU notion of abuse of law on the Italian tax legal system and the horizontal interaction of this latter system with other Member States' legislations. The first section of the paper illustrates the main features of the reverberation process; the second examines the impact of this process on the Italian tax legal system, with particular reference to the process of the codification of a national GAAR; finally, the third section attempts a comparison between Italian and English anti-abuse provisions to demonstrate an example of possible horizontal interaction between the two national systems.

The 'Reverberation Effect' of the EU Principle of Abuse of Law

The existence of an EU principle of abuse of law, along with the definition of its content and impact on the different Member States' national systems, is arguably one of the most disputed topics among EU lawyers. Yet, this topic has become popular among scholars only relatively recently: although the EU Court has been relying on the notion of abuse of law since the mid 1970s, for a long time the contours of these references were extremely vague and academic attention to this issue was scarce. The situation changed when the EU Court elaborated a clear notion of abuse of law in the Emsland-Starke decision, which was further refined in Halifax decision. In particular, the

---

1   de la Feria, R. & Vogenauer, S. (eds.), (2011), *Prohibition of Abuse of Law. A New General Principle of EU law?*, Oxford, Hart Publishing

latter decision incited an intense debate among tax experts about the meaning of the newly designated principle of abuse of law and the definition of its scope, with particular reference to its possible application to other areas of tax law beyond VAT taxation.

Probably the best synthesis of this debate is found in the volume edited by Professors Rita de la Feria and Stefan Vogenauer "Prohibition of Abuse of Law – A New General Principle of EU Law?". In the preface to this important book[2], Prof de la Feria relies on the metaphor of "reverberation" in order to account for the creation and development of an EU principle of abuse of law and its impact on the different Member States' national legal systems. The reverberation process described by Prof de la Feria encompasses three stages. In the first – the pre-cognisance stage – similar principles of abuse of law existed within the legal systems of many Member States: at their core, they expressed the same content, but their particular characteristics, such as scope and criteria for application, differed from Member State to Member State. Relying on these discrepancies, the Court was able to slowly elaborate, at the end of the cognisance phase, an autonomous concept of abuse of law epitomised in the two decisions, Emsland-Starke and Halifax. In the cognisance phase, the Court made repeated references to the notion of abuse of law in response to preliminary rulings by national courts. Nonetheless, at the early stage of this phase, the notion of abuse adopted by the Court was quite vague on account of the discrepancies among the different Member States' legal systems as to the scope, content and criteria for application of this notion. Then, with the Halifax decision in 2006, the Court was able to define an autonomous principle of abuse of law with an EU-specific meaning, scope and criteria for application, albeit initially limited to the area of VAT. The subsequent phase – the post cognisance phase – has produced the full reverberation effect, i.e. an intense interaction between levels and legal operators, both in vertical (between the EU Court, national courts, and legislatures of the Member States) and horizontal (between courts and legislatures of different Member States) directions. The application of the principle of abuse of law has quickly been extended by the EU Court to many other sectors of European Law beyond VAT and taxation, such as company law, free movement of goods, recognition of professional qualifications, competition, social policy and agricultural policy. Legal commentators have increased their attention to the issue of abuse of law broadly debating the legal nature, scope and content of the principle; national courts have started to apply the

---

2   de la Feria R. (2011), Introducing the Principle of Prohibition of Abuse of Law, in de la Feria R. & Vogenauer S. (eds.), *Prohibition of Abuse of Law*, cit., pp. XX ff.

EU notion of abuse of law to purely domestic situations; national legislation and case law has been emended as a result of the EU Court's decisions on abuse of law. As the principle of abuse of law is increasingly invoked across a greater diversity of contexts, the process of reverberation, in its post-cognisance stage, continues, so that many are of the opinion that it has developed into a fully-fledged general principle of EU law.

The "Reverberation Effect" in Italian Tax Law

This paper argues that the reverberation effect of the EU principle of abuse of law has been – and continues to be – especially strong in the Italian tax legal system. In particular, the progressive development of an EU-specific concept of abuse of law has prompted a close interaction between the EU Court and EU institutions on the one hand, and the Italian courts, legislature and academic tax community on the other. The main outcome of this interaction has been a fundamental amendment in Italian tax law: the codification of a written general anti-abuse clause (GAAR) in Italian legislation.

Until 2015, the Italian tax legal system had never envisaged a general provision forbidding abuse of law. For many years, the Italian tax legislature tackled the issue of abuse of law by introducing into the system special provisions which forbade specific cases of abuse of law. The main flaw with these special anti-abuse provisions was that, by addressing only specific transactions, they became outdated very quickly once tax planning practice developed new abusive behaviours not envisaged by these provisions[3]. In other words, given their specific content, the anti-abuse rules were unable to capture new abusive actions as they emerged in tax practice. In 1997, the legislature attempted to react to this situation by introducing a semi-general anti-abuse clause[4] providing, on the one hand, a general definition of abuse of law, which considered as abusive those behaviours devoid of valid economic basis aimed at circumventing tax legislation and obtaining an undue tax benefit or saving; but on the other hand limiting its application only to income taxes and, within this restricted domain, only to the specific transactions listed therein. Obviously, this semi-general anti-abuse clause paid lip service to the goal of overcoming the deficiencies related to the existence of many specific anti-abuse provisions in the Italian tax system; however, since its application was limited only to specific transactions, taxpayers were still free to carry out abusive practices which did not fall into the specific trans-

---

3   Gallo, F., (2015), La Nuova Frontiera dell'Abuso del Diritto in Materia Fiscale, *Rassegna Tributaria*, **6**, p.1315.

4   Article 37bis Presidential Decree no. 600 of 29 September 1973

actions listed, even though these behaviours met all the requirements envisaged in the general definition provided in the clause (behaviours devoid of valid economic basis aimed at circumventing tax legislation and obtaining an undue tax benefit or saving).

The publication of the Halifax decision in 2006 exerted a determinant reverberation effect in Italian tax law: the vertical interaction between the EU Court and the Italian Court of Cassation made possible, in a relatively short time-span, what had been impossible for many years in the Italian Parliament; namely the elaboration, initially via case law, of a domestic general principle of abuse of law in the Italian tax system. Immediately after Halifax, the Italian Supreme Court developed, in a series of decisions rendered between 2006 and 2008, a general anti-abuse principle applicable also to purely domestic situations and in all areas of taxation. In this first round of decisions, the Italian Court identified as basis for the domestic GAAR the EU principle of abuse of law. The Court held that, even though this principle had been elaborated by the EU Court in a domain – indirect taxation – falling within its competence, whereas direct taxation was left to Member States' jurisdiction, the notion of abuse of law amounted nonetheless to an interpreting criterion of the whole system[5]. Therefore, Member States should exert their exclusive jurisdiction in direct taxation in accordance with the fundamental principles and freedoms embedded in the EU Treaty, and abuse of law featured among those principles.

As to the content of the domestic anti-abuse clause, the Court initially adopted a very broad definition, considering as abusive those transactions aimed at obtaining any tax benefit or saving in the absence of clear and significant economic reasons for carrying it out. The first series of decisions stimulated wide debate among the Italian tax community. In particular, many voiced strong criticism against the idea of extending the EU principle of abuse of law to domains not covered by EU law; moreover, it was observed that the Italian Court, in transposing the Halifax test into the domestic system, had truncated one of its fundamental elements, the so-called frustration of purpose, i.e. the requirement that the granting of the tax benefit should be contrary to the purpose of the rule providing this benefit[6]. In the wake of this criticism, at the end of 2008 the Italian Court rendered three important decisions[7] in which it further clarified the contours of the domestic

---

5   Italian Court of Cassation, Decision No. 8772 of 4 April 2008

6   Zizzo,G., (2008) L'Abuso dell'Abuso del Diritto, *GT- Rivista di Giurisprudenza Tributaria*, 6, p.465.

7   Italian Court of Cassation, Decisions No. 30055, 30056 and 30057 of 23 December 2008.

GAAR. According to these decisions, it should be deemed as abusive the inappropriate use of legal arrangements which, although being formally in compliance with the law, are aimed at obtaining an undue tax advantage in the absence of significant economic reasons other than the expectation of obtaining that tax advantage. Furthermore, the Court identified as legal basis for the anti-abuse rule the "ability to pay principle", enshrined in Article 53 of the Italian Constitution, according to which all must contribute to public expenses in proportion to their respective ability to pay taxes. The mainstream interpretation always considered Article 53 of the Constitution as a provision aimed at protecting the taxpayer from excessive or in any way disproportionate taxation[8]. In contrast to mainstream interpretation, the Supreme Court held that any tax-planning scheme without sound purpose other than saving taxes constitutes per se a violation of the constitutional principle and of the duty of solidarity that inspired the fundamental charter. Therefore, the tax authority may disregard the application of any tax provision in transactions without a clear and significant business purpose, which appear aimed at obtaining a specific tax benefit and circumventing the law.

Since the leading cases mentioned above were published in 2008, many Italian scholars have expressed their concerns about the peculiar interpretation of Article 53 of the Constitution by the Supreme Court: reading this Article through the lens of the abuse of law doctrine would have increased the level of uncertainty of the tax system as never before, making business decisions remarkably uncertain and risky[9]. In particular, this interpretation was likely to confer upon tax authorities too wide a discretion in identifying abusive behaviours. In assessing the lack of valid economic basis, tax authorities could be entitled to question the strategic and entrepreneurial choices underlying the transaction concerned anytime the taxpayer was able to achieve a tax advantage. This was felt to be a blatant infringement of the principle of economic freedom enshrined in Article 41 of the Constitution.

These concerns were left unaddressed for many years. A number of drafts were put forward to reform the semi-general anti-abuse rule and turn it into a general anti-abuse rule codifying the case law developed by the Court of Cassation; yet, none of these projects managed to be approved by the Parliament. Another "external shock" was therefore needed in order to overcome this legislative impasse. This shock was given by a second "reverberation

---

[8] Greggi, M., (2015) *The Dawn of a General Anti Avoidance Rule: the Italian Experience*, ITAX Papers on Taxation, , retrived from http://ssrn.com/abstract=2709704, p.6

[9] Greggi M. (2015), *The Dawn of a General Anti Avoidance Rule*, cit., p.7.

wave" of the EU principle of abuse of law in the Italian tax system. This time the reverberation consisted in a vertical interaction between the EU Commission and the Italian Parliament and Government.

In December 2012 the EU Commission adopted, within the framework of the Action Plan to strengthen the fight against tax fraud and tax evasion, the EU Recommendation on Aggressive Tax Planning. This Recommendation urged Member States to adopt a number of measures aimed at counteracting aggressive tax planning, defined as the exploitation of the technicalities of a tax system or of mismatches between two or more tax systems for the purpose of reducing tax liability. Among these measures, the Recommendation contained a general anti-abuse clause, which Member States were encouraged to introduce in their domestic legislation, allowing tax authorities to ignore any artificial arrangement carried out for tax avoidance purposes and instead impose tax on the basis of actual economic substance. The model clause also provided guidance to help identify artificial arrangements.

In the wake of this Recommendation, in 2014 the Italian Parliament, within the framework of broad tax reform envisaged in Law no. 23 of 11 March 2014, charged the Government with enacting a general anti-avoidance provision replacing all existing special provisions on abuse of law. In conferring this task upon the Government, Parliament made express reference to the need to align the content of the national GAAR to the principles and criteria laid down in the EU Recommendation on Aggressive Tax Planning[10]. In executing its mandate, the Government approved in 2015 a decree containing the long-awaited national GAAR[11]. A quick glimpse at the text of this provision immediately shows that it is fully consistent with the model GAAR envisaged in the Recommendation. The national GAAR defines abuse of law as "one or more transactions without any economic substance that, while formally complying with tax law, are carried out essentially to obtain undue tax advantages". It also defines transactions without economic substance as "facts, acts and contracts, also linked to each other, that are not suitable for producing significant effects other than tax advantages". The model clause provided in the EU Recommendation states that:

> ...an artificial arrangement or an artificial series of arrangements which has been put into place for the essential purpose of avoiding taxation and leads to a tax benefit shall be ignored. National authorities shall treat these arrangements for tax purposes by reference to their economic substance.

---

10 Law no. 23 of 11 March 2014, art 5 par 1.

11 Legislative Decree n. 128, which added article 10 bis "Discipline of the Abuse of law or Tax Avoidance" to the law passed on July 27th 2000, n. 212 (Taxpayer's Bill of rights).

As we can see, the notion of abuse of law provided in the Italian GAAR encompasses two fundamental elements: 1) the lack of economic substance; and 2) the attainment of an undue tax advantage. In this respect, the Italian GAAR appears to depart from the definition contained in the model clause, which comprises three elements: 1) the artificial arrangement, which, as the same model clause clarifies, is another name for arrangement without economic substance; 2) the attainment of a tax benefit; and 3) the essential purpose of avoiding taxation, i.e. where the transaction defeats the object, spirit and purpose of the tax provisions that would otherwise apply.

Yet, this difference is only apparent because the third element (the frustration of purpose) is implied in the definition of undue tax advantages; this is provided for in the second paragraph of the Italian GAAR as those benefits, even if not immediately achieved, that conflict with the purpose of tax rules or with the principles of the tax system. Furthermore, the national GAAR provides a number of indicators to help identify transactions without economic substance; namely, the inconsistency of the legal characterisation of the single transactions of which an arrangement is consistent with the legal substance of the arrangement as a whole, and when the arrangement is carried out in a manner not consistent with reasonable and ordinary business conduct. In this respect, the Italian legislature implemented only the first two of the many indicators contained in the Recommendation, which appear to be more general in scope.

As a result of this short comparison, we can arguably conclude that the text of the Italian GAAR essentially mirrors that provided in the EU Recommendation. Accordingly, the recently approved GAAR places Italy among the first EU Member States to have introduced into its national system a piece of legislation fully compliant with the new European standards on abuse of law. In this respect, the Italian GAAR might potentially exert a horizontal reverberation effect acting as a model for those EU countries wishing to update their abuse of law legislation to these standards.

Compatibility of the UK GAAR with the EU notion of Abuse of Law

The Finance Act 2013 has, for the first time, introduced a General Anti-Abuse Rule into UK tax law. The stated purpose of the UK GAAR is to counteract "tax advantages" arising from "tax arrangements" that are "abusive". "Tax arrangements" are arrangements where, "having regard to all the circumstances, it would be reasonable to conclude that the obtaining of a tax advantage" was their "main purpose, or one of their main purposes". The "tax arrangements" are "abusive" if they do not pass the so-called "double reasonableness test", i.e. they cannot reasonably be regarded as a reasonable course of action.

In particular, following the approval of the Anti-Tax Avoidance Directive in July 2016, the issue of the compatibility of the UK GAAR with the European notion of abuse of law is increasingly becoming the object of much debate. Moreover, this despite the outcome of the referendum on Brexit: presumably, during the two year exit-negotiation period that follow the submission of an Article 50 TUE notification, the UK will continue to participate in the detailed day to day processes of the EU and be bound by its laws. Besides, it has been argued that the principles laid down in the Directive might find their way into UK law either as a result of the UK adopting very similar legislation domestically or as a consequence of any future deal to obtain access to the single market, or simply as part of its adoption of the OECD-G20 BEPS Actions (as stated in its Preamble, the aim of the Directive is to ensure a coherent and coordinated approach between Member States to dealing with BEPS issues following the publication by the OECD of its 15 Action Plans in October 2015).

This Directive requires Member States, among other things, to implement a general anti-abuse rule reflecting in most part the notion contained in the previous EU Recommendation. In particular Article 7 of the Anti- Tax Avoidance Directive defines abuse of law as "a non-genuine arrangement or a series thereof, carried out with the essential purpose of obtaining a tax advantage that defeats the object or purpose of the otherwise applicable tax provisions". The same Article also states that "an arrangement or a series thereof shall be regarded as non-genuine to the extent that they are not put into place for valid commercial reasons which reflect economic reality.

Concerns have therefore been expressed that this Directive would seem to require the UK to enact a broader GAAR, which would apply to any non-genuine arrangements carried out for the essential purpose of obtaining a tax advantage[12]. This is because the approach to abuse of law followed by the EU is considerably different from that adopted by the UK's General Anti-Abuse Rule. The former is an objective approach relying on economic substance as the key criterion for assessing abusive tax arrangements, whereas the latter relies on the subjective and very narrow double reasonableness test, which was carefully drafted in order to tackle only the most egregious

---

12 Luder, S., (2016) *Corporate Tax Avoidance and BEPS: the EU grasps the nettle*, Practical Law, February 25, retrieved from https://uk.practicallaw.thomsonreuters.com/Document/If11b4 2fddaf011e598dc8b09b4f043e0/View/FullText.html

schemes and not all forms of tax abuse[13]. Accordingly, some authors have even suggested that the current GAAR based on the highly controversial and subjective "double reasonableness test" should be replaced with a GAAR based on the objective "economic substance" test, independently of the approval of the EU Anti Tax Avoidance Directive. This reform would be required in order to reflect the need for a real tool to tackle all forms of tax avoidance that undermine the revenue of the government[14].

A Possible Horizontal Interaction between the Italian GAAR and the UK GAAR

Should the UK decide to update its current GAAR to the notion of abuse of law stemming from the EU Recommendation on Aggressive Tax Planning and the proposal for an Anti-Tax Avoidance Directive, it might look with interest at the Italian GAAR, which, as we have seen, is one of the first pieces of legislation to have been updated to the new European standards. A quick comparison between the two national GAARs shows that a number of provisions embedded in the Italian anti-abuse rule may help the UK tax system to overcome some of the weaknesses that have been found in its GAAR.

First, we have already underlined that the Italian GAAR provides a definition of abuse of law encompassing all the objective criteria envisaged in the EU model GAAR; namely, the lack of economic substance, the attainment of an undue tax advantage, and the essential purpose of avoiding taxation. Second, the Italian GAAR may provide possible solutions to some procedural aspects that have been considered as problematic in the UK GAAR, i.e., the counteraction of the abuse, the burden of proof, and the absence of a specific clearance system. Regarding the first aspect, the UK GAAR provides that, if it is determined that an arrangement is abusive, then the tax advantage that the arrangement sets out to achieve will be counteracted on a just and reasonable basis. This criterion, which is similar to the double reasonableness test, appears flawed by the same uncertainty and vagueness, with the consequence that the manner in which tax avoidance arrangements are to be countered remains quite unclear. By contrast, the Italian GAAR provides that abusive arrangements are not enforceable towards the tax authorities, which should disregard the tax advantages achieved by such arrangements, and compute taxes on the basis of the rules and principles that have been

---

13 Rayney, P. (2013), Mind the GAAR, *Accountancy*, September, retrieved from http://www.peterrayney.co.uk/pdfs/gaar.pdf

14 The Deficiencies in the General Anti- Abuse Rule, retrieved from https://www.tuc.org.uk/sites/default/files/GAAR.pdf

circumvented. This guidance, which appears even clearer than the one used in both the model GAAR and the Draft Directive ("tax liability shall be calculated by reference to economic substance in accordance with national law"), allows tax authorities to tackle tax avoidance in an objective fashion capable of being numerically assessed, because it limits the extent of tax avoidance to the rules and principles that have been circumvented.

Concerning the second element, the UK GAAR has been much criticised on the grounds that it places the burden of proof on whether an arrangement is abusive or not entirely on the tax authority: this requirement, while reversing the burden of proof from a normal tax appeal for apparently no reason, is viewed by some commentators an insurmountable obstacle to the effective application of the GAAR. In this respect, the Italian GAAR attempts to strike a reasonable balance between the tax authority's and the taxpayer's burden of proof: the former must prove the main elements of the notion of abuse (the lack of economic substance, the attainment of an undue tax advantage, and the essential purpose of avoiding taxation); whereas the latter must demonstrate that the transaction is justified by non-negligible business purposes other than of a tax nature. Therefore, according to the Italian GAAR, it is up to the taxpayer to prove that the arrangement is somewhat reasonable because it is justified by non-negligible business purposes, and thus corresponds to economic logic. By contrast, according to the UK GAAR, it is up to the tax authority to prove that the arrangement cannot be reasonably considered as a sensible course of action.

As to the third element, the lack of a clearance mechanism in the UK GAAR, which would allow the taxpayer to obtain from the tax authority prior agreement as to the abusive character or not of their proposed transactions, is felt to create unnecessary uncertainty in the system. A clearance mechanism would therefore help to clarify the GAAR's scope of application, ensuring that sufficient certainty about the treatment of tax transactions could be provided without undue compliance costs for businesses and individuals[15]. Also in this regard, the Italian GAAR provides a specific clearance scheme whereby taxpayers can submit a ruling application to the tax authority to verify whether any envisaged or already completed transactions are considered abusive. The request should be filed prior to the deadline for the filling of the relevant tax return, or for the completion of other tax obligations relating to the transactions.

---

15 The Deficiencies in the General Anti- Abuse Rule, retrieved from https://www.tuc.org.uk/sites/default/files/GAAR.pdf

It is nonetheless important to note that this possible interaction between the two national GAARs is not only one-way: the UK GAAR contains a number of provisions that deserve to be taken into careful consideration by the Italian legislature.

In particular, the UK GAAR provides a number of procedural requirements which have to be met before HMRC can invoke the GAAR. These are set out in Schedule 43 to FA 2013 and contain elements that are designed to act as safeguards for the taxpayer. The first is that only a designated HMRC officer – a senior official of HMRC specifically authorised to deal with cases where the GAAR may apply – can invoke the GAAR. It is envisaged that this would bring some consistency and uniformity in the application of the anti-abuse discipline. By contrast, according to the Italian legislation, the issue of abuse of law may be raised by any official in the course of an audit. This may actually generate inconsistency in the application of the GAAR because the assessment of the abuse is left to the discretion of any single official, no matter how experienced in the field he or she may be.

The second safeguard provided by the UK GAAR is that, before the designated officer may proceed to counteraction, the case has to be submitted for consideration to the GAAR Advisory Panel, a commission of independent experts with experience or expertise in the particular field of the transaction in question, who have to express their view as to whether the taxpayer's actions are reasonable (the "single reasonableness test"). It must be said that the effective impartiality of this panel has been seriously called into question, its members almost exclusively being drawn from the tax profession (i.e. the people who are by far the most likely to create, sell or use complex tax abuse schemes), with the exclusion of HMRC officials[16]. A similar panel – albeit with a mixed membership made up of both tax authority officials (possibly those specifically authorised to deal with anti-abuse cases according to their experience in the field) and exponents of the tax profession – may help build taxpayers' trust in the application of the Italian GAAR. Yet, it must be said that the IMF, when reviewing Italian tax reform, made express reference to the UK experience in order to suggest Italy introduce a similar Advisory Panel[17], but eventually the Italian legislature decided not to take this advice.

---

16 The General Anti-Abuse Rule is a step in the right direction, but we have a long way to go to beat tax avoidance, (2013, April ,16), retrieved from http://www.taxresearch.org.uk/Blog/2013/04/16/the-general-anti-abuse-rule-is-a-step-in-the-right-direction-but-we-have-a-long-way-to-go-to-het-the-attack-on-tax-avoidance-right/

17 IMF, Italy: The Delega Fiscale and the Strategic Orientation of Tax Reform, (2012, September), retrieved from http://www.tesoro.it/primo-piano/documenti/Italy_-_TA_Report_on_the_Delega_Fiscale_and_Strategic_Orientation_of_Tax_Reform.pdf.

The third feature of the UK GAAR deserving consideration is the Guidance which is periodically approved by the Advisory Panel. This document has two main purposes: the first is to give, in layperson's language, a broad summary of how the GAAR operates. The second is to be an aid to the interpretation and application of the GAAR, in particular by providing examples of abusive and non-abusive transactions, which must be taken into account by the courts. The publication of a similar guidance, which could include the Revenue Service's established practice as to what constitutes abusive behaviour and what is a reasonable course of action, would surely be welcome in the Italian tax system, as it would help create more certainty in the application of the GAAR, and assist taxpayers know in advance whether their tax arrangements are within or outside the GAAR.

Concluding remarks

The development of an EU principle of abuse of law exerted a strong reverberation effect in the Italian tax legal system, which culminated in the recent codification of a written general anti-abuse clause (GAAR) in Italian legislation. This reform has placed Italy among the first EU Member States to have introduced in its national system a piece of legislation fully compliant with the latest new European standards on abuse of law as enshrined in the EU Recommendation on Aggressive Tax Planning and the proposal for an Anti-Tax Avoidance Directive. In this respect, the Italian GAAR might potentially exert a horizontal reverberation effect acting as a model for those EU countries wishing to update their abuse of law legislation to these standards.

Bibliography

de la Feria, R. & Vogenauer, S. (eds.). (2011). *Prohibition of Abuse of Law. A New General Principle of EU law?*. Oxford: Hart Publishing

de la Feria, R. (2011), 'Introducing the Principle of Prohibition of Abuse of Law', in de la Feria, R. & Vogenauer, S. (eds.), *Prohibition of Abuse of Law*. Oxford: Hart Publishing

Gallo, F., (2015), La Nuova Frontiera dell'Abuso del Diritto in Materia Fiscale, *Rassegna Tributaria*, 6.

Greggi, M. (2015). *The Dawn of a General Anti Avoidance Rule: the Italian Experience*, ITAX Papers on Taxation. Retrived from ssrn.com/abstract=2709304

Keen, M., de Mooij, R. & Eyraud, L. (2012). The Delega Fiscale and the Strategic Orientation of Tax Reform. Retrieved from http://www.tesoro.it/primo-piano/documenti/Italy_-_TA_Report_on_the_Delega_Fiscale_and_Strategic_Orientation_of_Tax_Reform.pdf

Luder, S. (2016). Corporate Tax Avoidance and BEPS: the EU grasps the nettle. *Practical Law*. Retrieved from https://uk.practicallaw.thomsonreuters.com/Document/If11b42fddaf011e598dc8b09b4f043e0/View/FullText.html

Murphy, R. (2013). The General Anti-Abuse Rule is a step in the right direction, but we have a long way to go to beat tax avoidance. Retrieved from http://www.taxresearch.org.uk/Blog/2013/04/16/the-general-anti-abuse-rule-is-a-step-in-the-right-direction-but-we-have-a-long-way-to-go-to-het-the-attack-on-tax-avoidance-right/

Rayney, P. (2013). Mind the GAAR. *Accountancy*. Retrieved from http://www.peterrayney.co.uk/pdfs/gaar.pdf

Trades Union Congress. (2013). The Deficiencies in the General Anti- Abuse Rule. Retrieved from https://www.tuc.org.uk/sites/default/files/GAAR.pdf

Zizzo,G., (2008) *L'Abuso dell'Abuso del Diritto*, GT- Rivista di Giurisprudenza Tributaria, 6.

10 The EU Directive against Tax Avoidance (ATAD-1)

Marco Greggi

Abstract

The Anti-Tax Avoidance Directive (ATAD-1) is perhaps the most important achievement so far by the European Union in the struggle against international tax avoidance and evasion: it makes the most of the findings and recommendations by the OECD as summarised in the Base Erosion and Profit Shifting (BEPS) Action Plan. The goal of this paper is to compare the solutions adopted by the EU in the Directive with the domestic provisions already in force in some member states, including Italy and the UK.

The methodology chosen is comparative in its nature. Qualified anti-avoidance provisions – such as General Anti-Abuse Rules (GAARs) and Diverted Profits Tax (DPT) – already in force on a national scale have been tested to see whether they are compatible with the new European guidelines and rules. The first findings allow the interpreter to draw different conclusions depending on the national rules tested. While for some, such as the DPT, the consistency with OECD recommendations and EU law is uncertain, others, such as most of the national GAARs, appear to already be compliant with the new European standards. In the latter case, however, the influence of EU law will arguably be essential in terms of interpretation of the rules, and the widening or narrowing of its scope, together with the need to counterbalance the power of the tax administration with the protection of the fundamental rights of the taxpayer, rights that some administrations are reluctant to grant while making use of GAARs.

The conclusions also stress the 'double standards' approach of the EU legislation which has made use of different provisions, some more or less aggressive towards the taxpayer, depending on whether the tax structure is European or also involves third-party countries.

Setting the Framework: the BEPS Project and the contribution of the OECD

A new wind is blowing across Europe, and as yet it is too early to see whether it is going to bring a storm or just a small shower. In any case, taxation law on the Continent will not remain the same for much longer[1]. Inspired by the OECD and the increasing need to reconsider traditional rules in international taxation law, changes started with the 2013 BEPS Action Plan[2]. Principles set out in the mid-1920s by the League of Nations were considered no longer adequate to address the most complicated tax planning schemes enacted by multinational entities (MNEs), including the use of hybrid financial instruments, transparent entities and so on[3]. Current international literature has largely explored the most significant aspects of the BEPS Action Plan[4]. It was not expected that some of these policy guidelines would have already been transformed into legally binding rules by national legislators and, even more surprisingly, that each member state would be bound to them in a Directive passed by the European Council (2016/1164)[5].

Avoidance was indeed just one of the issues addressed by the BEPS Action Plan, and perhaps not even the most pertinent. The situation that prompted the BEPS project was the intolerable asymmetry that emerged over the years between the place where wealth is generated and the one where taxation occurs. The traditional symmetry between these two factors has been progressively eroded by the development of technology, mostly IT, and the consequent difficulties in assessing where value is created and how the value chain is structured[6]. According to the traditional or classical para-

---

1   Cohn, M. (2015). 'G20 Leaders Endorse OECD BEPS Tax Reforms'. *Accounting Today*. New York, November 17.

2   Saint-Amans, P. & Russo, R. (2013). *What the BEPS Are We Talking About?*, Paris.

3   Coates, W. H. (1924). League of Nations Report on Double Taxation Submitted to the Financial Committee by Professors Bruins, Einaudi, Seligman, and Sir Josiah Stamp. *Journal of the Royal Statistical Society*, **87**(1), 99–102.

4   Brauner, Y. (2014). 'What the BEPS?' *Florida Tax Review*, **16**(2), 55–115.

5   On June 21st the EU Council agreed on the final version of the Directive addressing tax avoidance practices (ATAD-1). The member states will have until December 31st 2018 to transpose the directive into their national laws (December 31st 2019 for the provisions concerning exit taxation). On May 29th 2017 the Member states agreed on another Directive (2016/0339 (CNS)) against tax avoidance extending the scope of ATAD-1 to other hybrid instruments and improving the accuracy of the anti-avoidance provisions when non-EU based entities or financial instruments are involved.

6   Heckemeyer, J. & Overesch, M. (2013). *Multinationals' profit response to tax differentials: Effect size and shifting channels*, ZEW-Centre for European Economic Research. See also Ault, H. J., Schoen, W. & Shay, S. E. (2014). Base Erosion and Profit Shifting: A Roadmap for Reform. *Bulletin for International Taxation*, **68**(6/7), 275–279.

digm, taxation should occur in the place where ability to pay is assessed or detected, generally in the place of residence of the taxpayer, or, alternatively, in the location where he/she operates through the permanent establishment of a business. Normally, taxation occurred in the place where the taxpayer was domiciled, whether as an individual or a legal entity. Mainstream literature therefore identified the combination "Seat versus Permanent establishment" as the most appropriate legal instrument to define the taxing power of the state, preventing possible double taxation and, potentially, double non-taxation as well[7].Other authors have observed that this connection has been progressively eroded by technological developments and, furthermore, that this trend has been accelerated by aggressive tax planning schemes[8]. Both of these issues pressed the OECD to address the BEPS phenomenon. However, while the first issue – technological development – is, to some extent, natural as it derives from the ordinary improvement of production and sales techniques, the second – aggressive tax planning schemes – is purely artificial as it originated within the law and was therefore not tolerable.

Despite differing interpretations of the BEPS Report, it appears reasonable to conclude that the project is aimed at addressing both of these situations, of which only the second can be considered "abusive" or an "avoidance of the law", as it is traditionally understood by academic literature. In other words, while most abusive operations result in base erosion, clearly not all erosions of a taxable base derive from avoidance of the law. This perspective is also helpful in comprehending why such strong resistance has been generated towards the BEPS project despite there being a preliminary consensus on the policy guidelines as they were originally delivered[9].

The distinction between the two aspects of the BEPS project is vital in order to understand the real impact of the European Commission's Directive 2016/1164 [10], which has boldly implemented some of the project's guidelines and, to some extent, can be considered the most relevant example so far of the large scale implementation of the BEPS recommendations. The Directive

---

7   Couzin, R. (2002). *Corporate Residence and International Taxation*. Amsterdam: IBFD. See also Kingson, C. I. (1981). The Coherence of International Taxation. *Columbia Law Review*, **86**(1), 1151–1289.

8   Kingson, C. I. (1981).

9   The various positions are reported in Schoueri, L. E. (2015). Transparency Under the BEPS Plan: What Holistic Approach? *Kluwer Tax Law Blog*. Retrieved from http://www.kluwertaxlawblog.com/blog/2015/06/24/13300/.

10 Presented on January 28th 2016. The text commented on in the following pages is the one delivered in Brussels on June 17th 2016 and eventually published here http://eur-lex.europa.eu/legal-content/EN/TXT/PDF/?uri=CELEX:32016L1164.

is justified in Art. 115 TFEU[11] and is deemed necessary as a more effective course of action to be taken by member states against avoidance, together with the necessity to support the OECD findings, which are clearly referenced in the preamble. The policy framework is therefore one of the most robust available to both the Commission and the Council, which relies on the conclusions reached in the OECD Report and the implicit consensus of the States, member or not, regarding the project.

On the other hand, however, some loopholes appear to be evident and will remain even if the ATAD-2 is eventually adopted[12]. Without mentioning the fact that legal transplants are rarely successful, even in terms of policy, some authors immediately pinpointed discrepancies between the concluding recommendations in the BEPS Report and EU law. Specifically, some of the approaches suggested by the OECD may not be applicable within the EU, considering the impact on fundamental freedoms and the need for the proportionality principle to be respected when considering the risk to be tackled and the means used to address it. The strengthening of controlled foreign corporations (CFC) regulations, as suggested by the OECD, is perhaps one of these situations. Conversely, European policy makers have witnessed an ever-increasing level of unilateral interventions by individual states on the issues addressed by the BEPS project, creating a situation that is intrinsically inconsistent with the OECD recommendations, which aimed at achieving a more holistic approach to the issues identified and a multilateral way of dealing with them[13]. Subject to these divergent pressures, the Commission proposed a Directive in January 2016 which aimed to strike a balance between them, while preserving European specificity. Although some measures were discarded during the subsequent debates at the Council of Europe – most notably, the so called "switch over" clause – the proposed Directive was eventually passed.

Besides the technicalities of Articles 4 and the following ones, the manner in which the Commission achieved the balance is interesting from a number of perspectives. The BEPS project aimed to address erosion and the shifting of taxable bases in a very broad way, eventually leading to an overall rethink of the traditional nexuses of source and residence by suggesting an alternative approach. In the view of the OECD, international tax avoidance is just

---

11 Treaty on the Functioning of the European Union (2007): TFEU, from now on.
12 Ault, H. J. et al. (2014). Base Erosion and Profit Shifting: A Roadmap for Reform. *Bulletin for International Taxation*, **68**(6/7), 275–279.
13 Greggi, M. (2015). Genuine Nexus or Perpetual Allegiance? (Some Considerations on the "Diverted Profit Tax" Proposal). *ITax*, **4**(1), 1–27.

one of the ways in which erosion may be determined, and may not even be the most important one. The approach by the Commission, on the other hand, is aimed at counteracting avoidance, leaving the broader issues unaddressed. It is difficult to understand the reasons why this choice has been made. The motivation can probably be found in the natural constraints of the decision-making process of the Council, and a possible predictive approach to the chances of the directive being passed, considering the very peculiar mechanism currently governing approval of directives and regulation of tax law within the Union.

An approach consistent with subsidiarity and with a limited scope has arguably been considered as the one having the most chance of success, even given its obvious weakness from a purely legal perspective. Subsidiarity may be used under the condition that the issue to be addressed falls under the jurisdiction of both the states and the EU. This is not yet the case in the field of direct taxation, where countries still maintain an exclusive power to legislate as consistent with the fundamental principles of the Treaty.

The Commission actually tried to find an adequate and reliable premise which would allow intervention in this field. Despite the criticism that the first draft of the text attracted, and the pessimistic forecasts concerning its final approval, it can nonetheless be considered a success in term of policy implementation by the Commission and the competence of the Commissioner in particular, who was brilliant in dropping the most contested provisions – namely, the switch over clause – thereby allowing the remaining ones to be passed[14].

Comparing Approaches to Tax Avoidance: the British DPT and the Italian GAAR

The decision to intervene in the field of international tax avoidance was taken by the European Commission for the reasons mentioned above and, arguably, also because some states had already begun to unilaterally and without coordination legislate on topics and issues addressed by the BEPS Action Plan. More precisely, in 2014/2015, during the latest BEPS stage, some states in the Union enacted new provisions to address the issue of tax avoidance, amongst them the UK and Italy.

---

14 Moscovici, P. (2015). 'Fighting Tax Avoidance: Commissioner Moscovici welcomes final adoption of international tax reform package'. Brussels. Retrieved from http://europa.eu/rapid/press-release_STATEMENT-15-5773_it.htm.

Despite differences in economic structure, tax systems and the overall philosophy inspiring their respective tax administrations and governments, the UK and Italy found themselves in similar positions regarding the implementation of new ways and means of securing tax revenue, particularly concerning the issue of international tax avoidance. Italy reacted to the challenges of international avoidance using both improved criminal law provisions as a way to pressurise the management of the multinationals via audit procedures, and anti-abuse regulations[15] by enacting GAAR legislation for the first time in recent history. The UK, apparently, made a bolder move with the Diverted Profit Tax.

Diverted Profit Tax as a unilateral anti-avoidance measure: some preliminary considerations

the Diverted Profits Tax suggests that income should be taxed where it is generated. To some extent, it appears to confirm the thesis posited by Reuven Avi Yonah some time ago[16] and to which he returned recently[17] writing in favour of a Destination-Based Corporate Tax (DBCT). According to DBCT, income 'is' where it is 'originated' and it should therefore be taxed in that location. In the past, this thesis was challenged on a number of bases and using a remarkable number of arguments[18]. Two of these arguments were particularly relevant: (1) the practical difficulty of calculating income liable to tax in the source state and (2) the possible confusion between 'income' and 'consumption' that might emerge if the first of the two is taxed in the place where it originates. The scope of the UK's DPT does not seem to be very far-reaching, as the application of it depends on the assessment of improper behaviour by the taxpayer, namely, the attempt to erode the taxable base in the UK. The academic proposal mentioned above is more systematic and not intended to solely address abusive operations.

The OECD has familiarised the scientific community worldwide with the notions of 'erosion' and 'profit shifting': nowhere in any paper, report or discussion draft by the Organisation for Economic Co-operation and Development have words such as 'diversion' or 'diverted' been used. Such words refer to qualified situations generated by the attempt of the taxpayer

---

15 Article 10 *bis* of Act n. 212 passed in 2000 as amended in 2015.
16 Avi-Yonah, R. (2012). Slicing the Shadow: A Proposal for Updating U.S. International Taxation. *Tax Notes*, **135**(10), 1229–1334.
17 Avi-Yonah, R. S. (2015). 'The Case for a Destination-Based Corporate Tax'. *SSRN Electronic Journal*. http://doi.org/10.2139/ssrn.2634391.
18 Altshuler, R., & Grubert, H. (2010). Formula Apportionment: Is it better than the current system and are there better alternatives?, *National Tax Journal*, December, **63**(4), 1145–1184.

to improperly minimize tax liability; 'diversion' seems to draw the distinction between these situations and the other types that normally occur using the argument of fairness and equity[19]. The words 'fair' and 'just' appear at least three times in the draft bill[20], making reference to the amount of income which is liable to tax in the UK despite the absence of a permanent establishment or the arrangements of the contract of the case.

'Diversion', at least to a non-native English reader and interpreter, appears to make reference to something that is different from what should or ought to be[21]: a deviation from the normality of taxation or the abandonment of a paradigm. From a theoretical perspective, the definition is indeed stimulating because the mention of 'diversion' should also entail the clarification of 'from what' and 'to where' the income or asset in question is moved. In this situation, it could be obvious to argue that 'diversion' is 'from' the tax liability in the UK 'to' a tax liability elsewhere; 'diversion' in this respect is similar to 'shifting', then, in the OECD's lexicon. Considering the UK tax system, a simple implementation of the OECD guidelines and recommendations in the framework of the BEPS Action Plan would be reductive and limitative.

From some perspectives, 'diversion' appears to be a more complicated term. This complexity is particularly evident when it is embedded in the notion of 'justice'[22] in taxation and 'reasonableness'[23] in the implementation of it. References to fairness and justice are not so frequent in the OECD reports; in the UK's definition, implicit reference to avoidance and abuse are present[24], even though they are not necessarily present in the BEPS reports addressing similar situations. In other words, 'diversion' occurs because of behaviour which is close to avoidance and abuse of law; 'erosion' and 'profit shifting' may be generated by business combinations or market decisions which do not necessarily qualify in this sense.

Evidence of this situation may be drawn from the text of the law (subsequent to the Discussion draft). To some extent, DPT is a punitive tax, as it is charged in its first version at a rate of 25%, which is higher than the ordinary

---

19 See the Consultation Draft on DPT, Part 1, Article 8 (3).
20 See also Consultation Draft on DPT, Part 1, Article 8 (6) (a).
21 "*Divert, v.*". Oxford English Dictionary Online. June 2015. Oxford University Press. http://www.oed.com/view/Entry/56070?redirectedFrom=divert (accessed August 10, 2015).
22 Consultation Draft on DPT, Part 1, Article 8 (3).
23 The principle of reasonableness is extended also to the foreign tax to be credited. See for instance Consultation Draft on DPT, Part 1, Article 19 (2).
24 See Consultation Draft on DPT, Part 1, Article 28 (1) extending to DPT Section 206(3) FA 2013 (as a matter of fact the general anti-abuse rule is applicable also to DPT).

corporate tax in 2015 in the UK of 20%. The British legislator decided to draft a brand new tax for companies falling into one of the cases covered by the law, while, at the same time, making the 'diversion' of profits much more expensive than ordinary taxation. Even if there are specific provisions aimed at addressing a potential international double taxation, there is no doubt that the conditions under which the tax is triggered are cases qualified as 'unjust' and 'unfair' by the legislator. Injustice and unfairness justify the higher tax ordinarily due and further fines if due.

DPT is applied in situations where the behaviour of the taxpayer, or its business model, defies the ordinary rules defining nexuses traditionally used to justify the power to tax in the source state: in this respect it is indeed an original and innovative tax, because it further extends the tax liability of offshore taxpayers. The first of the two cases covered by the DPT is the one related to 'hidden PE'. The basic assumption in this case is that a foreign taxpayer (non-resident in the UK) is developing an onshore business activity which is generating profits without matching any of the conditions currently listed in the Double Taxation Conventions in force between the UK and a third country empowering the first to tax it as the source state. The reference in this case is traditionally to Article 5 of the OECD Model Convention and the definition of Permanent Establishment[25] therein.

The quantitative element of the phenomenon, therefore, is perhaps one of the key elements that urged the UK legislator to react in this way. Indeed, it is the same factor on which the proposal by Italian Congressman Professor Boccia was based, when he tried to introduce a similar tax four years ago in the peninsula. In this respect, the British law made UK profits generated by a non-resident entity liable for tax if it appears clear that the latter has acted and developed its business in a way to prevent the existence of a PE[26]. This test is implemented so as to be consistent with the principle of reasonableness[27]; however, it dramatically increases the level of uncertainty for businesses, which has attracted criticism from the first commentators of the proposed law[28]. Increased uncertainty is, however, an unavoidable consequence

---

25 Frecknall Hughes, J., & Glaister, K. (2001). Electronic Commerce and International Taxation. *European Management Journal*, **19**(6), 651–658. http://doi.org/10.1016/S0263-2373(01)00090-1. See also Kobetsky, M. (2011). *International Taxation of Permanent Establishments*. Cambridge: Cambridge University Press.

26 Skaar, A. A. (2000). Erosion of the Concept of Permanent Establishment: Electronic Commerce. *Intertax*, **28**(5), 188–194.

27 Consultation Draft on DPT, Part 1, Article 2 (1) (c).

28 PwC. (2014). 'UK Diverted Profit Tax to be introduced'. London. [https://news.pwc.ch/wp-content/uploads/2014/12/pwc-uk-diverted-profits-tax1.pdf]

of widening the tax base beyond the taxation parameters traditionally listed by the OECD either in the Model or in the Commentary.

The second situation in which DPT is applicable is less peculiar than the first, as it makes reference to the taxpayer who intentionally pursues tax mismatches. Basically, DPT is triggered here on a transactional basis, and makes extensive reference to the transfer pricing rules and procedures, i.e. when the taxpayer:

1 Enters into one or more transactions devoid of actual economic substance with the purpose of diverting profits elsewhere from the UK and

2 Enjoys an aggregated lower taxation (the transaction of the case originates a cost tax deductible on UK resident company and a profits on a parent one resident in a low tax jurisdiction).

When these conditions are met the spread between what has been actually paid and what ought to is charged with the DPT in the UK.

The conditions under which 'diversion' is assessed are those identified using the principle of "just and reasonableness in taxation"[29] and in business planning. Any transaction devoid of a considerable business purpose or not in line with the "state of the art" of the business under review might trigger DPT if a tax saving occurs. DPT becomes another instrument similar to transfer pricing regulations with which it is now possible for HMRC to address cases in which the flow of revenue for the State is at risk.

The two instruments are not equivalent in any case, nor are their effects. On the one hand, in the case of TP, the prices of the transaction are adjusted in accordance with the 'arm's length principle'[30], and taxable income is increased in the UK. On the other hand, DPT accepts as correct the terms of agreement the parties entered into, but the spread between the amount paid and the amount which was supposed to be under arm's length negotiation is taxed under DPT. The first commentators, particularly from the business community[31], observed that while in theory this approach could seem to be reasonable overall, in practice it is much more complicated and uncertain

---

29 Consultation Draft on DPT, Part 1, Article 8 (3).

30 HMRC's Diverted Profit Tax: Guidance. Published on November 30th 2015, page 5. The document is accessible here https://www.gov.uk/government/uploads/system/uploads/attachment_data/file/480318/Diverted_Profits_Tax.pdf.

31 Hooper, C. et al. (2015). 'Diverted Profit Tax: Details Released'. London. [http://www.ey.com/Publication/vwLUAssets/EY-Finance-Bill-2015-Diverted-profits-tax-Details-released/$FILE/EY-Finance-Bill-2015-Diverted-profits-tax.pdf]

when the time comes for calculating "what income would have been if" for the purpose of DPT. In other words, the amount of the 'diversion' is anything but certain.

The new Italian GAAR, its application to cross border tax planning structures and its compatibility with ATAD-1.

In August 2015, after a considerable length of time, the Italian legislators finally approved and implemented a modern General Anti-Avoidance Rule (GAAR). It is probably the first example in the history of Italian tax law to have a provision of this kind with such a broad potential application, being suitable for implementation on not only income taxes and VAT but also on local duties and fees (only customs duties are excluded from its application). In this way, Italy has apparently followed the approach pursued by many other countries inside and outside the Union, which are one after another drafting similar provisions in the attempt to escalate the struggle against the common problem of tax avoidance. The development of an anti-abuse doctrine, which to some extent can be considered equivalent to a GAAR in its effect on the taxpayers' rights and duties, was facilitated in Europe due to the lack of specific, tailor-made anti-abuse provisions both in the Treaty and in derivative legislation, including regulations and directives.

In the development of EU law throughout the years, anti-abuse regulation was not considered a priority by the legislators in Brussels, an approach consistent with the subsidiarity principle. The EU left to each of the member states the power to regulate anti-abuse provision, with the only limitation being that of reasonableness and proportionality in its application. Italy had never previously experienced a GAAR, nor did academic literature strongly advocate it in the past, before the intervention by the European Court of Justice and the extension of it to direct taxes by the Italian Supreme Court. The Italian tax system has always been fragmented with an absence of general, overarching principles, such as no common procedural rules, different compliance duties and an unclear statute of limitation (as it changes tax per tax and according to the phase of activity by the Revenue service). In this respect, tax law has never been codified in the Italian legal experience, nor are there currently sound proposals to do so. The lack of common, shared rules applicable to different taxes makes addressing avoidance of direct taxes, VAT and local duties an impossibility. It is evident that in Italy the mainstream academic literature has always been critical of GAAR, albeit for varying reasons.

Certainty and predictability have been the main drivers that have inspired the Italian anti-avoidance rule applicable till August 2015. More to the point, the anti-avoidance provisions drafted in Article 37 bis DPR[32] n. 600/73 and applicable to income taxes for both individuals and corporations was limited to the situations listed in the law. It was, therefore, a sort of tailor-made rule, targeted at qualified circumstances. In the past, most of the anti-abuse provisions enacted in Europe were either based on judge-made law (such as in the case of VAT) or, alternatively, connected to beneficial ownership status in line with directives related to passive income, including "interest and royalties" and "parent-subsidiary" categories.

It is probably due to the efforts made by the OECD in this regard that the EU insisted on the necessity of having a more comprehensive tool made available to domestic legislators to tackle abusive situations, since unilateral domestic provisions in the past did not provide the best solution. The "Transparency Package"[33] also proved to be effective in creating the background conditions for this proposal to be passed by the European Council. The Cadbury Schweppes precedent[34] is a clear example of this unilateral inefficiency, with a domestic anti-abuse provision (actually a CFC regulation) found to be inconsistent with EU law and, precisely, with the freedom of establishment.

Council Directive 2015/121 rules that:

Member States shall not grant the benefits of this Directive to an arrangement or a series of arrangements which, having been put into place for the main purpose or one of the main purposes of obtaining a tax advantage that defeats the object or purpose of this Directive, are not genuine having regard to all relevant facts and circumstances.

Besides this, the Directive leaves room for member states to enforce their own unilateral domestic provisions where necessary and consistently with the principles of subsidiarity and proportionality. All in all, the wording of the Directive is not very different from the recently proposed GAAR in the Directive on Tax Avoidance. The Italian GAAR is no doubt an example of the unilateral provision of the kind mentioned above by Article 1, paragraph 4, just like the anti-abuse provisions enshrined in the treaties Italy entered

---

32 'DPR' stands for 'Decree of the President of the Republic'; in relation to the current analysis (and for what concerns its binding power on the taxpayer) is equivalent to an Act passed by the Parliament, although in the Italian Constitutional framework it is remarkably different.

33 Bhogal, S. (2016). 'The EU anti-tax-avoidance directive'. *Tax Notes International*, **83**(10), 881–884.

34 ECJ case C-196/04 decided on September 12th 2006.

into with a similar scope. The European provision is of course applicable only to the cross-border flow of dividends falling into the still somewhat narrow scope of the directive, but in this specific case, in theory, a business transaction could potentially trigger three different anti-abuse provisions: the domestic, the Directive's, and the Treaty-based ordinances.

The Possible Impact of the Directive against Tax Avoidance

ATAD-1 has the ambitious purpose of providing a common level playing field in the struggle against tax avoidance. This ambition was prompted by the fact that, on the one hand, avoidance is possible because some member states haven't got a sufficiently developed set of rules applicable to circumstances like these, or because the ones they have are not entirely consistent with the fundamental freedoms of the Treaty. On the other hand, the EU Commission observed at the opening of the Directive that the level of avoidance or base erosion within the EU and also from the EU to outside has reached a level that cannot be tolerated any longer. It is evident from the text of the Directive that the two phenomena are, however, treated differently. On one side, the Commission criticizes the profit shifting phenomenon within the EU while, on the other, it is more aggressive towards the one affecting the member states and involving countries that are not part of the EU. These two situations, not being identical under the law, are addressed with different means and ways in the text of the Directive. It is therefore appropriate to conclude that the European Union seems to take two different approaches to tax avoidance or, in other words, appears to have double standards regarding tax avoidance, depending on where the eroded profits are allocated: the anti-avoidance measures are tighter in the second case, more relaxed in the first. Arguably, the need to strike a balance between the implementation of the EU fundamental freedoms and the struggle against tax avoidance determined this approach. In other words, profit shifting is not considered entirely inappropriate if it occurs within the Union: it is a matter of legal perspective.

An analysis of the positive provisions suggested by the Commission makes it possible to identify five different tools which can be considered adequate to deal with international tax avoidance. They are: (1) a limitation on the possibility of deducting passive interests; (2) more comprehensive discipline on exit taxation; (3) a GAAR; (4) redefined CFC regulations and (5) some tools to deal with hybrid mismatches, basically, a 'tie-break' rule. The impact of the Directive is, therefore, selective and aimed at direct taxation. Apparently, neither VAT, nor customs duties or excises, are considered in the scope of it even if in these two latter fields the EU has a much broader power to intervene. The reasons for this are to be found in the fact that, ever since its first draft, the European text has been inspired by the OECD recommendations – which, for their part, are lacking in specific attention to the field of indirect taxation – so that other taxes were not considered as a priority or, as in the case of VAT, adequately addressed by judge-made law, or the abuse of law doctrine.

Limitation to passive interests deduction

Interest deduction has always been a sensitive issue in international taxation, possibly leading to the transfer of profits and improper allocation of taxable bases across member states. Easy as they are to reallocate, passive interests arouse the attention of tax systems of member states in various ways. In the past, different means have been used to limit their deduction for tax purposes to an amount considered acceptable and reasonable, i.e. consistent with the market value. Most notably, transfer pricing, 'thin capitalization' and overall limitation of the possibility of deduction have been implemented by the states in this respect.

While EU law has regulated interest taxation within the framework of the "Interests and Royalties" Directive[35], allocating taxing powers amongst source and residence states when they both belong to the EU, it has left unaddressed issues concerning excessive interest payments, and aggressive tax planning in connection with payment of interests on loans. This is the situation of the 'inflated' interests made reference to in the Directive on page 7 of the first draft proposal. The inflation of interests occurs in different ways: the parties agree on an excessive interest rate; a disproportionate amount of capital loaned vis-a-vis the needs of the financed company and, more precisely, in relation to the risk capital of it; or, an excessive rate in comparison to the business performance of the company. In the past, and currently on occasion, this issue has been addressed by member states individually.

The excessive interest payment is generally dealt with using the transfer pricing regulations, which are commonly applicable in this context. In this respect, in some countries such as Italy, courts have also extended control over financial activities of this kind, negating the possibility of deducting interest payments entirely by the permanent establishment resident in their territory if the payment is made to the company resident abroad. At the same time, the capital loaned may be considered as part of the functioning fund

---

35 Greggi, M. (2010). European Taxation of Passive Income. *Journal of the Australasian Tax Teachers Association*, 4(1), 39-54.

normally attributable to the permanent establishment. Such a position is very recent and consistent with the OECD's most recent guidelines in this respect, even if, in some circumstances, they have been applied retroactively.

Excessive capital loans were addressed in the past by thin capitalization rules, which were implemented by the member states in order to constitute an anti-base erosion measure *ante litteram*. In this field, the European Court of Justice observed in the precedent Lankhorst-Hohorst[36] that while prevention of base erosion is an essential goal for a state, nonetheless it must be pursued with ways and means consistent with fundamental freedoms. A thin-cap rule such as the German *ratione temporis* is incompatible with EU law if it addresses only cross-border operations, most notably those between companies resident in two EU states. The *Lankhorst* doctrine, and its *ratio decidendi*, can still be considered as one of the most delicate obstacles to be overcome while implementing the BEPS project on a European scale.

In the view of the Court of Justice of the European Union not all profit shifting cases have to be counteracted even when they occur consistently with tax planning schemes of an aggressive nature, if the base erosion takes place between two states of the Union. In other cases, such as Lasertec[37], the same conclusion was not reached, since the state considered the involvement of a third, non-member country – Switzerland – and the free movement of capital was used to make the final decision of the Court. The case law of the European Court of Justice long before the BEPS project appeared on the agenda, has somehow been prophetic of the risks and limitations incurred when the possibility of deducting interest is restricted to the EU. Traditional arguments, such as the proportionality test between the means used and the risks of revenue loss or, alternatively, cohesion of the tax system, appeared to be ineffective or, at least, not entirely considered by the Court[38].

According to the Directive, an overall limitation on the possibility of deducting interest is considered to be compatible with EU law if some quantitative limitations are satisfied, namely up to 30% of earnings before interest, tax, depreciation and amortisation (EBITDA) of the taxpayer in a given fiscal year. The Directive appears to be applicable in cross-border situations, while leaving states free to legislate on issues which are purely domestic. In any case, it is doubtful whether the Directive can be applied only to cross-border interest payments, as this may discriminate between domestic and

---

36 ECJ case C-342/00 decided on December 12th 2002.
37 ECJ case C-492/04 decided on May 10th 2007.
38 Zalazinski, A. (2007). Proportionality of Anti-Avoidance and Anti-Abuse Measures in the ECJ Direct Tax Case Law. *Intertax*, **35**(5), 310–321.

cross-border loans, which is not compatible with EU law according to the fundamental principles of the Treaty[39].

Mobility within the EU

Exit taxation has always been an issue in EU tax law; in the past, it has been addressed in many cases by the Court of Justice of the European Union with the application of fundamental freedoms of the Treaty together with respect for member states' freedom to legislate in tax and commercial law matters[40]. More precisely, owing to the silence of the secondary legislation and, to some extent, the double taxation conventions, the Court has intervened in an attempt to strike a balance between the taxing power of the state and the freedom of establishment of the taxpayer.

It is well known in the academic literature that exit taxation has long been considered incompatible with the free movement of individuals in case law of long-standing, but is yet somehow acceptable, under some conditions, when the transfer abroad involves corporations[41]. This distinction depends on the fact that corporations are fictitious creations of the legal system, with the only exception being the *Societas europaea* and the equivalent cooperatives that were virtually unaffected by exit taxation. Therefore, their mobility may, on some occasions, be limited under commercial law and hence under taxation law.

The most recent attempts to legislate on exit taxation (including the one in Italy) were aimed at finding a balance in terms of time of taxation for the exit country: a tax deferral has been considered the most appropriate legal instrument to regulate the situation in this respect. The accrued but not yet realized capital gain would have been taxed only at the time when the asset of the case was sold in the outbound state. This conclusion has been adopted by many states, including Italy, where the need to preserve the taxing right of the state was maintained by the legislator, but was not considered decisive, since a number of issues remained unresolved. Among the most important such issues are the calculation of the taxable base when the asset of the case had been actually sold at a lower price in comparison to the one it had at the moment of the transfer abroad and the assessment of the delayed capital

---

39 Ruiz Almendral, V. (2005). Tax Avoidance and the European Court of Justice: What is at Stake for European General Anti-Avoidance Rules? *Intertax*, **33**(12), 562–583.

40 Greggi, M. (2009). Riflessi fiscali della mobilità all'interno dell'UE: per un nuovo Nomos europeo. *European Tax Studies*, **1**(1), 1-21.]

41 Zernova, D. (2011). Exit Taxes on Companies in the Context of the EU Internal Market. *Intertax*, **39**(10), 471–493.

gain to be taxed. In some jurisdictions, taxation on a capital gain that never occurred would be incompatible with the ability to pay.

The Directive appears to cut the Gordian knot of exit taxation, making it applicable to outbound movements under some conditions[42], but allowing a deferred payment by the taxpayer who enjoys a kind of financial facilitation. On the one hand, it makes cross-border movements a bit more complicated and expensive, but on the other hand, introduces a symmetry rule[43], which contributes in a remarkable way to making the situation more transparent and efficient in terms of preventing possible double taxation. The duty for the inbound state to accept the market value attributed to the assets in the outbound country at the moment of exit is arguably the most efficient way to prevent double taxation on capital gains while at the same time minimizing the risks of any infringement of the ability to pay principle. The proposed solution is no doubt efficient, but is has to be carefully evaluated as to whether it could be considered consistent with the Treaty and the free movements protected by it, particularly in the case of individuals.

The equivalence between transfer and realization can be acceptable according to the (domestic, if any) ability to pay principle, but nonetheless makes transfers much more expensive when on a cross-border scale. The Directive, in this respect, seems not to diverge remarkably from the policy guidelines of the OECD which recommend the balancing of the need to preserve the power to tax with the opposite necessity of allowing the seamless movements of companies and, most notably, of individuals on a global scale. Arguably, this endorsement by the OECD should help in making the conclusion more acceptable within the EU.

General Anti-Avoidance Rule, the European Way

Article 6 of ATAD-1 presents the text of a possible GAAR which could be considered as a standard in Europe. The wording is actually not that different from the one used in many countries, such as Italy for example, and which has been recommended by the relevant authoritative academic literature. An analysis of the GAAR falls outside the scope of this brief research[44] and, interesting as it is, has been addressed at least in part above.

---

42 Article 5 (2) of the Directive.
43 Article 5 (5) of the Directive.
44 Freedman, J. (2004). Defining Taxpayer Responsibility: In Support of a General Anti-Avoidance Principle. *British Tax Review*, **4**, 332–357. Freedman, J. et al. (2009). Corporate Tax Risk and Tax Avoidance: New Approaches. *British Tax Review*, **1**, 74–116.

In defining avoidance, the Commission can be seen to have used traditional concepts such as "non-genuine arrangement" that should somehow "defeat the object or purpose ..." of the transaction as such. On one hand, the goal is noteworthy and ambitious but, on the other, there is no doubt that, notwithstanding the efforts made by the Commission, avoidance and abuse are reliant on domestic arrangements. Abuses occur according to national rules governing contracts, agreements, deeds and other obligations under civil law. Private or commercial law in every country in Europe (the same would arguably be true on a global scale) has its own background, its own tolerance of non-typical business arrangements, and different ways of understanding and interpreting the abuse of law or abuse of rights. In this respect, the introduction of a GAAR at European level is, to some extent, like building a pyramid starting from the top.

The outcome may not be the same if Article 6 is interpreted in a different way: a provision aimed at unveiling the potential of the domestic anti-abuse provisions already in force. It should make them, to some extent, more tolerable under EU law and prevent the ECJ from adopting an over-aggressive approach, such as in the Cadbury case. The reference in Article 6, § 1 to the "essential" and not "exclusive" scope may be considered significant in this respect, allowing member states to exercise more intrusive powers in the struggle against avoidance and making their domestic anti-abuse provisions more compatible with the Treaty. At the same time, Article 7 is potentially applicable to other taxes as well, such as VAT perhaps, making the GAAR overlap with the abuse of law doctrine and influencing the interpretation of the Courts in this field as well.

Controlled foreign companies legislation and transparency rule

Controlled foreign corporations (CFC) legislation has undergone remarkable changes in recent times due to the influence of several factors including the progressive success of the OECD in promoting an effective and reliable exchange of information between states. The improved possibility of exchanging information has made the approach to CFC based on a "Black list" principle outdated and insufficient to handle these corporations in the traditional way, that is, as an instrument to prevent tax avoidance or, more precisely, tax deferral. On the other side, the compatibility of CFC regulations with EU law has often been questioned by academic literature in Europe.

In the most recent developments in studies of CFC rules, it appears that the two approaches of the discipline cannot be reconciled easily. On the one side, CFC legislation is considered as a way to neutralize abusive behaviours somehow equivalent to tax avoidance (as observed above) and ultimately ending up in a tax deferral. This vision has been maintained in states where CFC regulations may be applicable under the condition that the resident parent company has control of the subsidiary abroad in terms of voting rights and therefore may actually delay the distribution of dividends. This is the most restrictive way to extend CFC and the one much more oriented to address the most serious pathologies of taxation. On the other side, CFC legislation has been considered also as a more comprehensive instrument, aimed at reallocating taxing powers in more appropriate ways. The efforts made to pierce the Mayan veil represented by the foreign subsidiary in this instance derives from the necessity to attribute a broader taxable base to the country the parent is resident in, irrespective of the power of the latter to enact the tax deferral.

In the earliest versions of CFC legislation in some jurisdictions, the attribution of profits was determined did not hold the majority of the voting rights in the ordinary assembly, and thus would be legally incapable of postponing the distribution of dividends. The US example is clear in this respect, with the CFC regulation applicable, *inter alia*, according to the qualified participation of a company in a non-resident entity. The Commission has two paradigms to decide between, with perhaps the first one being friendlier to the EU law experience in general, and to fundamental freedoms in particular. The steps taken in Article 7 – and Article 8 as well, where relevant to the calculation of the taxable base – are towards the abandonment of the "blacklist" approach. They open up the possibility of applying CFC rules only when the spread between the tax level of the home country and of the one the subsidiary is resident in overtakes a specific amount i.e. lower than 40% of the effective tax rate. Controlled companies in the EU may trigger CFC regulations only if they are wholly artificial. The Directive extends remarkably the opportunity to apply CFC rules outside the EU and EEC, but it also thwarts this possibility within the EU, where most of the situations actually occur. By doing so, it makes any other domestic regulation that extends the scope of the CFC rule to cases that are not covered directly by the Directive objectively inconsistent with EU law.

Hybrid entities, hybrid instruments and the need to allocate taxing rights

The hybrid nature of entities or contracts may actually lead to double international non-taxation[45]: This statement has been made by the OECD, in the

---

45 Kahlenberg, C.. (2016). Hybrid Entities: Problems Arising from the Attribution of Income Through Withholding Tax Relief – Can Specific Domestic Provisions be a Suitable Solution Concept? *Intertax*, **44** (2) 146–162.

framework of the BEPS initiative, but it has been well-known to academic literature long before that. In legal literature, and taxation law in particular, there are no hybrid entities or contracts: a hybrid nature in this sense derives from a mismatch of qualifications in the two tax legislations involved. Both the resident and source states have a clear rule applicable to the so-called "hybrid entity" or contract; the point is that the two interpretations diverge and neither treaties nor indeed EU law are of any help in this respect. Legal theory and taxation law already have the instrument to overtake this situation: the tiebreak rule is commonly applied when this uncertain qualification affects other characteristics of the taxpayer, such as residence[46].

In the case of hybrid entities or contracts, and divergent interpretations, the Commission has proposed a tie break rule that is probably the outcome of political discussions between states, and is not deprived of good common sense. According to Article 9, in the case of divergent interpretations, the qualification of the source state prevails, with the source state being the one where the payment occurs or where the deduction of the costs related to the entity or the contract must take place.

Understanding Tax Avoidance: European versus Non-European Tax Planning Schemes

The European Directive addressing tax avoidance, although addressing a number of situations different from each other in law and proposing remarkably divergent means to overhaul them (GAARs, tie break rules, and so on), draws the attention of academics and practitioners to avoidance and, more precisely, to feasible ways to implement in the EU the OECD-inspired BEPS project. The EU is perhaps the most adverse environment in which the BEPS project could be applied, since the continent is characterized by a number of different legal layers overlapping each other. In addition, there is a long-standing and robust European academic tradition on tax avoidance that has delivered remarkable results long before the BEPS project that are, in some cases, divergent from it. The concepts of tax avoidance and tax evasion have been analysed in the past by tax academics and practitioners from all round the world with remarkable results. Anti-avoidance rules are an outcome of the everlasting struggle between the principles of legal certainty on one side and freedom of business activity on the other, between the legal form of commercial operations and the substance of the aims pursued by the taxpayers.

---

46   The current analysis is limited to ATAD-1, while most of the issues raised by hybrids are actually managed by the ATAD-2.

Despite the differences, the common ground of all these issues relies on interpretation: dealing with tax avoidance or with "abuse of law" still depends nowadays both on the interpretation of statutory law in the light of the TFEU (and possibly in the future, of the proposed Directive) and on the constitution of the state (if any). Some authors have noted that a line should be drawn between avoidance considered as the outcome of loopholes in statutes and avoidance that is the result of different interpretations of statutory law or common law. This distinction is, however, based on the interpretation of the rule of law, and that understanding of the rule of law is an *a priori* condition when ascertaining any loopholes or gaps in the system. This requirement has been well known in the continental experience since the Middle Ages, when the debates about the notion of "abuse" of law and "avoidance" of statutory law arose for the first time, even if they did not initially involve tax issues. Perhaps it is no surprise that the problems faced by medieval commentators and lawyers in Italy and in other Europeans countries were not so different from the current ones. They had to strike a balance between the statutory laws of the Italian municipalities and the *ius commune* (what was left of the ancient Roman law) considered to be the legal background that was always applicable if not specifically derogated.

Nowadays we almost have to follow the same path while managing the relationship between national laws and EU law, with ATAD-1 becoming the *ius commune* in anti-avoidance practice. The only fundamental distinction relies in the overall trend of the evolution: in the Middle Ages the *ius commune* was progressively being substituted by the *particularisme* of the different municipalities, at least in Italy. In the 21st century, national law is progressively surrendering to EU law where necessary and the Directive is a clear example of this trend, urging states as it does to legislate against avoidance and abuse in the same way.

The EU law on direct taxation, based as it is on the fundamental freedoms of the TFEU, had to develop a different approach to the issue. In other words, it had to find elsewhere the reasons and the legal principles to oppose tax avoidance, if it wished to do so. After decades of discussion, the Directive seems to offer the first statutory answer in this respect: the protected asset from tax avoidance is the fair functioning of the market. It remains to be seen whether, and how, an EU-wide concept of tax avoidance would be suitable for implementation by the different member states, as the potential conflict could involve fundamental rights and duties of some member states (see below on this). The opposite is also true. It has happened in the past that the need to battle against tax avoidance was used by member states to justify limitations to EU fundamental freedoms, with various cases appearing before the ECJ.

Generally, the need for anti-tax avoidance provisions is not a *conditio per quam* as a derogation to the EU freedoms is allowed: the ECJ has always asked for something more or tested the presence of tax avoidance under its own standards – such as in the Cadbury case, where the "wholly artificial arrangement" was needed – something that is now regulated in the proposed Directive. This could potentially constitute another field of conflict between the national experience in combating tax avoidance and the different necessities of the European Union. Some anti-avoidance provisions introduced to enforce the economic solidarity among citizen taxpayers could not work in an EU framework: they could be considered as disproportionate or unreasonable in the light of the communitarian approach, which is why the directive is essential in setting the benchmark according to which the proportionality test may be run.

Arguably, the domestic provisions in force will survive the implementation of the Directive, since the European legislation will work mostly, although not exclusively, at an interpretive level. According to this approach, the national anti-avoidance provisions must pass several tests in order to qualify as consistent with EU law. The first condition is that the specific circumstances of the case might fall into the scope of one of the fundamental freedoms mentioned above, as far as the conflict between national anti-avoidance rules and EU law arises only where the second is theoretically applicable. In this respect, it was noted that the real purpose of the taxpayer – namely, the subjective approach to avoidance – is now absolutely irrelevant, as the proposed Directive states. The ECJ has always judged the application of a fundamental freedom without taking into account the purpose followed by the taxpayer in the specific case, at least in this first stage of the inquiry[47]. While the subjective aspect is underestimated by the Court of Justice of the European Union, the objective aspect plays a more relevant role. The economic activity for which the taxpayer asks protection must be effective and genuine, and it must not constitute a mere device by which to qualify for the protection of the Treaty. In other words, the business activity must be actual and not artificial: the exercise of the freedom must be consistent with an economic interest of the taxpayer.

It is self-evident that, at first glance, the "rule of reason" seems to constitute an ideal concept capable of distinguishing the use from the abuse of a

---

47 Zalazinski, A. (2007). Proportionality of Anti-Avoidance and Anti-Abuse Measures in the ECJ Direct Tax Case Law. *Intertax*, **35**(5), 310–321.

right, and therefore capable of identifying avoidance. However, from a more practical standpoint, it is difficult for everybody, and for the Court of Justice of the European Union in particular, to assess in some cases the existence of reasonableness in a business activity carried on by a European taxpayer. The second feature of the "rule of reason", as it emerges from the Directive, is so evident that even in recent papers and seminars some influential authors have stressed the fact that the Court of Justice of the European Union to be losing the direction it has followed in recent years, deciding on tax avoidance cases (both in direct taxation and in VAT) without a clear general picture. The situation may be different from the one represented in the past: the Court of Justice approach has not changed throughout the years; rather the objects of judgement of many recent cases are taking the Court into the maelstrom of harmonising its tax approach on an issue that may also be unclear within a national context .The supranational approach cannot but emphasise divergences, and some decisions reached are, of course, hard for member states to accept, as the most recent case law clearly shows.

The basic assumption of this research is that the notion of tax avoidance and abuse of tax law must be understood and interpreted according to what happens in other fields of a given national legal system[48]. The historical evolution of each of them, and of Roman law, can clarify when abuse has taken place. This perspective has supported the idea that avoidance is not an "eternal problem" in tax law, but an issue that arises when legal provision collides with other sets of rules of a non-legal nature; of course, this conflict depends on the national background and on the strength, real or perceived, of the non-legal rules. When the Court of Justice, or in this case the Commission, tries to harmonise the different tax systems as far as is allowed by the Treaty, they progressively have to solve the same problems faced by various national states across the decades. However, in every member state, abuse is always a judgement of comparison between an individual right, not necessarily of the taxpayer, and other principles enshrined in the legal system, such as ability to pay, solidarity, social justice. In Europe, these principles and values are not yet accepted and protected as they are domestically or as they would have been with the European Constitution proposal rejected in 2007 right after the French and Dutch *referenda*.

---

48 Douma, S. (2011). *Optimization of Tax Sovereignty and Free Movement*. Amsterdam: IBFD.

Bibliography

Altshuler, R., & Grubert, H. (2010). Formula Apportionment: Is it Better than the Current System and are there Better Alternatives? *National Tax Journal*, **63**(4), 1145–1184.

Ault, H. J., Schoen, W., & Shay, S. E. (2014). Base Erosion and Profit Shifting: A Roadmap for Reform. *Bulletin for International Taxation*, **68**(6/7), 275–279.

Avi-Yonah, R. (2012). Slicing the Shadow: A Proposal for Updating U.S. International Taxation. *Tax Notes*, **135**(10), 1229–1334.

Avi-Yonah, R. S. (2015). The Case for a Destination-Based Corporate Tax. *SSRN Electronic Journal*. http://doi.org/10.2139/ssrn.2634391

Bhogal, S. (2016). The EU Anti-tax-avoidance Directive. *Tax Notes International*, **83**(10), 881–884.

Brauner, Y. (2014). What the BEPS? *Florida Tax Review*, **16**(2), 55–115.

Coates, W. H. (1924). League of Nations Report on Double Taxation Submitted to the Financial Committee by Professors Bruins, Einaudi, Seligman, and Sir Josiah Stamp. *Journal of the Royal Statistical Society*, **87**(1), 99–102.

Cohn, M. (2015). G20 Leaders Endorse OECD BEPS Tax Reforms. *Accounting Today*, New York. Published on November 17.

Couzin, R. (2002). *Corporate Residence and International Taxation*. Amsterdam: IBFD.

Douma, S. (2011). *Optimization of Tax Sovereignty and Free Movement*. Amsterdam: IBFD.

Frecknall Hughes, J., & Glaister, K. (2001). Electronic Commerce and International Taxation. *European Management Journal*, **19**(6), 651–658.

Freedman, J. (2004). Defining Taxpayer Responsibility: In Support of a General Anti-Avoidance Principle. *British Tax Review*, **4**, 332–357.

Freedman, J., Loomer, G. T., & Vella, J. (2009). Corporate Tax Risk and Tax Avoidance: New Approaches. *British Tax Review*, **1**, 74–116

Greggi, M. (2009). Riflessi fiscali della mobilità all'interno dell'UE: per un nuovo Nomos europeo. *European Tax Studies*, **1**(1), 1-21.

Greggi, M. (2010). European Taxation of Passive Income. *Journal of the Australasian Tax Teachers Association*, **4**(1), 39-54.

Greggi, M. (2015). Genuine Nexus or Perpetual Allegiance? (Some Considerations on the "Diverted Profit Tax" Proposal). *ITax*, **4**(1), 1–27.

Heckemeyer, J., & Overesch, M. (2013). Multinationals' Profit Response to Tax Differentials: Effect Size and Shifting Channels. ZEW Centre for European Economic Research. *Discussion Papers*, 13-045, 1-37.

Kahlenberg, C. (2016). Hybrid Entities: Problems Arising from the Attribution of Income Through Withholding Tax Relief – Can Specific Domestic Provisions be a Suitable Solution Concept? *Intertax*, **44** (2) 146–162.

Kingson, C. I. (1981). The coherence of international taxation. *Columbia Law Review*, **86**(1), 1151–1289.

Kobetsky, M. (2011). *International Taxation of Permanent Establishments*. Cambridge: Cambridge University Press.

Moscovici, P. (2015). Fighting Tax Avoidance: Commissioner Moscovici welcomes final adoption of international tax reform package'. Brussels. Retrieved from http://europa.eu/rapid/press-release_STATEMENT-15-5773_it.htm

Ruiz Almendral, V. (2005). Tax Avoidance and the European Court of Justice: What is at Stake for European General Anti-Avoidance Rules? *Intertax*, **33**(12), 562–583.

Saint-Amans, P., & Russo, R. (2013). What the BEPS Are We Talking About? Paris. Retrieved from http://www.oecd.org/forum/what-the-beps-are-we-talking-about.htm.

Schoueri, L. E. (2015). Transparency Under the BEPS Plan: What Holistic Approach? *Kluwer International Tax Blog*. Retrieved from http://www.kluwertaxlawblog.com/blog/2015/06/24/13300/

Skaar, A. A. (2000). Erosion of the Concept of Permanent Establishment: Electronic Commerce. *Intertax*, **28**(5), 188–194.

Zalazinski, A. (2007). Proportionality of Anti-Avoidance and Anti-Abuse Measures in the ECJ Direct Tax Case Law. *Intertax*, **35**(5), 310–321.

Zernova, D. (2011). Exit Taxes on Companies in the Context of the EU Internal Market. *Intertax*, **39**(10), 471–493.

11 Key Stakeholders' Perceptions of Introducing a General Anti-Avoidance Rule (GAAR) for Tackling Aggressive Tax Planning in Indonesia

Niken Evi Suryani and Ken Devos

Abstract

A number of studies have explored aggressive tax planning practices in developed countries. However, there are fewer studies that have examined aggressive tax planning in developing countries such as Indonesia. Those studies have concluded that the Specific Anti-Avoidance Rules (SAARs) in Indonesia have been inadequate in dealing with inappropriate tax-related practices. This raises the issue of whether a General Anti-Avoidance Rule (GAAR) should be introduced in tackling aggressive tax planning in Indonesia. This paper addresses this issue and research gap by specifically exploring key stakeholders' perceptions as to whether aggressive tax planning is a problem in Indonesia; whether the current Indonesian SAARs are sufficient to combat aggressive tax planning; and whether a GAAR should be introduced as a result.

This paper makes a contribution to the literature by employing a qualitative research methodology to address the research questions. Key informants from the Directorate General of Taxes (Indonesian tax authority), Tax Court judges, taxpayers, and tax advisors were interviewed. It is envisaged that the primary data gathered from the interviews provide a comprehensive picture of key stakeholders' opinions in Indonesia with regards to enacting a GAAR. Thirty two interviews were conducted encompassing all key stakeholders. Following an examination of the interview data, the paper provides preliminary evidence for the introduction of a GAAR to tackle aggressive tax planning. Consequently, this evidence could act as a basis for developing a GAAR in Indonesia.

Introduction

The problem of tax avoidance has been present since ancient times. Dating as far back as 6,000 years ago in Mesopotamia and more recently in 17th century England, tax avoidance has caused significant problems for tax authorities (Orow, 2000). Tax avoidance has become a serious concern for both developed and developing countries although the latter are regarded as more vulnerable because of a lack of resources in recognising tax avoidance transactions (Lampreave, 2013).

As a developing country, Indonesia currently faces the same problem of tax avoidance as evidenced by 70% of foreign direct investment companies not paying taxes as a result of reporting losses that were generated through the use of tax avoidance schemes, such as transfer pricing (Rahayu, 2008). In 2005, the Indonesian Minister of Finance stated that 750 Controlled Foreign Companies (CFCs) avoided taxes by reporting losses in five consecutive years (Supriyanto and Ika, 2005). This practice remained prevalent in 2016, according to the Minister of Finance who recently stated that around 2,000 foreign investment companies did not pay their corporate income taxes over the past 10 years with the estimated loss in government revenue of Rp 500 trillion or around US$37.53 billion (Sipahutar, 2016).

According to data from the Directorate General of Taxes (DGT), from 2001-2006, the percentage of taxpayers registered in the Foreign Investment Tax Office who did not pay corporate income taxes was 70.64% of the total 12,738 taxpayers (Lestari, 2008). Their losses were generated as a result of aggressive tax planning in the form of transfer pricing[1]. These practices resulted in tax losses amounting to £16.5 billion and US$50 billion each year respectively in the United Kingdom and the United States of America, whereas in Indonesia, the estimated tax gap is only Rp 2 trillion each year from foreign investment companies (Lestari, 2008). Considering the estimated tax gap[2] and the impact on national revenue of which 70% comes from taxes, the gravity of the problem of aggressive tax planning in Indonesia becomes apparent.

The aim of this paper is to address three research questions. First, investigate whether aggressive tax planning is in fact a problem in Indonesia.

---

1   The use of a pricing system with respect to the transfer of goods and services within a large organization. When used by multinational corporations, there have been suggestions that such systems have been used to transfer tax liability from higher-taxed countries to lower-taxed countries. (S. James, *A Dictionary of Taxation*, 2nd ed, Edward Elgar, 2012, p.278).

2   The difference between actual tax revenue and that which would be received if there were 100% compliance on the part of taxpayers (S. James, *A Dictionary of Taxation*, 2nd ed, Edward Elgar, 2012, p.258).

Second, examine whether the current Indonesian Specific Anti-Avoidance Rules (SAARs) are sufficient to combat aggressive tax planning. Third, consider whether a General Anti-Avoidance Rule (GAAR) should be introduced in Indonesia.

The remainder of this chapter is organised as follows. The next section reviews the key literature with respect to aggressive tax planning and the GAAR. The third section briefly outlines the research design. The paper follows with a discussion and analysis of the interview findings from key stakeholders. Finally, the chapter concludes with a summary of the main findings, tax policy implications, the study's limitations and suggestions for future research.

Literature review

Definition of aggressive tax planning

Multinational Entities (MNEs) employ tax planning to achieve a lower worldwide tax rate. However, tax planning can range from acceptable business planning to something that may be considered aggressive. Tax planning can vary from a choice to secure a less complex tax outcome to one considered as tax avoidance (Karimeri, 2012). For example, if a company makes a donation, it will incur an expense which will entitle it to claim a tax deduction. On the other hand, if a company creates artificial transactions to increase a deduction, this may be characterised as aggressive tax planning.

Aggressive tax planning involves exploiting tax laws thus creating a risk that the tax saving or tax benefit achieved may be challenged by the tax authority. For example, Murphy (2004, p.310) defined aggressive tax planning as "the situation where there is a reasonable probability that a particular tax return stance will not be upheld by an audit and subsequent legal challenge". Similarly, the Organisation for Economic Cooperation and Development (OECD) referred to aggressive tax planning as:

> Planning involving a tax position that is tenable but has unintended and unexpected tax revenue consequences and taking a tax position that is favourable to the taxpayer without openly disclosing that there is uncertainty whether significant matters in the tax return accord with the law. (OECD, 2008, p.87)

Moreover, the Canada Revenue Agency (CRA) defined aggressive tax planning as follows:

> In Canada, it involves transactions, arrangements or events that are normally fully disclosed but undertaken to achieve a tax result that is not supportable within specific anti-avoidance provisions or the overall scheme of the Income Tax Act, Excise Tax Act, or Income Tax Conventions. Typically, the transactions, arrangements or events lack economic substance and commercial reality and would not have materialized except for the tax result sought. The transactions, arrangements or events result in: sheltering income and capital gains that should be reported; creating or inflating tax deductions and losses, including capital losses that would not otherwise exist; misusing treaty provisions; or accessing tax incentives, credits and exemptions in an offensive manner. Aggressive tax planning undermines the integrity of tax laws and the tax base. (Larin et al., 2008, p.145)

Aggressive tax planning may be considered similar to tax avoidance. Orow (2000, p.3) points out that "aggressive tax planning would often be indistinguishable from tax avoidance". Therefore, aggressive tax planning should no longer be classified as acceptable tax planning, but as unacceptable tax avoidance. When a transaction results in a difference between the purpose and the literal interpretation of the tax law, tax avoidance can occur (Karimeri, 2011).

However, the distinction between what is regarded as acceptable tax planning and unacceptable tax avoidance depends on a country's tax law. In some cases, Finnerty et al., (2007) found that legal tax planning will be considered to be unacceptable tax avoidance because there is no generally accepted meaning of tax avoidance. Tooma (2008) indicated that the distinction is largely based on the taxpayer's motive and purpose which is ascertained from the circumstances and the nature of transactions. Therefore, it is important to clearly distinguish between defensive tax planning, which adopts a more conservative approach and aggressive tax planning which may lead to unacceptable tax avoidance.

Aggressive tax planning which leads to unacceptable tax avoidance is a general problem faced by tax authorities globally. Ordower (2010) believed that tax avoidance and aggressive tax planning also existed in civil law jurisdictions although seemingly found more in common law jurisdictions. According to Rohatgi (2007), unacceptable tax avoidance is more likely to be employed in jurisdictions that have complex legislation, unfair tax laws, unreasonably high rates of tax and complex and cumbersome tax rules.

Characteristics and Features of Aggressive Tax Planning

Lapidoth (2006) has identified five characteristics of aggressive tax planning. The first characteristic is that the transactions have tax avoidance or tax reduction as the primary objective with only insignificant economic objectives. Second, it complies with the relevant tax legislation, if interpreted through a literal statutory method, but contravenes it if the legislation is interpreted in a purposive manner. Third, it is sometimes considered unacceptable by the general business community. Fourth, it involves erudite and complex tax minimisation and lastly, it will presumably be challenged by the tax authorities (Lapidoth, 2006). Similarly, these characteristics could also be found in unacceptable tax avoidance.

There are several features related to aggressive tax planning. Lisowsky (2010) discovered that the likelihood that an American company will employ tax shelters, which is the most extreme type of tax aggressiveness, is positively related to the existence of these factors: subsidiaries located in tax havens, foreign-source income, inconsistent book-tax treatment, litigation losses, promoters' use, profitability, and size. Another finding was that book-tax difference was significantly related to tax sheltering, thus, a larger book-tax difference indicated more aggressive tax behaviour (Lisowsky, 2010). Furthermore, Frank et al., (2009) found a strong positive relationship between tax aggressiveness and financial reporting aggressiveness in American companies. This indicates that companies with aggressive financial reporting behaviour are more likely to engage in an aggressive tax planning, resulting in a larger book-tax difference. In relation to companies in Indonesia, Rahayu (2008) indicated that the common practices of tax avoidance conducted by the foreign direct investment subsidiaries were schemes of transfer pricing, thin capitalization[3], treaty shopping[4], controlled foreign corporation[5] (CFC), with all schemes involving the use of tax haven[6] countries.

---

3   The practice of financing foreign operations through debt rather than equity where this can shift tax liability from high tax countries to low tax countries. (S James, *A Dictionary of Taxation*, 2nd ed, Edward Elgar, 2012, p.274).

4   The situation where a person who is not entitled to the benefits of a tax treaty makes use – in the widest meaning of the word – of an individual or of a legal person in order to obtain those treaty benefits that are not available directly (B Larking (ed.), *IBFD International Tax Glossary*, 5th ed, IBFD, 2005, p.426).

5   This term is generally used in the context of tax avoidance rules designed to combat the diversion by resident taxpayers of income to companies they control and which are typically resident in countries imposing low or no taxation (B Larking (ed.), op.cit. IBFD, 2005, p.92).

6   Countries or areas where tax rates are substantially lower than those to which a taxpayer would be subject elsewhere (S James, *A Dictionary of Taxation*, 2nd ed, Edward Elgar, 2012, 258).

Strategies Employed in Tackling Aggressive Tax Planning

General strategies

Several strategies have been recommended to counter aggressive tax planning. For example, nine strategies to tackle aggressive tax planning have been offered by Braithwaite (2005). The first four focus on tax advisors and their roles in designing aggressive tax schemes for their clients. These include: the strategy of imposing heavy penalties on the promoters of aggressive tax planning schemes, promoting restorative justice[7], targeting the clients of big promoters, and banning contingency fees (Braithwaite, 2005).

Braithwaite (2005) also suggested two further strategies targeted at taxpayers which involved the employment of a strict liability regime and promoting shelter disclosure and book-tax disclosure for corporations. Braithwaite's last three strategies related to tax authorities that can recruit from the private sector and vice versa to enable more integration between private and public markets for tax advice. He also suggested that investors should be educated on the risks of engaging in aggressive tax planning schemes and corporate certification of continuous improvement in tax integrity should be promoted (Braithwaite, 2005).

The OECD Recommendations

The OECD (2011) has also recommended several strategies to deal with aggressive tax planning which include: data collection improvement, restrictions application, economic impact evaluation, policy analysis, effectiveness measurement[8] of the strategies to detect and respond to aggressive tax planning, cooperative compliance programmes, and disclosure initiatives.

In addition, the OECD offers specific strategies which deny or limit tax benefits by employing approaches which interpret tax statutes, general anti-avoidance rules, and specific anti-avoidance rules. An example of the interpretation of the relevant tax provisions is the arm's length principle which is usually imbedded in the domestic tax laws and can deny tax losses resulting from transfer pricing transactions (OECD, 2011). Most pertinent for present purposes is the OECD's conclusion that GAARs have been shown to be beneficial when the relevant tax laws are difficult to apply and when there is a lack of relevant SAARs to tackle the illicit transactions (OECD, 2011).

---

7   For more detailed explanation of restorative justice, see for example J. Braithwaite, (2006) Narrative and Compulsory Compassion, *Law and Social Inquiry* **31**(2), 425-46 and J. Braithwaite, (2013) Flipping Markets to Virtue with Qui Tam and Restorative Justice, *Accounting, Organizations and Society* **38** (6-7), 458-68.

8   For example, additional revenue or enhanced compliance.

Definition of a GAAR

Given the various strategies employed to combat aggressive tax planning, anti-tax avoidance measures can generally be divided into two broad categories: SAAR/TAAR (Targeted Anti Avoidance Rule) and GAAR. Finnerty et al., (2007, p.207) define a GAAR as "domestic rules that allow the tax authorities to re-characterize a transaction or a series of transactions that have been entered into with the (sole or main) purpose of obtaining undue tax benefits". Similarly, Cooper (1997, p.25) defines a GAAR as "a tool for combating tax avoidance, is an anti-avoidance rule." Furthermore, Pagone (2010, p.3) indicates that the fundamental aspect of a GAAR is "to nullify tax advantages brought about by avoidance arrangements".

Cooper (2001), Tooma (2008), Prebble (2009), and Freedman (2014) have all indicated that a GAAR could be the solution to tax avoidance schemes. Specifically, Tooma (2008, pp.26-27) indicated that:

> *While SAARs may be progressively enacted to combat avoidance schemes after they have been identified, a broader, all-embracing GAAR is required, to ensure that the revenue base does not shrink on account of the failure of the legislature to keep pace with newly emerging tax avoidance schemes. By definition, SAARs accept that there will be a certain level of avoidance schemes that the legislature finds unacceptable, before these schemes can be shut down by the specific provisions in the legislation. On the other hand, GAARs attempt to strike down avoidance that was not envisaged when the GAAR provisions were drafted.*

In practice, the application of a GAAR varies between countries. One common feature of a GAAR application is the power of reconstruction given to the tax authority to re-characterise abusive transactions, which is stated explicitly in the legislation.

Benefits of a GAAR

According to Cooper (2001), many countries have benefited from implementing a GAAR in their tax system. Cooper (2001) has drawn attention to the fact that although a GAAR is not a panacea to solve all tax problems or correct flaws in the tax system, it is a powerful tool to combat artificial transactions or schemes designed to obtain tax benefits. On the other hand, having a GAAR will not put tax advisors' jobs at risk as feared by many. Rather, a GAAR can change taxpayers' perception of their ability to create tax avoidance schemes. For example, Brown (2012) indicates that after China introduced its GAAR in 2008, tax advisors took great care in planning MNEs tax strategies to ensure that the schemes have economic substance and were not simply created to pursue tax benefits or avoid taxes.

Tooma (2008, p.9) indicates that "there is evidence that taxpayers engage in tax avoidance schemes believing that other taxpayers are engaged in tax avoidance schemes as well". According to Tooma (2008, p.9), "where avoidance is perceived as being widespread, taxpayers feel less inclined to pay tax while they believe that other taxpayers are actively engaged in tax avoidance schemes". Hence, tax avoidance in turn leads to further tax avoidance. Tooma (2008) thinks that it is necessary to have a GAAR when other measures in combatting tax avoidance are deemed insufficient and taxpayer morale is low. According to Li (2010), one virtue of a GAAR is that it sends a signal that the tax authority views tax avoidance as a serious problem and that accordingly taxpayers must arrange their transactions to adhere to the GAAR.

Challenges of Introducing a GAAR

Challenges in designing a GAAR

There are many challenges in designing a GAAR. In order to tackle sophisticated and novel artificial schemes, a GAAR must be drafted in a very broad manner. This will generate uncertainty for taxpayers as they will frequently be unaware as to the precise tax consequences of their transactions. This confers on tax authorities' significant power and discretion in determining whether specific transactions constitute tax avoidance. As indicated by Cooper (2001, p.85), in practice:

> *A GAAR will usually become just another part of the tax landscape which practitioners and the judiciary negotiate in much the same way they do any other area involving ambiguity and uncertainty.*

According to Orow (1998), to overcome different structure and jurisprudence between tax jurisdictions, the design of GAARs must be examined using the generally accepted criteria for evaluating tax systems. These include the following five criteria[9]: certainty, the rule of law, equity, efficiency and neutrality, and the right of taxpayers to organize their affairs within the law.

Also, in relation to GAAR design, Atkinson (2012) highlighted the need to balance certainty for taxpayers and preventing tax avoidance for the gov-

---

9   There are other criteria in evaluating a GAAR although not considered in this paper, for example, those suggested by J. Freedman (2014) 'Designing a General Anti-Abuse Rule: Striking a Balance', *Asia Pacific Tax Bulletin*, May/June 167-73 at 167; and G. Aaronson (2012) 'GAAR Study, a Study to Consider Whether a General Anti-Avoidance Rule Should Be Introduced into the UK Tax System', http://www.tax.org.uk/Resources/CIOT/Documents/2012/01/111111_GAAR_final_report.pdf

ernment. A GAAR should be able to provide guidelines which are consistent in distinguishing between acceptable and unacceptable tax arrangements (Atkinson, 2012).

Challenges in enacting a GAAR in the tax law

Enacting a GAAR in the tax law would be a lengthy process and can take a long time in Indonesia. Essentially, tax law is a form of laws ("Undang-Undang") made by the House of Representatives (DPR) in consensus with the President which binds the public (Law Number 12, 2011). There are several phases to enact the laws, which include planning, drafting, elaborating, approval and enactment (Law Number 12, 2011, Article 1). A bill must be supported by an academic report (Law Number 12, 2011, Article 43). However, there is no definite timeline in the aforementioned phases until the approval of a bill. After a bill is approved, the President must sign it in 30 days or the bill would self-enact (Law Number 12, 2011, Article 73). Therefore to have a statutory GAAR enacted in the tax law could take several years.

Challenges of the economic impact

A GAAR enactment in a country also poses economic risks, particularly relating to foreign investment. For example, Kaur and Susarla (2011) concluded that a GAAR is not necessary in Indonesia because its uncertainty may reduce Indonesia's attractiveness in doing business. They indicated that Indonesia had already far-reaching rules preventing tax haven usage and treaty shopping (Kaur and Susarla, 2011).

Tax avoidance and anti-avoidance rules in Indonesia

However, there is evidence that aggressive tax planning is currently practiced in Indonesia. For example, Lestari (2008) conducted an empirical study which provided evidence that Foreign Controlled Companies[10] (FCC) avoided taxes by reporting corporate losses due to transfer pricing manipulation schemes. Lestari employed a quantitative study using taxpayers from the Foreign Investment Tax Office as samples and compared certain variables (i.e. capacity, financial performance, affiliated transactions, and losses) with Indonesian Controlled Companies[11] (ICC). The study concluded that there was evidence of FCC avoiding taxes through transfer pricing in Indonesia (Lestari, 2008).

---

10 Companies owned by non-residents of Indonesia (foreign investment companies).
11 Companies owned by residents of Indonesia (domestic companies).

However, Prebble (2009) indicated that tax avoidance in Indonesia would not be sufficiently tackled by the existing SAARs and the substance over form principle alone. Prebble (2009) suggested that a GAAR should be introduced to operate more generally and also serve to highlight the importance of the substance over form principle in Indonesian tax law.

Rahayu (2008), Alhunieska (2008), Martatilova (2009), and Prebble (2009) have also recommended that the Indonesian government enact a GAAR. For example, in her dissertation Rahayu (2008) examined tax avoidance practice of foreign direct investment in Indonesia in the form of subsidiary company (PT PMA). Rahayu's research indicated that tax avoidance schemes which were commonly used by PT PMA were in the form of transfer pricing, thin capitalisation, treaty shopping, controlled foreign corporation (CFC), and the use of tax haven countries (Rahayu, 2008). Importantly, Rahayu found that the Indonesian Anti-Tax Avoidance policy contained many loopholes which could be exploited in tax avoidance schemes. Consequently, Rahayu (2008) suggested that Indonesia should have a GAAR to complement its SAARs.

Martatilova (2009) also recommended a GAAR for Indonesia after undertaking a study of Indonesian anti-avoidance rules from a normative juridical view. The study concluded that the SAARs should be complemented with a GAAR and suggested that Indonesia should enact a statutory GAAR which contains definitions of the following crucial concepts (so as to provide greater guidance to both taxpayers and tax authorities): tax avoidance, acceptable tax avoidance, and unacceptable tax avoidance (Martatilova, 2009).

A similar finding was found in a study by Alhunieska (2008) who analysed anti-tax avoidance measures in Indonesia from an intelligence perspective. Alhunieska (2008) concluded that the SAARs embedded in the Income Tax Law No. 36 of 2008 are insufficient in combatting tax avoidance because there are loopholes that still exist which could be exploited by taxpayers to avoid taxes. From an intelligence perspective, the SAARs were regarded as tactical intelligence measures which responded to the current tax avoidance schemes, whereas a GAAR was considered as strategic intelligence measure which responds not only to the current aggressive tax planning schemes but also counters potential future schemes. This strategic measure in the form of a GAAR is necessary because of the complexity and rapid development of business transactions which are moving more quickly than the ability of the tax authority to counter the tax avoidance schemes (Alhunieska, 2008).

Overall, Rahayu (2008), Alhunieska (2008), Martatilova (2009), and Prebble (2009) have recommended that Indonesia should enact a GAAR to combat tax avoidance. However, those recommendations were not based on empirical evidence. This paper aims to provide that evidence and contributes to the debate of introducing a GAAR in Indonesia. After reviewing the literature, the next section outlines the research design implemented in addressing the research questions by providing evidence from the perspective of key stakeholders.

Research design

Research methodology

As evidenced above, there is a vast literature on aggressive tax planning and the GAAR but arguably the literature is less developed in Indonesia. A previous empirical study on tax avoidance in Indonesia adopted a mixed-method approach by applying quantitative and qualitative methods (Rahayu, 2008).

This paper embarks on a similar approach in researching aggressive tax planning and makes a further contribution to the literature by interviewing the key stakeholders involved in the regulation and administration of anti-avoidance provisions. Specifically, the research involved collecting primary data from four categories of stakeholders, i.e. tax advisors, taxpayers, tax officials, and tax judges.

Interview sample

A sample of thirty two participants was interviewed, which consisted of eleven tax advisors, eight tax officials, seven taxpayers, and six tax judges. In general, participant recruitment in this study followed a snowballing sampling technique in order to obtain an information-rich sample. Creswell (2013) points out that this sampling strategy identifies cases of interest based on a chain of participants. The researcher recruited new participants by asking the interviewees whether they knew of people who might be interested in participating in the recruitment of tax advisors, taxpayers (represented by the tax managers of large businesses in Indonesia), and tax judges.

The research took place in Jakarta, which was chosen as it is the capital of Indonesia and is also the city where the majority of taxpayers conduct their business. Furthermore, it is where the head offices of tax firms, tax officials, and tax judges, are located.

In selecting the sample, the profiles of the interviewees were initially examined to access the most experienced participants. The researcher relied heavily on the internet and social media, such as Linkedin, to recruit tax managers. After viewing the profiles of potential participants on the internet, the researcher attempted to contact them via email.

In recruiting tax advisors, the researcher retrieved their emails from their tax firms' websites. The tax advisors interviewed represented all of the big four tax accounting firms and medium tax firms present in Indonesia. Finally, in recruiting tax officials and tax judges, a formal request was made to conduct research in each institution. The participants recruited had a minimum of 10 years' experience in the taxation field and included partners in the tax firms and CEOs. Their extensive knowledge was highly beneficial in conducting this research.

Interview protocol

The interviews followed a semi-structured format and were conducted from July to October 2015. The semi-structured interview is a strategy to gain an understanding of the situation from the perspective of those who have experienced it (McKerchar, 2008). Employing this method allowed the participants to elaborate on their answers and enabled the researcher to expand on the questions based on the participants' answers.

Semi-structured interviews of approximately 45-90 minutes duration were conducted which allowed interviewees to elaborate and expand upon their responses and provide any further comments they had. All interviews were transcribed by the researcher and a thematic analysis (Bryman, 2012 and Boyatzis, 1998) was employed in evaluating the interview transcripts.

Discussion and Analysis

Existing anti-avoidance rules in Indonesia

Before examining the interview data, a brief overview of the existing anti-avoidance rules is provided. Indonesia has several SAARs but opinions are divided regarding a GAAR. The general view is that Indonesia does not presently have a GAAR in its tax system and this is based on the country reports by tax consultants such as Ernst & Young (EY, 2013), Deloitte Touche Tohmatsu Limited (Deloitte, 2014) and KPMG (2013). However, Nakayama (2013) suggested that Indonesia already has a GAAR in the form of Income Tax Law (ITL) Article 4:

> *Taxable object is income, which is defined as any increase in economics capacity received by or accrued by a taxpayer from Indonesia as well as from offshore, which may be utilized for consumption or increasing the taxpayer's wealth, in whatever name and form, including ... (Income Tax Law, 2008, Article 4).*

Further evidence is in the form of Income Tax Law (2008, Article 23) which stated, "The following income, in whatever name and form, paid, apportioned to be paid, or on the due date of payment by ... shall be subject to withholding tax of ...", and Income Tax Law (2008, Article 26) stated, "The following income, in whatever name and form, paid, apportioned to be paid, or on the due date of payment by ... to foreign taxpayers ... shall be subject to withholding tax of ...".

In this case, the emphasis of Nakayama is on the wording "in whatever name and form" as a GAAR in Indonesia based on substance over form principle. However, these Articles in the ITL serve mainly as a guide in determining income tax and withholding tax. That is, the articles only provide guidance in determining income based on substance over form. This so-called GAAR is insufficient because there are several ways to avoid tax, not only by disguising income, but also by devising deductions and deferrals. Furthermore, these articles are deficient with regard to designing a GAAR, which typically comprises four elements: the provision to invoke a GAAR, the definition of tax benefit, the reconstruction power, and the tax administration issue (Cooper, 2001).

Indonesian Specific Anti-Avoidance Rules are predominantly found in Article 18 of ITL and include references to controlled foreign companies in paragraph 2, thin capitalization rules in paragraph 3, transfer pricing in paragraph 3, advance pricing agreements[12] in paragraph 3(a), special purpose company[13] related transactions in paragraph 3(b), conduit companies[14] in tax haven countries in paragraph 3(c), and international hiring out of labour[15] in paragraph 3(d).

---

12 An agreement between a multinational company and one or more tax authorities on the methods used to determine appropriate prices in transfer pricing situations (S James, *A Dictionary of Taxation*, 2nd ed, Edward Elgar, 2012, 8).

13 A company established for a special purpose as a mean to conduct tax avoidance by the parent company. A taxpayer who purchases shares or assets of other entity through a special purpose company can be deemed as the real party who conducts the transaction, provided that such taxpayer is the affiliation of the special purpose company and the price of the transaction is unfairly settled (Article 18 of the *Income Tax Law 2008* (Republic of Indonesia).

14 A company through which earnings from foreign countries can be channelled to a holding company in a country with lower tax rates or in a tax haven (S James, *A Dictionary of Taxation*, 2nd ed, Edward Elgar, 2012, 60).

15 The amount of income that an individual resident taxpayer has received from an employer which is the affiliation of non-resident's entity may be adjusted by tax authority, in case of the employer transfers the payment in forms of expenses or other expenditures which is paid to his affiliation (Article 18 of the *Income Tax Law 2008* (Republic of Indonesia)).

Other SAARs cover beneficial ownership[16] rules which tackle tax avoidance using treaty shopping schemes. The provision is found in Article 26, paragraph 1a, of the ITL which specifies that the domicile country of the foreign taxpayer, other than those conducting business or performing business through a permanent establishment[17] (PE) in Indonesia, is the country where the foreign taxpayer resides or where he or she actually receives benefit from that income (beneficial owner) (Income Tax Law, 2008, Article 26). Also, in support of these laws, there are operational regulations from the Minister of Finance Regulations and the Director General of Taxes (DGT).

Interview Findings in Indonesia

Interview findings in relation to aggressive tax planning

In examining the interview data and distinguishing between participants, a code was used to guarantee anonymity. For example, tax advisors were coded with 1a to 1k, tax managers were coded with 2a to 2g, tax officials were coded with 3a to 3h, and tax judges were coded with 4a to 4f.

In the interviews, tax advisors and taxpayers indicated that aggressive tax planning is solely a term used by tax officials. Generally, tax advisors and taxpayers stated that they only undertook tax management. They considered tax as a cost which needed to be efficient. Generally speaking, in the absence of a specific provision that made a particular type of transaction taxable, taxpayers and their tax advisors were led to believe that the activity in question was tax-free. However, when there was a difference between their tax treatments and the tax officers' assessment, a dispute could occur.

The issue of tax compliance was predominant throughout the interviews. Taxpayers indicated that they must comply with tax rulings but found it difficult to find the balance between the cost of compliance and the cost of doing their business. However, compliant taxpayers would manage their tax planning in a way that is within the law. Tax manager 2a argued that when a company invests more in compliance cost, they tend to be more compliant. For example, a company which hires special staff to handle tax matters is more compliant than a company which has the same staff doing tax matters along with other matters, such as accounting and finance.

---

16 The person who benefits from an asset. This might be different from the legal owner, who may be a nominee (S James, *A Dictionary of Taxation*, 2nd ed, Edward Elgar, 2012, 30).

17 A distinct fixed place where business is carried on and which usually leads to tax liability in a particular jurisdiction (S James, *A Dictionary of Taxation*, 2nd ed, Edward Elgar, 2012, 199).

Most participants concurred that aggressive tax planning and tax avoidance are similar and are used by taxpayers who want to take advantage of the loopholes in the tax laws. Aggressive tax planning was considered as unacceptable tax avoidance. However, the majority of interviewees indicated that the line between acceptable and unacceptable tax avoidance and the difference between defensive and aggressive tax planning should be defined by the tax authority.

Basically, taxpayers believed that they only undertook tax management, and had not been involved in aggressive tax planning or tax avoidance. They indicated that aggressive tax planning and tax avoidance were tax office jargon. They believed that a company whose tax affairs were well-managed would not undertake aggressive tax planning.

The difference between aggressive tax planning and acceptable tax planning lies in the motive or purpose of taxpayers. As tax manager 2a stated:

> *Generally a company wants to increase its profit from its generic business by increasing productivity or creating business innovation, but not from tax minimization. If the motive of its tax planning is not driven by business purposes then I will call it aggressive tax planning.*

This opinion is consistent with the literature which indicated that aggressive tax planning usually has no business purpose (Lapidoth, 2006). This is also in line with the definition of aggressive tax planning provided by the CRA (Larin et al., 2008).

Interestingly, the terminology has also changed over time. For example, tax advisor 1c said that:

> *Tax avoidance is legal, tax evasion is illegal; it seems to me that the thinking has changed somewhat that tax avoidance itself now seems to be a bad thing. And perhaps the terminology is wrong because I think what is and what should be legitimate and should stand up even from an ethical or moral viewpoint is that where options are available to taxpayers they are allowed to choose the option which results in the lowest tax ability. That is surely the approach that we always take with our advice. If you call it aggressive tax avoidance then certainly in terms of current thinking that is moving into the kind of maybe not quite illegal but maybe immoral or not really in the spirit of how taxes are supposed to be applied.*

Several participants indicated that aggressive tax planning, although legal, was unethical. Aggressive tax planning was perceived as a practice which is within the law but against the morality of a nation. On the one hand, taxpayers have the freedom to arrange their tax matters, but, on the other hand, taxpayers are expected to act ethically. However, aggressive tax planning is still in the context of tax planning itself which is not against the law. Therefore, it is not a fraud and cannot be categorised as tax evasion. Tax judge 4b emphasised this notion by stating that, "Avoidance is not legally wrong, but must be battled, because it causes improper tax saving".

Almost all participants agreed that aggressive tax planning is not a phenomenon limited to developed countries, but also occurred in developing countries such as Indonesia. Generally, aggressive tax planning involved cross border transactions which correspond with multinational companies, both inbound and outbound investments. Consequently, as the world economy becomes more integrated and there are different tax rates between countries, it is suggested that aggressive tax planning is more likely to exist.

It was evident from the interviews that aggressive tax planning can take the form of various schemes but generally falls into four types of schemes which usually involve the use of tax haven countries. This finding is consistent with the study of Rahayu (2008) which found that the following schemes are used by foreign controlled companies to avoid taxes. The first scheme is controlled foreign companies (CFCs) where companies can easily transfer their profits to their subsidiaries abroad and never distribute dividends to the parent companies in Indonesia. The subsidiaries are taxed on territorial income,[18] not worldwide income, so their profits are not taxed abroad which leads to double non-taxation.

The second scheme, thin capitalisation, usually happens when companies acquire loans from abroad with a significant interest and loan amount which surpasses the equity. In an arm-length transaction this can still occur, but in an affiliated transaction, this kind of scheme is more common. This scheme is considered by tax officers as aggressive tax planning because it can cause a profitable company to make a loss after the income is reduced by interest deductions attributable to the loan.

The third scheme is treaty abuse, which is conducted in the form of treaty shopping. Taxpayers use treaty facilities to minimise tax or to avoid tax in Indonesia. For example, where a company established a CFC in the Netherlands, the tax treaty between Indonesia and the Netherlands states that a loan from the Netherlands is exempted from tax when the duration of the loan exceeds two years. This facility is used by taxpayers who want to give loans to Indonesian companies so that the interest income is never taxed and the

---

18 Territorial income means taxpayers are taxed based on their income generated solely in the country; while, a worldwide tax system levies tax from all source of income worldwide.

Indonesian companies can minimise tax by deducting the interest expense. This is a concern for the tax authority and the treaty between Indonesia and the Netherlands has now been renegotiated to change that clause.[19]

The interview data also indicated that another example of treaty abuse is related to combined royalty and management fee payments. Also included in this scheme is a transaction which is in the nature of a royalty payment but stated as a management fee in the contract. The management fee is a business profit which can only be taxed in Indonesia as a source country, provided there is a PE. When there is no PE involved, then the profit cannot be taxed. In this case, when examined thoroughly, the management fee is actually a technical fee, which is a royalty.

Another example of a royalty case is assigning the intellectual property in a country which gives the most preferable tax rate in the treaty. In substance, the company does not have the capacity to develop the intellectual property nor to generate one. This is also a concern for tax officials to ascertain that a tax treaty is not exploited to obtain tax benefits. Therefore, as stated by tax official 3a, the tax authority is constantly developing regulations to be more optimal in dealing with treaty abuse cases.

A fourth scheme is transfer pricing. Although transfer pricing is not illegal, in substance, it distorts business competition and fairness. With a transfer pricing scheme, taxpayers can easily shift profits from a country with high tax rate to a country with low or more preferable tax rate. Transfer pricing is a worldwide tax issue which also exists in Indonesia. This is further illustrated by tax official 3a who stated:

> In essence, transfer pricing is the easiest and most effective way in tax planning which some countries find it hard to handle, ..., to quote from OECD research, transfer pricing is the most effective way to avoid tax. However, the Indonesian tax authority thinks that transfer pricing is normal as long as there is no intention to avoid tax.

The interview data also indicated that aggressive tax planning can occur domestically. It is usually related to non-deductible expenses and deductible expenses. For example, a non-deductible expense can be treated as deductible (e.g. donations disguised as marketing expenses). Consequently, acceptable tax planning can be differentiated from aggressive tax planning, which occurs to solely acquire tax benefits.

---

19 This treaty had been ratified and the tax charged shall not exceed 5 per cent of the gross amount of the interest (Article 2 of Protocol Amending the Agreement between the Government of the Republic of Indonesia and the Government of the Kingdom of the Netherlands for the Avoidance of Double Taxation and the Prevention of Fiscal Evasion with Respect to Taxes on Income and Its Protocol).

In order to identify the aforementioned schemes, the quality of human resources to deal with aggressive tax planning is crucial. One issue identified by tax judge 4b was that officials need have the ability to identify aggressive tax planning schemes. Judges, in particular, need to have the skills to identify the schemes, determine whether the schemes are unacceptable, and determine the substance of the transactions.

It is evident from the interviews that in dealing with aggressive tax planning, tax officials adhere to existing tax regulations. When there are no rules governing a particular scheme, tax officials generally consider international best practices and accepted principles under the OECD guidelines.

Interview findings in relation to the adequacy of SAARs

Regarding SAARs in Indonesia, the majority of participants agreed that the current rules were insufficient to combat aggressive tax planning. Tax official 3a stated that regulations regarding transfer pricing maybe adequate but were poorly implemented. Further, tax manager 2a agreed that the SAARs need to be supported by clearer rulings and consistent implementation.

One issue raised by some of the interviewees was concerned with the different tax treatment by tax officials in assessing similar transactions by taxpayers. Tax advisor 1c, for instance, pointed out that:

> *The problem that I see from my perspective and that of my clients, is that the application of that theory (SAARs) by the Indonesian tax authority is not necessarily in the spirit of what is intended... For example, if they're investigating a taxpayer and decide there's a transfer pricing issue, under the regulations, they're supposed to carry out the full study themselves to establish what the result should be. I think it's very rare that they're able to do that. They just make the adjustments and then walk away and let somebody else decide whether it's the correct adjustment or not. Usually they actually say to taxpayers don't argue with us, let the Court decide and the problem is that the Court will only decide at least two years later than the point when the assessment is made and quite often that the Court doesn't even make a decision so taxpayers are left with an unfavourable result. So, the theory is reasonably fair but the practice is not.*

This kind of behaviour has resulted in an increasing number of Tax Court cases. As tax judge 4c indicated, the number of outstanding tax cases has reached an overwhelming level.

The differing applications of SAARs is arguably caused by the unclear wording of the provisions. Tax judge 4b indicated that it could also be a result of the drafting of SAARs which is too general and thus some articles need more explanation. He stated that, "For taxation, it can't be too general, that's my opinion, because the application will be too loose, the boundary must be clear".

However, very prescriptive wording of the provisions could cause another problem. Tax advisor 1c explained that:

> I think one leads to the other because the regulations are, either they're not clear or they are too clear. I mean for example in transfer pricing the current Indonesian regulations are very prescriptive in that they say that companies must fall into a specific category, either must be a fully- fledged manufacture, limited risk, toll or contract manufacture, they have to fall in one of the other categories. Whereas in reality a lot of companies are somewhere in between; it's not in this box or that box, there's a mix of arrangements and so there's a lot of scope for companies to be wrongly categorized and adjustments need to be made accordingly because they have to fit into a box that doesn't necessarily reflect the reality.

The evidence implies that the government should be more aware of taxpayers' real business conditions when drafting regulations.

In order to secure a more consistent application of SAARs, most participants also suggested developing further training for tax officials, especially tax auditors. Tax auditors should be required to keep up with the changing business process of taxpayers. Several tax judges stated that specialised training, for example, training in international taxation, is required to enable tax judges to stay up-to-date with current tax regulations in deliberating cases in order to improve the quality of their rulings.

Interview findings in relation to introducing a GAAR

The majority of participants agreed that Indonesia needs a more comprehensive GAAR to combat aggressive tax planning as distinct from Article 4. Tax advisor 1a indicated the importance of introducing a GAAR was "to reduce the practices of aggressive tax planning. This means Indonesia as a source country will incur less harm by the profit shifting pressure".

This finding is consistent with the study of Cooper (1997) which indicated that a GAAR is a powerful tool to combat artificial transactions or schemes designed to obtain tax benefits. This conclusion also concurs with the OECD (2011) recommendation regarding aggressive tax planning.

There is a view that Indonesia already has a GAAR which is stipulated in Article 4 ITL which defines "taxable income" as "any increase in economic capacity ... in whatever name and form ..." that contains the substance over form principle. However, the interviews clearly illustrated that it is inadequate in its operation. As one of the interviewees from the tax authority stated:

> So it [the Article 4 ITL] is just a regulation which is never been implemented. Substance over form is within our tax laws but it is still challenged in the Tax Court. I think we should define the GAAR, not implicitly, in a certain Article. There should be a special Article which rules the GAAR. So, it is explicit not implicit.

Therefore, if the GAAR was introduced, it should be explicit to give the tax authority the legal framework to execute it.

All participants indicated that if Indonesia introduces a GAAR, it should be stipulated in the tax law provision and supported by more detail regulations. Tax manager 2b indicated that, "If the government wants to implement a GAAR then it should be stipulated in the tax law. As long as the policy is evaluated and its effect is fully calculated, the taxpayers basically support what is regulated in the tax law".

A GAAR should be enacted in a legislation rather than merely contained in a ruling by the Director General of Taxes. According to Law No. 12 (2011), the legislation is the highest law which binds the people with the highest power; therefore, it is advisable that Indonesia has a statutory GAAR.

The majority of participants indicated the importance of certainty and clarity of tax law provisions. Generally, taxpayers and tax advisors will comply with the tax laws provided they are clear and consistent. Tax manager 2c noted that, "Initially taxpayers will abide with the rules as long as they are clear, consistent and can be easily implemented".

This concurs with the study of Atkinson (2012) which highlighted that a GAAR should be able to provide guidelines which are consistent in distinguishing between acceptable and unacceptable tax arrangements.

A further issue raised during the interviews in introducing a GAAR is its interaction with tax treaties. Currently, Indonesia has an extensive network of tax treaties with nearly 70 countries. A GAAR as a domestic rule will be effective as long as it does not contradict the existing tax treaties. In Indonesian tax law, a tax treaty is a "lex specialis", meaning that it can overrule domestic tax law. In this case, OECD Base Erosion and Profit Shifting (BEPS) Action Plan Action 15 (OECD, 2013) could be adopted where a multilateral agreement can overrule tax treaties that have deficiencies or require amendments. With the large number of tax treaties, it would require a lot of work to rectify the articles in the tax treaties one by one. Harmonisation of different tax laws across countries is less likely to work because each country must have its own domestic interest. Instead, the government could opt to initiate a multilateral agreement to address the problem of aggressive tax planning. Consequently, the multilateral exchange of information is crucial for combatting aggressive tax planning.

On the contrary, tax judge 4c suggested that instead of introducing a statutory GAAR, Indonesia should focus on replacing tax treaties that provided loopholes to be utilised in aggressive tax planning. Another way is to add a Limitation on Benefits (LOB) clause into the tax treaties.

The OECD BEPS Action Plan will help reduce aggressive tax planning, as indicated by tax advisor 1c :

> Well, I certainly think that it's going to make it very difficult for the multinationals to apply some of the arrangements that they had in the past, and I think most of what I understand or I read about in Action item 15, I think are very good and very fair and should lead to a more equitable result in terms of where taxes are paid. The danger is always that multinationals, and perhaps their advisors, are a bit more flexible than the government and may be one step ahead, so I don't know whether the implementation to the extent that it can be applied is going to cover everything, but I certainly believe that it should wipe out quite a lot of the practices that happened in the past.

Based on this evidence, it is suggested that in Indonesia, the DGT needs to scrutinize the OECD BEPS Action Plan carefully before deciding what to adopt.

The challenge in introducing a GAAR in Indonesia lies in convincing the investors that there will be sufficient safeguards to ensure that the power granted to the tax authority is not abused. Interestingly, most taxpayers and tax advisors agreed that a GAAR should be in place to ensure a level playing field in doing business. They also indicated that there should be appropriate guidelines in enacting a GAAR. As long as the regulation is clear and can be easily implemented, taxpayers and tax advisors fully support the introduction of a GAAR in Indonesia.

Conclusion

Summary of the main findings

A summary of the main findings based on the above analysis reveals the following. First, aggressive tax planning is a problem in Indonesia, possibly not so much in number and complexity as in more developed countries, but taxpayers nevertheless will try to exploit the loopholes either way. Aggressive tax planning is considered as unacceptable tax avoidance which creates artificial schemes without any business substance. However, taxpayers believe that the tax authority should clearly distinguish between what is acceptable and unacceptable tax avoidance.

Second, the current SAARs in Indonesia are inadequate to combat aggressive tax planning on an ongoing base, given that there are new schemes which are not covered by the SAARs. Taxpayers will always be one step ahead of tax officials in devising schemes that are not covered by the existing tax laws. Likewise, the application of existing SAARs should also be improved to provide consistent tax treatment.

Third, a GAAR should be introduced in Indonesia as an option to combat aggressive tax planning. The interviews indicate that the substance over form principle and Article 4 of ITL are inadequate and insufficient to effectively clamp down on unacceptable tax avoidance. In addition, a GAAR will attempt to strike down aggressive tax planning that is not envisaged at the time of drafting.

Tax policy implications

Following on from the recommendation to introduce a GAAR in Indonesia, there are some tax policy implications that flow from the above analysis. First, as a consequence of implementing a GAAR, there should be adequate training provided to tax officers as well as tax judges to familiarise themselves with the new law. The DGT needs to ensure that they have the necessary resources to enact a GAAR and provide adequate training for tax officials when applying the GAAR.

Second, the application of the GAAR should be supported by detailed rulings. Since the tax law only contains a fundamental concept of the GAAR, further breakdown of the regulation will provide guidance on the GAAR application. These rulings should also be reflective of taxpayers' real business conditions.

Third, the OECD BEPS Action Plan Action Item 15, which is a mandate for the development of a multilateral instrument on tax treaty measures, should be adopted (OECD, 2013). Considering the vast network of tax treaties currently in place, the Indonesian government should think about adopting the OECD BEPS Action Plan Action 15 concerning multilateral cooperation with some adjustments for Indonesian conditions. With this instrument in place, Indonesia should have a robust solution should there be a conflict between a GAAR and a tax treaty.

Limitations

It is acknowledged that this study is not without its limitations. For example, this research focuses only on large taxpayers which are usually handled by large and medium tax firms. Consequently, this study did not take into account small and medium taxpayers which might also be affected by the introduction of a GAAR. Second, the field work only took place in Jakarta, which is the centre of government and business in Indonesia, which excluded other areas of the country where the findings may have been different.

Further research

However, despite the limitations, this study is part of ongoing research which will incorporate further legal and archival components to complement the qualitative component of the research. It is envisaged that this and further research will support the argument of a GAAR being introduced in Indonesia to tackle aggressive tax planning in future years.

References

Alhunieska, F. (2011) Analisis terhadap Ketentuan Anti-Tax Avoidance dalam Undang-Undang Nomor 36 Tahun 2008 sebagai Upaya Pencegahan Pengindaran Pajak Internasional [The Analysis of the Anti-Tax Avoidance Provisions in Act No. 36 of 2008 as An Effort to Prevent International Tax Avoidance] (Master Thesis, The University of Indonesia).

Aaronson, Q. C., Bartlett, J., Freedman, J., Henderson, S. L., Nowlan, H., & Tiley, J. (2011). GAAR Study: A Study to Consider Whether a General Anti-avoidance Rule Should be Introduced into the UK Tax System. Retrieved at http://www.tax.org.uk/Resources/CIOT/Documents/2012/01/111111_GAAR_final_report.pdf

Atkinson, C. (2012). General Anti-Avoidance Rules: Exploring the Balance between the Taxpayers' Need for Certainty and the Government's Need to Prevent Tax Avoidance. *Journal of Australian Taxation*, 14(1), 1-56.

Boyatzis, R. E. (1998). *Transforming Qualitative Information: Thematic Analysis and Code Development*. Thousand Oaks, CA: SAGE Publications.

Braithwaite, J. (2005). *Markets in Vice Markets in Virtue.* Annandale, N.S.W.: Federation Press.

Braithwaite, J. (2006). Narrative and Compulsory Compassion. *Law and Social Inquiry,* **31**(2), 425-446.

Braithwaite, J. (2013). Flipping markets to virtue with qui tam and restorative justice. *Accounting, Organizations and Society,* **38**(6), 458-468.

Brown, K. (2012). A Comparative Look at Regulation of Corporate Tax Avoidance. Dordrecht, New York: Springer.

Bryman, A. (2012). *Social Research Methods Fourth Edition.* Oxford: Oxford University Press.

Cooper, G. (1997). *Tax Avoidance and the Rule of Law.* Amsterdam, Netherlands: IBFD Publication.

Cooper, G. (2001). International Experience with General Anti-Avoidance Rules. *SMU Law Review,* **54**, 83-130.

Creswell, J.W. (2013). *Qualitative Inquiry and Research Design: Choosing Among Five Approaches.* Thousand Oaks, CA: SAGE Publications.

Deloitte. (2014). *Taxation and Investment in Indonesia 2014.* Retrieved from http://www2.deloitte.com/content/dam/Deloitte/global/Documents/Tax/dttl-tax-indonesiaguide-2014.pdf

EY. (2013). GAAR Rising Mapping Tax Enforcement's Evolution. Retrieved from http://www.ey.com/Publication/vwLUAssets/Mapping_tax_enforcement%E2%80%99s_evolution/$FILE/GAAR.pdf

Finnerty, C.J., Merks, P., Petriccione, M. and Russo, R. (2007). *Fundamentals of International Tax Planning.* Amsterdam, Netherlands: IBFD Publications.

Frank, M.M., Lynch, L.J. and Rego, S.O. (2009) Tax Reporting Aggressiveness and Its Relation to Aggressive Financial Reporting. *The Accounting Review,* **84**(2), 467-496.

Freedman, J. (2014). Designing a general anti-abuse rule: Striking a balance. *Asia Pacific Tax Bulletin,* May/June, 167-173.

Income Tax Law (2008) Republic of Indonesia.

James, S. R. (2012). *A Dictionary of Taxation.* Edward Elgar Publishing.

Karimeri, R. (2011). A Critical Review of the Definition of Tax Avoidance in the Case Law of the European Court of Justice. *Intertax,* **39**(6-7), 296-316.

Kaur, D. and Susarla, K. (2011). Anti-Avoidance Developments in Selected Asian Jurisdictions. *Asia-Pacific Tax Bulletin,* **17** (4), 256-277.

KPMG. (2013). Indonesia Tax Profile. Retrieved from https://www.kpmg.com/Global/en/services/Tax/regional-tax-centers/asia-pacific-tax-centre/Documents/CountryProfiles/Indonesia.pdf

Lampreave, P. (2013). Anti-Tax Avoidance Measures in China and India: An Evaluation of Specific Court Decisions. *Bulletin for International Taxation,* **67**(1), 49-60.

Lapidoth, A. (2006). New Legislative Measures in Israel to Counter Aggressive Tax Planning. *IBFD Bulletin,* June, 255-260.

Larin, G., Duong, R. and Jacques, M. (2008) Policy Forum: Responses to Aggressive Tax Planning – A Study Framework. *Canadian Tax Journal*, **56**(1), 143-159.

Larking, B. (2005). *IBFD International Tax Glossary*, 5th edition, IBFD.

Law No. 36 of 2008 on Income Tax (Republic of Indonesia).

Law No. 12 of 2011 on Formation of Laws (Republic of Indonesia).

Lestari, D. (2008). Kajian Empiris Metode Tidak Langsung terhadap Modus Penghindaran Pajak melalui Transfer Pricing: Studi Kasus di KPP PMA [Empirical Study on Indirect Method of Tax Avoidance Schemes through Transfer Pricing: Case Study at Foreign Investment Tax Office] (Master Thesis, The University of Indonesia), 5.

Li, J. (2010). Tax Transplants and Local Culture: A Comparative Study of the Chinese and Canadian GAAR. *Theoretical Inquiries in Law*, **11**, 655-685.

Lisowsky, P. (2010). Seeking Shelter: Empirically Modeling Tax Shelters Using Financial Statement Information. *The Accounting Review*, **85**(5), 1693-1720.

Martatilova, LPA. (2009). Kajian Normatif Yuridis mengenai Peraturan Anti Penghindaran Pajak (Anti Avoidance Rule) menurut Peraturan Perundang-undangan Perpajakan di Indonesia [Normative-Juridical Study of Anti-Avoidance Rule According to Indonesian Tax Laws] (Master Thesis, The University of Indonesia).

McKerchar, M. (2008). Philosophical Paradigms, Inquiry Strategies and Knowledge Claims: Applying the Principles of Research Design and Conduct to Taxation. *eJournal of Tax Research*, **6**(1), 5-22.

Murphy, K. (2004). Aggressive Tax Planning: Differentiating Those Playing the Game from Those Who Don't. *Journal of Economic Psychology*, **25**, 307-329.

Nakayama, K. (2013). General Anti-Avoidance Rules in Asian Countries. Retrieved from https://www.imf.org/external/np/seminars/eng/2013/asiatax/pdfs/nakayama.pdf

OECD (2008). *Study into the Role of Tax Intermediaries*. Paris: OECD.

OECD (2011). *Corporate Loss Utilisation through Aggressive Tax Planning*. Paris: OECD.

OECD (2013). *Action Plan on Base Erosion and Profit Shifting*. Paris: OECD.

Ordower, H. (2010). The Culture of Tax Avoidance. *Saint Louis University Law Journal*, **55**(1), 47-128.

Orow, N. (1998). Part IVA Seriously Flawed in Principle. *Journal of Australian Taxation*, **1**, 57-78.

Orow, N. (2000). *General Anti-Avoidance Rules A Comparative International Analysis*. Bristol: Jordan Publishing Limited.

Pagone, G. T. (2010). *Tax Avoidance in Australia*. Annandale, N.S.W.: Federation Press.

Prebble, Z. (2009). Approaches to Tax Avoidance Prevention in Seven Asian Jurisdictions – A Comparison. *Asia-Pacific Tax Bulletin*, January/February, 22-39.

Rahayu, N. (2008). Praktik Penghindaran Pajak (Tax Avoidance) pada Foreign Direct Investment yang Berbentuk Subsidiary Company (PT. PMA) di Indonesia (Suatu Kajian tentang Kebijakan Anti-Tax Avoidance) [The Practice of Tax Avoidance by the Foreign Direct Investment in the form of Subsidiary Company (PT. PMA) in Indonesia (A Study in the Anti Tax Avoidance Policy] (Doctoral Thesis, The University of Indonesia).

Rohatgi, R. (2007). *Basic International Taxation. Volume 2*: Practice. London: BNA International Inc.

Sipahutar, T. (2016). Foreign Firms Targeted for Tax. *The Jakarta Post*, March, 29. Retrieved from http://www.thejakartapost.com/news/2016/03/29/foreign-firms-targeted-tax.html

Supriyanto, A. and Ika, S. (2005). Menteri Keuangan Serahkan Daftar 750 PMA Mangkir Pajak ke DPR (Minister of Finance Hands the List of 750 Multinationals Paying No Taxes Over to the House of Representatives). Tempo.Co, November, 24. Retrieved from http://www.tempo.co/read/news/2005/11/24/05669675/Menteri-Keuangan-Serahkan-Daftar-750-PMA-Mangkir-Pajak-ke-DPR

Tooma, R.A. (2008). *Legislating Against Tax Avoidance*. Amsterdam: IBFD.

12 Cooperative Compliance in Action:
A UK/Dutch Comparison

Dennis de Widt and Lynne Oats

Abstract

This chapter explores cooperative compliance models used to regulate large business taxpayers in the Netherlands and the UK. Both jurisdictions were early adopters of the model and have remained enthusiastic proponents. Since their inception in 2005 and 2006 respectively, the landscape has shifted significantly and tax authorities, large business taxpayers and their advisers are under unprecedented scrutiny. Although modelled on the same basic premise of closer collaboration, there are differences in the two models. In the Netherlands participation in the programme is voluntary and the mode of engagement effectively formalised. The UK by contrast is characterised by incremental adaptation over time and applies to all large businesses. There are considerable benefits to be gained from comparing different models of cooperation, but it is important that the economic and institutional context is well understood as a backdrop to evaluating how the models work in practice in different settings.

Introduction[1]

Cooperative compliance, as a regulatory mechanism, covers a range of arrangements centred on a core notion of collaboration for mutual benefit. Its emergence and adoption has been patchy across countries, with considerable variation in the operational detail. Formerly known as "enhanced relationships", a term coined by the OECD's 2008 intermediaries study, co-operative compliance mechanisms are most commonly focused on large business taxpayers who have long been recognised as posing significant risk to tax authorities in terms of potential revenue loss. There is no universal cooperative compliance model, but features most commonly seen include:

---

1   The authors gratefully acknowledge research funding from the EU's Horizon 2020 research and innovation programme 2014–2018 (Grant Agreement No FairTax 649439). The authors would also like to express their gratitude to the interviewees for their generous time.

- Risk assessment procedures that identify those taxpayers in need of closer monitoring, as distinct from those who for various reasons can be 'trusted' to be compliant;
- Real time working under which discussions between taxpayers and tax authorities are ongoing and proactive, rather than ad hoc and reactive, as is the case with more traditional command and control models of tax regulation; and
- Mutual understanding, whereby both parties to the arrangement invest in developing a more nuanced appreciation of the context and constraints under which the other is working.

The emergence of cooperative compliance arrangements can be traced back to developments in the late 20th century in which regulators more broadly began to appreciate the benefits of adopting a more responsive stance towards regulatees (Ayres and Braithwaite, 1992; Parker, 2013). The OECD (1988) had acknowledged the merit of a responsive approach to regulation. At its crudest, responsive regulation in the tax administration context entails recognising the factors influencing compliance behaviour of taxpayers, categorising them through risk segmentation and formulating strategies to manage these various categories. Such strategies depart from the traditional 'detect non-compliance and punish it' approach by embracing more supportive techniques with the aim of encouraging voluntary compliance with tax obligations.

The need for new approaches to encourage a move away from traditional adversarial interaction towards a more collaborative approach heightened in the wake of the large corporate scandals of the later 1990s and early 2000s. In 2005, three jurisdictions, the Netherlands, the United States and Ireland, initiated specific programmes designed to secure higher levels of cooperation from large corporate taxpayers. The UK also embarked on a series of initiatives that collectively could be described as cooperative compliance, but were not overtly labelled as such at the time, indeed the UK took the lead in the OECD 2008 Intermediaries study in which the term 'enhanced relationship' was first used.

Impetus for these changes did not only stem from the desire of tax authorities to better manage their relationships with large corporate taxpayers, but also from the taxpayers themselves, who were increasingly frustrated by delays and deficiencies in tax authority interactions and placed a high value on securing certainty in relation to their tax liabilities. The progress of implementation of cooperative compliance arrangements worldwide was investigated by the International Fiscal Association (IFA) in 2010, which published a report in 2012 that highlighted the need for taxpayers and tax authorities to work together for mutual benefit, while conceding that there was, at that time, considerable variation in the appetite for enhanced relationships. The IFA report identifies a number of common features of enhanced relationships and attempts a definition as follows (IFA 2012, p.18):

The Enhanced Relationship concerns a specifically defined institutional relationship, based on mutually expressed intentions and not on detailed rules, that [taxpayers] and [tax authorities] voluntarily enter into above and beyond their basic legal obligations, which relationship is based on mutual understanding, respect and true co-operation, and has as aim the administration of tax laws to the TP's business in the most efficient and timely matter, assuming full, timely and reciprocal disclosure of relevant tax related information (including positions taken) and leading to the assessment of the correct amount of tax taking into account the spirit and purpose of the tax law (rather than merely the letter of the law) while respecting each parties' rights and obligations under procedural laws in case of disagreement on what constitutes the correct amount of tax.

The IFA report showed support for continued global discussion about the merits and practicalities of enhanced relationships, which around this time began to be referred to as cooperative compliance relationships, given that the notion of enhanced relationships did not sit well with contemporaneous accusations of special treatment for large corporations, which ultimately led to the OECD's Base Erosion and Profit Shifting (BEPS) project. A follow up to the OECD's 2008 Intermediaries study was led by the Netherlands in 2012, culminating in a report published in 2013, which noted that cooperative relationships were becoming embedded in risk management strategies and recognised several challenges in implementation. The influence of the Netherlands on the 2013 OECD report is reflected in the emphasis on tax control frameworks which form the backbone of the version of cooperative compliance adopted by the Dutch National Tax and Customs Agency (NTCA). A subsequent OECD report (OECD, 2016), published by the Forum on Tax Administration's Large Business Programme and produced with the cooperation of the Business and Industry Advisory Committee to the OECD (BIAC) and members of large accounting firms acting as advisers to multinational businesses, provides guidance on the design and operation of tax control frameworks.

The conclusions of the 2016 report are (OECD, 2016, p28):
- The value to both a taxpayer and the tax administration of a fully developed and monitored internal control system that includes a robust tax control framework (TCF) is well demonstrated;

- A common understanding about a TCF, its essential features, and how it is deployed in practice underpins the successful operation of a cooperative compliance relationship;
- In circumstances where both parties have agreed to be transparent, a fully developed TCF provides a verifiable assurance to the taxpayer and revenue body that tax risks generally may not arise because of a lack of control and a poor understanding of the tax risks on the part of the enterprise itself;
- Although it is not possible to prescribe a one size fits all system of internal control, six principles or building blocks were identified. They are: tax strategy established; applied comprehensively; responsibility assigned; governance documented; testing performed; assurance provided;
- To form an opinion on the effectiveness of a particular TCF, the revenue body needs to assess and test its scope and effectiveness;
- Revenue bodies may also have mandatory disclosure regimes designed to ensure disclosure of tax risks to obtain greater assurance about the reliability of an enterprises (sic) tax risk management system; and
- To assure external stakeholders that the revenue body is impartial, tax officials must remain impartial and professional to retain a critical attitude towards the taxpayer and the information and tax risks that it discloses.

Cooperative compliance in the Netherlands[2]

The Netherlands arguably has one of the most structured cooperative compliance models, introduced in 2005 in an environment in which regulatory pressures more broadly were felt to be increasingly onerous in Dutch society and in which self-regulation was promulgated to ease this pressure. As was the case in other jurisdictions, the corporate scandals, which included the Dutch retailer Ahold, raised calls for heightened expectations for internal control mechanisms and led to the Corporate Governance Code in 2004 requiring a statement as to their effectiveness to be included in corporate annual reports. At the same time, the NTCA was coming under criticism for adopting a 'them and us' mentality (Stevens et al., 2012, p28) in which an antagonistic relationship led to increasing resource requirements for both taxpayers and the tax administration. Pressure for change was also brought to bear in the form of negative media coverage of the NTCA in the wake

---

2 This section draws heavily on De Widt (2017).

of the 'De Vinkenslag' incident in which agreements with taxpayers were found to be contrary to the law, leading to a reduction in the discretion allowed to NTCA officers.

In a letter of June 2004 from the Secretary of State for Finance to the Dutch House of Representatives, the term horizontal monitoring (HM) was introduced to describe a differentiated approach to supervision according to the risk profile of taxpayers, consistent with responsive regulation. These events form the backdrop to the introduction of horizontal monitoring formally in 2005 with a pilot group of twenty large, primarily listed, companies.

According to the Netherlands Tax and Customs Authority (NTCA, 2013, p.22), the horizontal monitoring system focuses upon increasing "trust, transparency and mutual understanding" between the tax administration and corporate taxpayers. The first pilot was extended to another twenty companies in 2006. The pilots were evaluated by means of a survey among corporates and the NTCA's processing teams, and found to be positive, leading to the rollout of the programme to the rest of the NTCA's Very Large Business segment in 2007, then to the Medium Sized Business Division in 2008. In 2013, the NTCA's Very Large Businesses Division was merged with the largest businesses from the Medium-Sized Businesses Division to form the Large Business Division, currently, comprising around 9,600 companies (De Widt and Oats, 2017). While the initiative originated from within the NTCA, both corporates and the Dutch employers' association (VNO-NCW) were actively involved in promoting the model.

The Dutch horizontal monitoring relationship is voluntary and corporations can apply to be part of the programme with acceptance being at the discretion of the NTCA. For corporations that are not accepted into the programme, traditional methods of interaction continue to apply. For both companies inside and outside of horizontal monitoring, a dedicated tax administrator is appointed as first point of contact. The key difference with those corporations inside the horizontal monitoring programme is that a covenant is concluded to outline the future working relationship. The features of these covenants are described by De Widt (2017) as follows:

- The covenant applies to the entire business group, or at least those business units which are engaged in the core activities and over which the Dutch management exercises a controlling influence. This should prevent cherry picking – i.e. where one part of the entity participates, the rest does not.

12: Cooperative Compliance in Action: A UK/Dutch Comparison

- The tax administration and business articulate the wish to build an effective and efficient working relationship, based upon "mutual trust, understanding and transparency".

- Rights and duties of taxpayers remain unchanged, with the outcome of the taxation of taxpayers participating in HM neither more nor less favourable than the outcome of the taxation pursuant to other forms of supervision.

- The corporation puts effort in developing a system of internal and external control, known as Tax Control Framework (TCF). The TCF is aimed at filing acceptable tax returns and should be adapted to the characteristics of the business. The tax administration, in its turn, customises its supervision based upon the quality of the company's TCF.

- The company ensures it settles its tax debts in time, while the tax administration ensures it pays any tax refunds in time.

- Real-time working is promoted by both sides. The company actively provides the NTCA with an insight into all facts and circumstances relevant for its fiscal position, as well as the standpoints and the company's perception of the resultant legal consequences. The NTCA, in turn, undertakes to provide rapid certainty in the event of requests to adopt a standpoint. Real-time working should enable fast processing of tax returns, which, in turn, will increase legal certainty for taxpayers, and optimise use of administrative capacity in both the tax administration and corporate tax divisions.

- HM is not limited to corporation tax, but includes all taxes for which a business might be liable.

- Companies remain free to execute transactions that received negative judgement from the tax administration during the preliminary consultations. The company, however, must explicitly label these transactions in its tax returns, and the tax administration is then likely to apply corrections on those returns. The company is subsequently able to litigate against these corrections, with similar objection and appeal procedures available to covenant companies as for non-covenant companies. Albeit the similarity in legal options available to companies in and outside HM constituted a discussion point during the introductory phase, it has since then become a core principle of HM (also known as "agree to disagree").

- The covenants are concluded for an unlimited period of time. If one of the parties wishes to terminate the compliance agreement, it must

provide a written statement to the other party of its reasons for doing so. Within the tax administration, the account management team must always consult with the NTCA's management and professional specialists before taking any decisions that may lead to the termination of HM relationships.
- Periodic evaluations of the compliance agreements are undertaken. In theory, these are conducted once a year with very large businesses and once every two years for other large businesses.

The entry process into horizontal monitoring comprises three phases, the first being a feasibility analysis where the steps required to be taken by the corporate are explained, the attitude of the corporate towards compliance is evaluated and a client profile drafted outlining the current relationship including outstanding disputes. The second stage is a compliance scan conducted by the NTCA to review the feasibility of horizontal monitoring through interviews with key personnel to gauge whether "the organisation is willing to gain tax control (in the longer term) and is transparent about tax issues" (NTCA, 2013, p.19). This will include evaluation of internal controls including IT systems and external monitoring and advice received by the taxpayer. Assuming that the compliance scan does not reveal any fundamental problems and both parties remain positive, the relationship is confirmed in a standard covenant, from which variations are not possible given the institutional requirement to maintain legal equality. Entry into the programme allows for resolution of outstanding issues, to clear the way for prospective real time working (NTCA, 2013; Van der Hel-van Dijk and Poolen, 2013)

The key requirement is the company's level of fiscal control, as evaluated by the NTCA. Corporate taxpayers who conclude a covenant must demonstrate a higher level of control over their fiscal affairs or a willingness to improve control. Evaluation is heavily based on self-assessment and it is the taxpayer who is responsible for its tax control framework and to develop, if necessary, an action plan to move towards the required level of control.

In 2012, the Stevens Committee, named for its chair, conducted an evaluation of horizontal monitoring and while concluding that the concept of horizontal monitoring remained appropriate, in particular for large corporate groups, it identified a lack of empirical data on which to base an evaluation, observing that 'intuition' appeared to guide its introduction rather than rational considerations (NTCA, 2013). The findings of a subsequent survey of 350 large corporates from inside and outside horizontal monitoring was published in 2017 (Belastingdienst, 2017). The results of the study give mixed and partly inconclusive support to the idea that a good working relationship increases fiscal compliance behaviour.

Trust is an important component of horizontal monitoring; the NTCA trusts corporates that are fiscally transparent, in control of their fiscal affairs and have an appropriate strategy in place (NTCA, 2013). These concepts, particularly that of fiscal control, are explained in published guidelines. The trust relationship is perceived to be undermined if the corporate engages in aggressive tax planning and the NTCA may terminate a covenant if a company displays an unacceptably aggressive stance. In a letter to Parliament from the Secretary of State for Finance in 2010, it is stated that "In case a taxpayer uses fiscally aggressive structures and is not (fully) transparent therein, the covenant will be eliminated. Moreover, it does not fit into a covenant relationship when a taxpayer is constantly engaged in sophisticated tax avoidance activities."[3] The trust approach may not suit all companies, particularly those with foreign ownership or connections in jurisdictions with more adversarial tax administrations, such as the US.

One question that has arisen is why the NTCA is reluctant to provide guidance in the form of a blueprint for the tax control framework, to give corporate taxpayers more clarity about expectations. The reasons given include that the circumstances of each company will be different and so each tax control framework will be unique. Understandably, the NTCA is reluctant to impose a structure on corporations that may subsequently prove to be problematic.

In the introductory period, horizontal monitoring was considered to be beneficial from an efficiency perspective for both the NTCA and large corporates. The number of companies participating increased over time, and this became a measure of the success of the programme. The popularity of horizontal monitoring has led to resourcing problems for NTCA which may threaten the sustainability of the programme in the longer term, notwithstanding the tangible benefits such as the decline in the number of disputes. Other benefits include the speedier resolution of issues under real time working and apparently reduced compliance costs for corporate taxpayers, although the current climate of increasing distrust in the wake of BEPS and scrutiny of national tax arrangements by the European Commission may undermine these benefits.

---

3   Letter of the Secretary of State for Finance, 1 July 2010, nr. DGB2010/2996U, p.3.

Cooperative compliance in the UK

The UK has a long history of a risk-based way of working and in 2003 a New Compliance Process was introduced for corporation tax with a pilot group of 17 large businesses from a range of industries (Oats and Tuck, 2008; Tuck, 2007). The merger of the two UK revenue bodies into a single unit, Her Majesty's Revenue and Customs (HMRC), paved the way for a holistic Client (later Customer) Relationship Management (CRM) model to be implemented by the newly created Large Business Service (Tuck, 2010). Speaking in 2003, then Chairman of the tax authority, Sir Nicholas Montague said of the creation of the LBS "This has enabled us to devote some of our best technical experts to helping the customer organisations get and keep their affairs in order, and also to policing them effectively and detecting things going wrong, or risks, at an early stage" (Montagu, 2003). Two things are noteworthy in this statement, the first is the use of the term "customer" instead of taxpayer which at the time was a radical departure but has subsequently become embedded in the UK (see Tuck, 2010, 2013). The second is the mention of "risk", which referred to the development of a formalised risk assessment process in relation to large business customers. The risk assessment process was an outcome of a 2001 consultation that culminated in the Hartnett Report (Inland Revenue, 2001) and was part of a modernisation programme to achieve efficiencies in resource utilisation.

Dave Hartnett, who became Commissioner of Revenue and Customs in 2005 and Second Permanent Secretary for Tax from 2008 until his retirement from HMRC in 2012, was instrumental in the development of the UK's large business strategy. Hartnett's contribution includes an intensive campaign to raise the profile of tax on the agenda of corporate boards through the Tax in the Boardroom Agenda (HMRC, 2006a; Hartnett, 2008). The introduction of the disclosure of tax avoidance rules in 2004 was another early indication of a new direction; an overt attempt to change the dynamics of the market for tax avoidance schemes.

The programme in the UK applies to all companies within the purview of the Large Business Service, renamed Large Business Directorate in 2016. Several reviews of relationships with large business took place between 2006 and 2013 (e.g. HMRC, 2006b). Initially approximately 700 groups were subjected to the cooperative compliance programme. This was extended to some 2,000 in 2014 (Knott, 2015).

Risk rating is a prominent feature of the UK programme, but the methodology has received criticism from businesses, especially for its focus on company size, complexity and attitude to tax planning, rather than its openness and transparency with HMRC (Freedman, Loomer and Vella, 2007; HMRC, 2007; HMRC, 2016; De Widt and Oats, 2017). A former director of the Large Business Directorate, writing in 2015 (Knott, 2015), described CRMs as "experienced and highly trained tax professionals who 'man mark' ... complex and potentially high-risk businesses." Dealing with issues in real time is seen to be a key benefit of the UK model; this includes discussing proposed transactions in advance so as to clarify, and hopefully agree, the appropriate tax treatment. Knott (2015) further notes that this also allows HMRC to "identify problems and loopholes quickly, so that ... policy colleagues can ensure ... legislation remains robust". Board level engagement is another key feature of the UK system, which HMRC see as a mechanism for influencing businesses to move towards being low risk.

The Senior Accounting Officer (SAO) legislation introduced in 2009[4] is unique in that it creates an obligation on a named individual to attest to the veracity of the tax computations. It is different to the US SOX requirements, which apply to internal controls more broadly, and is part of the evolving picture of making large corporates more aware of the need to manage tax affairs carefully and transparently; effectively an extension of the 'tax on the boardroom agenda' movement referred to earlier. The introduction of SAO responsibilities has focussed attention on internal controls as well as providing HMRC with the ability to conduct more robust risk assessments.

The customer relationship management approach has, on the whole, created an environment in which large businesses are better placed to manage their tax affairs more speedily and with greater certainty. Freedman (2011) observes that there is a difficult balance between encouraging trust and voluntary compliance and the maintenance of consistency across all taxpayers.

The UK programme has been highly politicised with the intervention of the Public Accounts Committee in 2013 and subsequent National Audit Office inquiries (NAO, 2012) in relation to allegations of special arrangements for large corporates ('sweetheart deals') (James, 2013).

A number of legislative and other regulatory measures have been implemented subsequently, which water down the spirit of collaboration to some extent. In 2012, HMRC launched a high risk corporates programme to deal with dispute resolution for very large business. HMRC (2012) state that the key elements of this programme are the following:

---

4 For a contemporaneous discussion of its introduction, see Freedman (2009).

- Board to Board engagement;
- A very high level of governance under the monthly cross-directorate Programme Board;
- Rigorous investigation and debate of technical issues with customers, face-to-face, and a detailed agreed project plan where possible;
- Effective partnership working across directorates and with external counsel and others;
- Resolution decisions fully in line with the Litigation and Settlement Strategy.

HMRC's formal approach to dealings with large corporates is outlined in two documents released in 2014 (HMRC, 2014a; HMRC, 2014b). In 2015, a further new measure requires large corporates to make public their "tax strategy". The implementation of extra assurance processes within HMRC has reduced the ability of tax administrators to provide early certainty to corporates.

Both the Dutch and UK models reflect the growing sophistication of risk management in tax authorities. In the next section, we canvass the literature on meta-regulation in order to better understand the impact generated by risk-based regulatory arrangements in the corporate tax domain.

Reflections on risk based regulation

Research on risk-based regulation has increased considerably in recent years[5]. In the academic literature, categorisations of risk are produced that frequently dichotomise it, for example, into internal and external risk (Black, 2005) societal and institutional risk (Rothstein et al., 2006) primary and secondary risk (Power, 2004). These binary categorisations of risk identification are not consistent among scholars and take different perspectives, for example, the focus of Power's work is on the regulatees whereas for Black and Rothstein et al. it is the regulator.

Black's (2005, p.543) distinction is pertinent in the current context. Internal risks are those which the regulator (tax authority) itself understands and perceives as its own risks and so implements internal control systems to manage them. These internal risks are conceptually different to the external risks, which are those of the regulatee (here large corporate taxpayer) and are therefore of interest to the regulator. If the regulatee does not have correct procedures to manage its own operational risks, this can then create

---

5   The ensuing discussion draws in part on Mulligan, Oats and Tuck (2009).

or exacerbate the regulator's own, internal risks. Therefore, the regulator is interested in and concerned about the robustness of the internal controls of the regulatee, a phenomenon referred to as "meta-regulation".

Power notes that risk-based internal control systems have become "an increasingly significant regulatory object" (2004, p.27) in the post-Enron environment. In addition, growing pressures on resources have incentivised regulators to apply a meta-regulation approach as an alternative to traditional, command and control based regulation. Although lacking a universally agreed-upon definition, the element of indirect regulation, or regulated self-regulation, returns in definitions of meta-regulation (Braithwaite, 2003; Coglianese and Mendelson, 2010; Power, 2004). For example, Hutter (2006) defines meta-regulation as "the state's oversight of self-regulatory arrangements", while Parker and Braithwaite (2004) characterise "institutional meta-regulation" as "the regulation of one institution by another". Morgan (2003) argues that meta-regulation "captures a desire to think reflexively about regulation, such that rather than regulating social and individual action directly, the process of regulation itself becomes regulated".

Despite similarities with self-regulation, Coglianese and Mendelson (2010) emphasise the differences between self-regulation and meta-regulation. While self-regulation occurs when the regulator issues commands that apply to itself, meta-regulation refers to "ways that outside regulators deliberately – rather than unintentionally – seek to induce targets to develop their own internal, self-regulatory responses to public problems". By commands, Coglianese and Mendelson (2010) refer to instructions that regulators give to regulatees (their targets), in which case they can choose to either specify means standards or ends commands. Means standards outline ways in which regulatees should realise compliance, and are most appropriate when the regulator understands what actions are needed to achieve compliance. Instead, ends commands – usually called performance standards – do not require any particular means but direct the regulatee to achieve (or avoid) a specified outcome related to the regulatory goal.

One advantage of meta-regulation and self-regulation is the degree of discretion they afford to regulatees. By exploiting regulatee's information advantages through leveraging the regulatee into the task of regulating itself, regulators are expected to be able to reduce their monitoring activities. Increased discretion will allow regulatees to find the most cost effective way to achieve compliance. In addition, compliance may also be higher under meta-regulation as regulatees may perceive their own rules to be more reasonable than those imposed by outsiders (Coglianese and Mendelson, 2010, p.153). The consequences of non-compliance will influence the effectiveness of meta-regulation – and consequences can vary in their size, direction (negative ones – such as fines, or positive ones – such as reputational benefits), and level of certainty (May, 2003).

As observed in De Widt and Oats (2017), Braithwaite (2003) explicitly talks about meta-regulation in the context of tax administration. "The conventional approach by tax administrations has comprised merely analysing more closely the risks faced by the organisation." Braithwaite suggests, however, that a further stage is required for tax authorities to try to influence the risk management systems of regulatees. In a later work, Braithwaite (2005) describes meta-risk management in the tax administration context as consisting of a shift from "inside out" to "outside in" design. By this, he means that the tax authority needs to move away from the traditional approach of designing tax systems to suit administrative purposes and then requiring taxpayers to comply with it, to an approach that engages taxpayers by finding out what "natural systems" they already use, and then shaping the tax system to "go with the grain of user systems" (De Widt and Oats, 2017). Power (2004) suggests, along similar lines, that meta-risk regulation entails providing a central role for internal control systems and being responsive to the way in which regulatees self-organise.

Meta-regulation, however, also contains risks. Black (2006) expresses concern about how risk-based regulation has "the potential both to expose and obscure key socio political and socioeconomic choices". These choices relate to, for example, the amount or types of regulatory failures that a regulator will tolerate. A second risk, which has been identified in relation to the Sarbanes Oxley regulations, is that meta-risk regulation may lead to an environment of over-regulation that could impede business progress and innovation (Shadab, 2008). However, regulators and others will argue that due to continued tax avoidance activity, meta-risk regulation should in fact be developed and increased (Mulligan et al., 2009). Another risk of meta-regulation is that regulators might become captured by the regulated entity (Coglianese and Lazer, 2003).

In thinking about co-operative compliance as risk-based regulation, a number of questions arise. What should be the focus of regulation for the tax authorities? Does meta-regulation allow for monitoring internal processes of regulatees only, or provide a mechanism for influencing, even controlling, regulatees? (De Widt and Oats, 2017).

Conclusion

In both the Netherlands and the UK, growing tensions between the tax administration and corporate taxpayers, combined with increasing regulatory pressures, incentivised the introduction of non-traditional forms of monitoring. In both countries, it was primarily the leadership of the tax administration that took the initiative for implementing risk-based regulatory arrangements, even though this move was partly in response to feedback from corporate taxpayers. Individuals in the tax administration's leadership, such as HMRC's Permanent Secretary for Tax, acted as policy entrepreneurs and have been critical to initiating and helping to secure resources and political backing for the new monitoring approaches. More than a decade after the first initiatives were implemented, closer scrutiny of tax authority behaviour is putting increasing pressure on cooperative compliance and the resources required to maintain the programmes. Inequality of service level between those taxpayers within a cooperative compliance programme and those outside it is problematic in both the Netherlands and the UK.

Despite strong similarities as to their origins and current challenges, this chapter identifies important differences regarding the institutional design of cooperative compliance in the UK and the Netherlands. In contrast to the programme structure of the Dutch system, cooperative compliance in the UK demonstrates an incremental development over time, without having an overarching programme design as in the Dutch case. Second, UK cooperative compliance arrangements automatically apply to all large corporates, while corporates in the Netherlands voluntarily decide whether they want to join horizontal monitoring. Partly due to this, the Dutch model provides a clear incentive for corporate taxpayers to improve their internal fiscal control mechanisms, giving them greater control over their tax affairs and facilitating trust by the tax authorities. The legal status of the covenants entered into on entry into horizontal monitoring creates some uncertainty, although they are viewed by most participants as equivalent to a private contractual agreement that sets out the commitments of both parties without having any direct legal implications in the event of non-fulfilment. This low level of legality provides horizontal monitoring with flexibility, but has also left the process vulnerable to criticism.

As the tax behaviour of large corporates receives increasingly negative publicity around the world, the long-term viability of less formal arrangements is now in question. The benefits of cooperative compliance models in terms of efficiency gains and decreased uncertainty must be weighed against these resource requirements. Transparency about the differences in interest between the tax administration and businesses, and how the regulatory regime deals with these differences, is critical to make cooperative compliance systems more robust.

References

Ayres, I. and Braithwaite, J. (1992). *Responsive Regulation*. Oxford: Oxford University Press.

Belastingdienst (2017). *Rapport Onderzoek Grote Ondernemingen*. Utrecht: Belastingdienst/Centrum voor Kennis en Communicatie.

Black, J. (2005) The Emergence of risk-based regulation and the new public risk management in the United Kingdom, *Public Law*, 512-549.

Black, J. (2006) Managing Regulatory Risks and Defining Parameters of Blame: A Focus on the Australian Prudential Regulation Authority. *Law and Policy*, **28**(1), 1 – 30.

Braithwaite, J. (2003) Meta Risk Management and Responsive Regulation for Tax System Integrity *Law and Policy*, **25**(1).

Braithwaite, J. (2005), *Markets in Vice, Markets in Virtue*, Oxford University Press, Oxford.

Coglianese, C. and Lazer, D. (2003). Management-Based Regulation: Using Private Management to Achieve Public Goals. *Law and Society Review*, **37**, 691.

Coglianese, C. and Mendelson, E. (2010). Meta-regulation and self-regulation. In R. Baldwin, M. Cave and M. Lodge (Eds.), *The Oxford Handbook of Regulation*. Oxford: Oxford University Press.

De Widt, D. (2017) *Dutch Horizontal Monitoring: The Handicap of a Head Start*, FairTax Working Paper No 13, available at: http://umu.diva-portal.org/smash/get/diva2:1142129/FULLTEXT01.pdf

De Widt, D. and Oats, L. (2017). Risk Assessment in a Co-operative Compliance Context: A Dutch–UK Comparison. *British Tax Review* (2), 230-248.

Freedman, J. (2009) Legislative Comment: Finance Act Notes: Section 93 and Schedule 46 – duties of senior accounting officers of large companies, *British Tax Review*, 620.

Freedman, J. (2011a) Responsive Regulation, Risk and Rules: Applying Theory to Tax Practice *University of British Columbia Law Review*, **44**(3), 627-662.

Freedman, J. (2011b) Tax Risk Management and Corporate Taxpayers – International Tax Administration Developments. In Bakker, A. and Kloosterhof, S. (Eds.) *Tax Risk Management; From Risk to Opportunity*, Amsterdam, IBFD, 111-134.

Freedman, J., Loomer, G. and Vella, J. (2007). *Moving Beyond Avoidance? Tax Risk and the Relationship between Large Business and HMRC*, Report of the Oxford University Centre for Business Taxation, Oxford: Said Business School.

Hartnett, D. (2008). The Link between Taxation and Corporate Governance. In Wolfgang Schön (Ed.). *Tax and Corporate Governance*. Berlin: Springer, 3-8.

HMRC (2006a). *Tax on the Boardroom Agenda: The Views of Business*.

HMRC (2006b). Review of Links with Large Business. London: The Stationary Office. Available at http://webarchive.nationalarchives.gov.uk/20140206161013/http://www.hmrc.gov.uk/large-business/review-report.pdf (Accessed 8 August 2017).

HMRC (2007). *HMRC approach to compliance risk management for large business*. London: The stationery Office. http://www.hmrc.gov.uk/budget2007/large-business-riskman.pdf (Accessed 8 August 2017).

HMRC (2012) *Large Business: The High Risk Corporates Programme*. Available at https://www.gov.uk/guidance/large-business-the-high-risk-corporates-programme

HMRC (2014a) *Large Business: Customer relationship management model*. Available at https://www.gov.uk/government/publications/large-businesses-customer-relationship-management-model/large-businesses-customer-relationship-management-model (Accessed 8 August 2017).

HMRC (2014b) *Large Business Strategy*. Available at https://www.gov.uk/guidance/large-business-strategy (Accessed 8 August 2017).

HMRC (2016). *Tax Compliance Risk Management*. https://www.gov.uk/hmrc-internal-manuals/tax-compliance-risk-management (Accessed 8 August 2017).

Hutter, B. (2006). Risk, Regulation, and Management. In P. Taylor, Gooby and J. Zinn (Eds.) *Risk in Social Science*, Oxford: Oxford University Press, 215

Inland Revenue (2001) *Review of Business Links* (The Hartnett Report), http://www.inlandrevenue.gov.uk/pbr2001/businesslinks.pdf

International Fiscal Association (IFA) (2012). *Key Issues Report: Imitative on the Enhanced Relationship*. https://www.ifa.nl/publications/enchancedrelproject/pages/default.aspx (Accessed 8 August 2017)

James, M.D. (2013) Cutting a good deal – UK Uncut, Goldman Sachs and the challenge to administrative discretion. *Journal of Applied Accounting Research*, **14**(3), 248-267.

Knott, J. (2015). Q&A: The View for HMRC's Large Business Directorate. *Tax Journal* 1284.

May, P. (2003). Performance-Based Regulation and Regulatory Regimes: The Saga of Leaky Buildings. *Law & Policy*, **25**, 381.

Montagu, N. (2003) The Inland Revenue – Strong on support, strong on revenues, speech, the Chartered Institute of Taxation 9 January. Available from https://www.scotsman.com/news/the-changing-face-of-the-taxman-1-1382124 (Accessed 8 August 2017).

Morgan, B. (2003). *Social Citizenship in the Shadow of Competition: The Bureaucratic Politics of Regulatory Justification.* Aldershot: Ashgate Publishing, 2.

Mulligan, E., Oats, L. and Tuck, P. (2009). *Meta risk management and tax accounting.* Paper presented at the Interdisciplinary Perspectives on Accounting conference, Innsbruck.

National Audit Office (NAO) (2012). *Press notice 31/12, Settling large tax disputes, 14 June 2012.* http://www.nao.org.uk/press-releases/settling-large-tax-disputes-2/ (Accessed 8 August 2017).

NTCA (2013). *Supervision Large Business in the Netherlands.* Netherlands Tax and Customs Administration.

Oats, L and Tuck, P. (2008). *The Relationship between HM Revenue & Customs and Large Corporate Taxpayers: The Changing Role of Accountants.* London: ICAEW.

OECD (1988). *Administrative Responsiveness and the Taxpayer.* Paris: OECD.

OECD (2008). *Study into the Role of Tax Intermediaries.* Paris: OECD.

OECD (2013). *Co-operative Compliance: A Framework. From Enhanced Relationship to Co-operative Compliance.* Paris: OECD.

OECD (2016). *Co-operative Tax Compliance: Building Better Tax Control Frameworks.* Paris: OECD.

Parker, C. (2013) Twenty years of responsive regulation: An appreciation and appraisal, *Regulation and Governance*, 7(1), 2-13.

Parker, C. and Braithwaite, J. (2004) Conclusion. In C. Parker, C. Scott, N. Lacey, and J. Braithwaite (Eds.) *Regulating Law*. Oxford: Oxford University Press, 283.

Power, M. (2004). *The Risk Management of Everything: Rethinking the Politics of Uncertainty*, Demos Publishing.

Rothstein, H., Huber, M. and Gaskell, G. (2006) A Theory of Risk colonisation: the spiralling regulatory logics of societal and institutional risk, *Economy and Society*, **35**(1), 91-112.

Shadab, H. (2008). Innovation and Corporate Governance: The Impact of Sarbanes-Oxley. *Journal of Business Law*, **10**, 955.

Stevens, L., Pheijffer, M., Van den Broek, H., Keijzer, T. and Van der Hel-van Dijk, L. (2012). *Tax Supervision – Made to Measure*. The Hague: Committee Horizontal Monitoring Tax and Customs Administration.

Tuck, P. (2007). *A Study of the Changing Relationship between Large Corporates and the Inland Revenue*, unpublished PhD thesis, The University of Warwick.

Tuck, P. (2010). The emergence of the tax official into a T-shaped knowledge expert. *Critical Perspectives on Accounting,* **21**(7), 584–596.

Tuck, P. (2013). The Changing role of tax governance: remaking the large corporate taxpayer into a visible customer partner, *British Journal of Management,* **24**, 116-131.

Van der Hel-van Dijk, E. C. J. M. and Poolen, T. (2013). Horizontal Monitoring in the Netherlands: At the Crossroads. *Bulletin for International Taxation* **67**(12), 673-678.

Lightning Source UK Ltd.
Milton Keynes UK
UKHW020500090519
342370UK00005B/273/P